ANN R MCNICOL

# Before I Was Mom

*Reading The World Differently, A Memoir Of Dyslexia,*
*Discover & Science*

*This story covers a lifetime, about seventy years. I've reconstructed some events and conversations to capture the emotional truth when my memory was hazy. While most names are accurate, I've changed a few because I couldn't recall the originals.*

*The following are pseudonyms: Mrs. Maxwell, Mr. Keaton, and Dr. Stimson.*

*First edition*

*ISBN (paperback): 979-8-9886932-4-6*
*ISBN (hardcover): 979-8-9934413-0-6*

*This book was professionally typeset on Reedsy.*
*Find out more at reedsy.com*

*Dedicated To:*
*The mentors and teachers who guided me.Thank you.*
*A special thank you to the librarians –*
*who sparked my curiosity and opened up the world.*

*And as always, to my husband, Ken McNicol*
*and my children, Robin and Bernard McNicol,*
*who support my compulsion to write.*

"There's power in allowing yourself to be known and heard, in owning your unique story, in using your authentic voice. And there's grace in being willing to know and hear others."

Michelle Obama

# Contents

# Foreword

# Chapter 1 ~ Prologue

Mr. Groff paced in front of the blackboard. He was a thin man in his forties, with receding hair and glasses, wearing a dress shirt and tie. Everything about him said "teacher." He turned and wrote the phrase, *I am a...* on the board and waited while we copied the topic into our notebooks.

It was late afternoon, and as usual, the heat made it hard to concentrate. Even with the windows open, very few breezes made their way from the courtyard into the classroom. I thought I could hear the sounds of snoring. A few students were slumped over with their heads on the desks. This was my creative writing class, and the writing topic was always provided on Friday, so we had the weekend to work on it. Mr. Groff surveyed the class.

When no one said anything, he asked, "Questions?"

"Can you give us more to work with? I'm not sure I understand the assignment," I said.

He was standing next to John, who was indeed snoring. Mr. Groff tapped on John's desk until he lifted his head.

Then Groff said, "If I needed to wake my son from a nap, I might put my hand on his shoulder or ruffle his hair. In other words, I behave differently with my children than I do with my students. I'm your teacher, but when I go home, I'm a father and a husband."

John's face was red. Clearly, he wasn't enjoying the attention. There were chuckles and even a few claps.

"Okay, let's finish this," Mr. Groff said. "Your assignment is to write 250 words on the topic, 'Who am I?' Capture the way you see yourself and how others see you. As usual, make sure your work is neat. Spelling and grammar count."

The bell rang, and we gathered our belongings and filed out the door into a hallway filled with noisy teenagers ready for the weekend.

It was an age before computers and digital records. I can't look back to see my essay, but I have a clear memory of my writing points: I was a student, a daughter, a sister, a friend, a science fiction fan, and a guitar player. Those were the essential constants of "me" in 1971, my senior year at Norland.

This wasn't my first year in Mr. Groff's class. He was my tenth-grade English teacher, and I loved his class. He switched teaching assignments the next year, and fate handed me the bonus of a second year with him. My senior year, he offered an elective class in creative writing. I signed up without hesitation.

Mr. Groff's high school classes were a long, long time ago. *How much of the "me" from high school remains after fifty-five years?*

I was a student then, and I'm a student now. I've returned to my role as a student repeatedly throughout my thirty-six years working in science and science education. My parents never attended college, and neither did my older brother. Somehow, I ended up with three college degrees and still take classes.

I played guitar when I was a kid and was in a band for a while in junior high. But my obsession grew when I lived in Washington, DC, working for the National Institutes of Health. There was a vibrant folk community filled with like-minded young professionals. My evenings and weekends were spent playing in folk clubs and folk events. Years later, while attending graduate school in Australia, I gravitated to Australian folk music clubs and festivals. I took a job playing music in a local restaurant. No one listened, but that was fine. I earned money for practicing. Guitar was central to who I was.

I'm no longer a guitar player. When I was pregnant with my first child, the folk band I was in suggested we take a break. Maybe they didn't like the optics, or maybe they were nervous about having a very pregnant guitar player on stage. I thought we would restart the band after my baby was born. It didn't happen. I was working full-time in a physiology lab and caring for a newborn infant. It left little time for practice or performing. By the time my child was older, I had changed careers. Other interests captured all my time and energy. I still have my guitar and keep hoping one day to rekindle my old passion.

Science Fiction? My house overflows with books spanning a lifetime of reading. My tastes have always leaned toward hard science fiction rather than fantasy, but I've made exceptions. In recent years, my appetite for books, fueled by free time and the ease of online shopping, has grown to a frightening level. Check: I'm still a science fiction fan.

It took me fifty years to venture into writing science fiction. I think Mr. Groff would understand the complicated set of reasons it took so long, and he would be pleased it finally happened. I am sorry my mother and father passed away before I published my first book. They were both avid readers and would have been thrilled that my life included writing and publishing.

Yes, I'm still a daughter. My parents loved me unconditionally and supported everything I turned my hand to. Although they are no longer here, they still influence me. That first book grew to a three-book young adult science fiction series. Somewhere along the way, I decided my life journey was worth writing about, hence, this memoir.

# Chapter 2 ~ Window To the World

The light came in from the attic window of my bedroom. Beyond the window, squirrels scurried along the branches of our oak tree. My baby brother was asleep in his crib under the slanted part of our attic bedroom. I dressed quietly and closed the door behind me. I knew today was special, but I couldn't remember why. I was about halfway down the stairs when Dad called up to me from the living room floor.

"Sweetie, how old are you today?"

I held up my hand, showing five fingers, and said, "Five." That's when I remembered. Today was my birthday, and Mom was going to bake my favorite cake. Richard was still sleeping. I heard sounds from the kitchen, so maybe Mom was working on the cake. I rushed down to see.

"Good morning, princess. Happy birthday," she said.

"Are you making my cake? " I asked.

"Not yet, but I will."

I sat down at the table, and Mom put a bowl of cereal in front of me. I ate, then headed off to play with my slinky, making it walk down the stairs. There was a noise from outside, and Dad opened the front door and stepped outside. I watched as a truck maneuvered into our driveway. Two men carried a large piece of furniture into the living room and placed it against the wall.

Mom came in from the kitchen with furniture polish and removed smudges from the shiny tan wood surface.

"It's a television," Dad said, pointing to what looked like a dark window. "I'll show you what it can do once we have it set up."

He plugged the television into a wall socket and turned it on. Crackling sounds filled the room. A window in the center came to life, bright white, with lines and fuzzy images. Dad moved dials and arranged the antenna, deep in concentration. I soon lost interest and went outside to play.

The television wasn't *for* me, but it made my birthday memorable. Most evenings, my parents watched the *Jackie Gleason Show*. Richard and I would watch for a while. But the shows were boring, so we went outside to play. None of the houses had fences, so the backyards formed one enormous area where we could explore and see who else was around.

We came inside once the sun set. Richard disappeared into his room. He built plastic model airplanes from kits, painting them and adding decals. His miniature air fleet was displayed as if ready to take flight from the shelves on the wall. He liked to work alone. Because I shared a room with Jim, I had to be quiet, but I could color or read without waking him.

Six months later, I walked into the house and found Mom and Dad had arranged all the chairs from the kitchen and dining and all our living room furniture like a theater around the television.

"What's this for?" I asked.

Dad said, "They're launching Explorer I from Florida tonight. We invited the neighbors in to watch."

Shortly after dinner, the doorbell started ringing, and people started filling the room. Mom brought platters of food out, and Dad put glasses out so people could fix a drink. Mom put Jimmy to bed.

Richard and I were supposed to be in bed, but we hung out at the bottom of the stairs, where we could see the television, trying to avoid being noticed. We watched the television image of the rocket on the launch pad. When the announcer said, "We are T-minus 60 seconds," thick clouds of smoke formed at the base of the rocket. There was a hush of anticipation in the room. No one said a word as we all watched the clouds and smoke on the television.

Dad clinked his drink and said, "Count down!" as numbers flashed to the right of the rocket. *Sixty, fifty-nine, fifty-eight.*

We all started counting with the announcer.

Then it was up, rising into the dark sky. We heard cheering and clapping from the television set. Soon, the adults in our living room were clapping and cheering with them. Richard and I stayed still and watched until Dad came over.

"Time for bed," he said.

"That was cool," Richard said.

"Yes, it was. Now up to bed."

We climbed the stairs and went to our rooms, but it took me a long time to get to sleep. The rocket was incredible. I marveled at what I'd just experienced right in my own living room. It was as if my family and my whole neighborhood had been transported to Cape Canaveral to see the launch. My family's world had wonderfully expanded.

Space launches weren't all we watched. Dad loved ball games and often took Richard to Yankee Stadium. But now, he could watch ball games played in other cities. But we watched every single televised launch. Dad helped me clip articles from the newspaper and make a scrapbook.

But the launches were the favorites and were on everyone's mind.

We couldn't watch the Russian launches, but everyone talked about them, saying things like, "Russia is using satellites to spy on us."

The country was science crazy. Every parent wanted their child to grow up to be a scientist. Mom and Dad gave Richard and me chemistry sets and Meccano building kits for holiday and birthday gifts, which were very cool.

One of my chemistry sets had a plastic rocket. When I mixed baking soda and vinegar and sealed the chamber, it would launch. I hit the ceiling a few times. Then my New Jersey cousin caused a fire in her walk-in closet, where she had her makeshift lab. Uncle Chuck and Aunt Marian were furious; there was smoke damage on the entire first floor. I really wanted to know what she had been doing and using when the fire started.

Mom and Dad lost their enthusiasm for chemistry sets and switched to less exciting science gifts. They were always fun, but never as good as a chemistry set. I remember walking home with my best friend, David. I was five. Dave asked what I wanted to be when I grew up.

I didn't hesitate at all. "A scientist."

# Chapter 3 ~ My Town

Our neighborhood was a suburban paradise for kids; houses had big backyards without fences. We treated the combined backyards as an enormous park, playing hide and seek, running bases, and climbing trees. In winter, we found front yards with hills and fearlessly pulled our sleds to the top, tempting fate as we raced down to the sidewalk and the six-lane highway beyond. Well, we all survived, so no harm.

Behind my house sat a sandbox, a swing set, and a log cabin playhouse. One year, Richard decorated the log cabin with colorful crepe paper streamers. The next day, we found the log cabin without the decorations, but bits and pieces of the streamers were all over the yard.

"Who would do this?" he asked.

I shrugged, lacking any answer.

He put more streamers up, and we spent hours watching to see who was coming into your yard. As the sun set, the cabin was attacked by squirrels that leaped about, shredding the paper in a furious dance. Richard laughed so hard he almost fell over. The next day, he decorated the log cabin again just to watch them in action.

The swing was nothing special, a metal unit from Sears that Dad assembled, but I loved it. I would pump hard on the swing, going fast and reaching as high as it would go. Then at the top of the arc, I'd release the chains, traveling high in the air and making a game of how far I could go before landing. It was my early exploration of the laws of motion. Little did I know, I'd end up teaching physics.

The backyard called to me, even when I wanted quiet time. I'd sit on the swing with my school "Flutophone," a white plastic recorder with nine holes and a mouthpiece. The school had a Flutophone band for teaching students music notation. The plastic instruments were inexpensive, indestructible, and my favorite part of school.

Twice a week, our teacher would march us all to the school music room. She would play a recording of a new piece of music so we could hear what it should sound like. Then she would work with us on our part.

The backyard swing was my retreat, a place where Richard wouldn't make rude comments about noise and my lack of skill. I'd start by practicing the school assignment, and then just make up tunes for fun. But I'd always make sure I had my assigned piece perfect for music class.

The first time we had a combined rehearsal was magic. My class lined up on the first row of the stage. Then the third graders came in, standing behind us on a riser. When the teacher raised her baton and played, it was amazing. The third graders had smaller Flutophones and were playing different music that fit in with ours. I had to concentrate on my part because the combination of sounds made me want to stop and just listen. Later that month, we had our first recital, opening the evening before the school band played. I can still hear the applause when I think of that night.

Other than our music class, there was little for me to look forward to in my classes. No matter how hard I tried, my handwriting was illegible. Even in second grade, I was failing spelling tests, appearing unable to learn even the simplest words. For math lessons, we worked with flash cards, drilling simple addition and multiplication. Teachers quickly decided I either couldn't or wouldn't learn.

My best school memories are from recess and the hour lunch break. In winter, teachers sprayed water on the basketball courts. We brought ice skates from home and spent recess on the ice. In warm weather, the playground stayed open all the time. Sometimes, I stayed after school to play, walking home instead of taking the school bus.

The school was only half a mile from my house. I took the school bus when it was cold, snowing, or raining. In nice weather, I walked home with my friend David. One time, we got carried away exploring, talking, and goofing around. By the time we got home, our parents were furious. David's mom and my mom flew out of our front door as we walked into the yard.

"Where the hell were you!" Mom demanded. Her hair was disheveled, and her face was flushed.

David and I looked at each other, trying to figure out what to say.

"Walking home," David answered, but it sounded weak.

His mother grabbed his arm, dragging him off.

"We were so worried we called the police," Mom said.

I wasn't sure I believed her, but felt suitably miserable and apologized repeatedly. Soon after the incident, Dad gave me my first watch and said I was to be home before four p.m. on school days.

David and I were inseparable. On Saturday mornings, I crossed the big street to David's house, and we watched *Diver Dan* and *Captain Kangaroo*, then played in the yard on a tire swing and climbed over piles of leaves. Dave's mom was a good cook, and in their kitchen, I learned spaghetti didn't come from a can and that you add sauce to white noodles.

In the middle of October, as the leaves were turning orange and red, David came down with the mumps. He missed school for two weeks. I was devastated when Halloween came, and he was still contagious. His mom must have understood my angst because she handed me his decorated bag and UNICEF box.

"Can you collect for David?" she asked. "I'm sure it would make him feel better."

Dressed as a black cat, in a costume from Aunt Naomi, I walked up to each door, rang the bell, and called, "Trick or Treat."

At each house, the door opened, and a neighbor looked skeptically at my two bags.

"I'm collecting for David; he has the mumps," I dutifully said.

My neighbors put generous amounts of candy into both bags and said they hoped David would be better soon. At the end of Trick or Treat, I had two staggeringly heavy bags of candy and two filled UNICEF boxes to bring to school and turn in. It was the best Halloween ever.

That was my last Halloween in the old neighborhood. We moved to Florida the following year. David wrote me a letter, and I tried to write one back. Writing was so hard for me that my letter looked like a toddler wrote it, and I didn't send it.

My family visited New York in 1964. We went to the World's Fair and visited our old neighborhood. I apologized to David and explained my problem with writing letters. We exchanged phone numbers and promised to keep in touch. But three years is a long, long time for young kids, and we had grown apart. We had a good visit, and I enjoyed hearing about what he was into, like The Monkees But we weren't close like we had been. We had drifted apart.

*Was Hewlett as idyllic as I remember?* Maybe not. But we could walk home from school feeling safe, and everyone knew me. It felt like people looked out for each other, even if they didn't know them. That was nice.

# Chapter 4 ~ Paradise

Mom and Dad bundled us into the back of the station wagon long before the sun was up. We were traveling from Long Island to South Florida to spend the holidays with Grandma Jean, Grandpa Paul, and Uncle Bob.

The folded-down back seat was covered in thick blankets. Richard, Jim, and I slept on our makeshift bed for the first couple of hours, waking up as daylight arrived. We had a deck of cards and spent the morning playing War and Go Fish. When we got tired of cards, we'd drive Mom and Dad crazy with games like I Spy. Around two in the afternoon, they'd find a roadside motel with a swimming pool, and we'd check in. We'd wear ourselves out swimming and jumping in the pool. The next day, we did it all again.

Grandpa's heart problems prompted a move to Miami for the warmer weather, making this our yearly visit to see the Miami family.

Mom was Grandma's oldest child, but Bob, her youngest, was one year older than me. I loved the visits because Uncle Bob felt like a brother or a good friend. Mom's other brother, Uncle Mike, was away at college.

Their apartment on Treasure Island was commuting distance to their dry cleaning store in the elegant Roney Plaza, a landmark Miami Beach hotel. We stayed at the Waldorf, a less expensive hotel that was so close we could easily walk over to their store and visit.

Grandma Jean had dirty blond hair, laced with gray. She adored gladioli and always had a vase of them in her living room. Grandpa Paul's hair was entirely gray. He loved parakeets, and they had two that would perch on his shoulder when he opened their cage. Paul played the mandolin. He had a natural musical talent and could play any tune he heard.

I loved to swim, and the Waldorf had a high board where Richard, Bob, and I would climb the ladder and jump into the deep end. On time, while I was on the board, I saw Jimmy tumble off the edge and tumble into the pool. Mom was sitting near him, but hadn't seen him fall.

"Mom," I screamed.

She'd been chatting with an older man when she abruptly shoved him aside and plunged into the deep end of the pool. I watched Mom pull Jim up to the surface. Afterward, she told me that when she'd found him, he was still at the bottom, sucking his thumb. She said he didn't even seem bothered.

Jim wasn't upset, but Mom was. She started Jim on swimming lessons as soon as we got home.

Bob was the perfect older brother, even if he was actually my uncle. He knew the best places to explore, and the hotel staff all knew him by name. We spent our days moving from pool to beach, drifting from the Waldorf to the Roney Plaza, where we walked on the boardwalk, explored gardens, and goldfish ponds. Bob treated the beach and the surrounding area like an extended backyard.

The Miami ocean water was Caribbean blue and crystal clear. Small fish dashed about in the shallow water where waves crashed onto the sand. We jumped the waves, worked our way into deeper water, and dove into the ocean world while Mom played with Jim on the sand, keeping a watchful eye on him.

Bob and I had "play boats" when we were kids. Mine was just a blue plastic tub. Bob's was a Styrofoam triangle with a net seat, so his legs always dangled in the water. We each had wooden paddles. With the sun shining and the cool water around our feet, we'd push off and leave the shore behind, going past the waves and the swimmers into deeper water, where paddling was easier.

One day, the ocean was unusually calm, and I'd drifted further from shore than usual, distracted by trying to spot fish. Bob was quite a distance away from me. He struggled to move, since his legs slowed him down. I paddled back to him and saw that he looked unhappy.

"I think we should go back," Bob said.

I looked back at the shore. We were a long way out. For the first time, I wondered how deep the water was. I couldn't see the bottom.

"Yeah, we should turn back," I agreed.

It took longer than we expected and lots of paddling to reach shallow water where people were standing. We were both tired when we got there, embarrassed to find that people were watching us, and vocal about their disapproval.

"You shouldn't go out that far!" one lady said as we passed her on our way into shore.

"Where are your parents?" a man called out.

We didn't answer her. Grandma was in the dry cleaning shop. Mom was with Jim by the pool. They trusted us at the beach.

We ventured out again and again that week. But we never went as far from shore as we did that first day. Even I knew we were out much further than we should have been.

Every summer, we'd visit Miami, and I always felt a pang of sadness when it was time to return to New York. Part of it was the joy of vacation, where our family truly connected and we put aside the usual to-dos of everyday life. And, Miami just had a certain magic to it. New York had beaches and the ocean, of course, but they never felt as vibrant, and the water never seemed as inviting.

# Chapter 5 ~ Nomads

Fall came, summer ended, and the school year began. I was in third grade at Hewlett Elementary. Richard was in sixth grade, and this would be his last year of elementary school. He started playing trombone and was on a baseball team. He was almost pleasant to be around. Jimmy was getting older and could play games. He even had a really cool battery-operated go-kart that he zoomed around the house with.

It was a few months into the school year when I noticed Mom was distracted. She kept misplacing her purse, her cigarettes, or even her car keys. She seemed always to be looking for something. Day was also distracted and seemed angry. Something was wrong, but I didn't know what. Then Mom dropped the news over dinner.

"We're moving to Florida," Mom announced.

"Why?" I asked

Dad said, "ABC trucking closed. We're having problems keeping up with the house payments. Your grandparents offered us a place to stay while we get on our feet."

Mom said, "I'm thinking of it as an opportunity. I'd like to be closer to Grandma and Grandpa. We will be staying with them for a while."

"Are Grandma and Grandpa okay?" I asked.

"They're fine," Mom said.

I wondered what house payments meant. At the store, Mom gave money to the woman at the cash register. How did you make a "house payment?"

"Can we come back when we can make a house payment?" I asked.

Mom and Dad were silent. Dad looked away.

"Sweetie, we will make house payments again sometime soon, but we will get another house in Miami."

I blurted out, "I'll miss playing with David."

"I know," Mom said. "But you love playing with Bob, and we'll be near the ocean."

Richard didn't say anything. He was four years older than I was, and I expected he understood the seriousness of the situation better than I did.

Dad said, "Sometimes things change, and you need to make adjustments. Try to be positive."

The conversation shifted to details. Richard and I would go first, taking an airplane to Grandma's at the start of Christmas break. Mom and Dad would stay and pack up the house. Dad's trucking friends would help us move. Jim, age three, would stay with Mom and Dad.

"Why can't I stay and come with you? I can help," Richard asked.

Mom said, "It would be best for you to be in Miami and start at your new school at the start of the new semester."

In the months leading up to the move, Richard stayed in a perpetual mood. If he wanted to play catch, none of his friends were around.

"I need gray number five for the Spitfire," he said one night.

"It should be in the box," Mom said.

"It isn't. I don't know what happened to it. Can we go to the shop and get a bottle?"

Mom tried to be supportive, but she nearly lost it with that request. It didn't help that whatever was for dinner "sucked."

I stayed out of Richard's way.

For me, the hardest part was saying goodbye to my best friend Dave.

We were in his backyard, playing on his tire swing on the day before Richard and I were to leave.

"I wish you weren't going," he said.

The words stung.

"Me too," I said.

Dave's Mom came out, bringing us cookies and lemonade.

"Miami is a long way from here, but you can write. And, this will give us a reason to visit Miami Beach."

We brightened at the thought, but I was skeptical. Miami was a three-day drive. It was a big deal.

As Mom and Dad planned, Richard and I went by plane as school broke for the Christmas holiday.

Richard had on a dress shirt and black slacks, and I wore an olive-green dress. And I carried a birdcage with Pete, our pet parakeet.

"Put these on," the flight attendant said, handing us lanyards with an *unaccompanied minor* badge.

We slipped them over our heads.

When the announcer called for early boarding, I hugged Mom and promised not to fight with Richard. Then, the attendant came and walked us onto the plane,

Richard took the window seat, and I sat in the center with Pete in his cage on the center seat. It was my first time in a plane, and I stared past Richard at the runway as we taxied into position and accelerated down the runway. I didn't take my eyes from the window until we were above the clouds.

"You're a brave bird, Pete. I can't wait for you to meet Grandpa," I whispered into the cage.

"You know he doesn't understand, don't you?" Richard said.

"How do you know?" I asked.

"He's a bird!"

"Don't listen to him, Pete," I said.

The attendants came by with food and drink. Passengers walking by our seats said nice things about Pete and asked about us traveling alone. We landed and waited for the passengers to leave, then the attendant walked us off the plane and handed us over to Grandma and Grandpa. Bob was with him, and he jumped up and down when he saw me.

"We have a house with a backyard!" Bob said.

I thought about my own backyard; that wasn't mine anymore. "That's great. I can't wait to see it."

"When did you move?" Richard asked as Grandpa put our bags in the back of the car, and we climbed into the back seat.

"September. It's a longer drive to work, but it's nice to have a house again," Grandma said.

Grandpa pulled up in front of a pink house with palm trees in the front yard. "Here we are."

He unloaded our bags while we followed Grandma into the living room, carrying Pete in his cage. I recognized the furniture from their apartment in Treasure Island. The cool curved sofa and a console record player. White Gladiolas in Grandma's favorite vase stood gracefully on a table behind the curve of the couch.

Bob showed me his bedroom. The next room was the den with a bunk bed against the wall.

"This is where you and Richard will be sleeping," Grandma said.

"I have the top bunk," Richard said, tossing his backpack onto it.

"Okay." I sat down, looking around the room.

It was a small house with two bedrooms, a living room, a den, and a screened-in porch. Mom and Dad took the big bedroom, and my grandparents took over Bob's bedroom. They added bunk beds and cots to the den, converting it to a bedroom for Bob, Richard, Jimmy, and me. The eight of us crowded the cottage of a house.

It felt like one big sleepover party, and that was kind of fun. But more than once, I woke up in my bunk bed to find a giant fuzzy wolf spider crawling above my head on the bottom of Richard's upper bunk. I took to sleeping with a flashlight.

The house had a patch of undeveloped land behind the backyard. There were scrub palmetto, butterfly weeds, and trees covered in vines that dangled from branches, perfect for us to swing on and play Tarzan. It was like having a jungle for a backyard, hence the spiders, palmetto bugs, and occasional snakes that made their way into the house.

Grandpa showed us how to collect and open coconuts, and they had a banana tree in the yard. *Who knew bananas grew on trees?* Walking through the neighborhood, we came across tortoises, snakes, and even peacocks. This was a side of Florida that was different from the beach and from my neighborhood in New York. I think Bob enjoyed having company.

They put me in the same third-grade classroom as Bob to help me adjust to the new school. I missed the Flutophone band, but it was cool being in Bob's class.

Dad had a punching bag in the house, and Richard practiced. He teased Bob and me until we agreed to "fight," then took our allowance. We both hated it and were more than a little afraid of his bullying. I'm sure Richard missed Hewlett, his friends, and having his own bedroom. But his behavior was hard to take.

* * *

At dusk and dawn, the buzzing of mosquitoes announced the presence of the insatiable blood-sucking flying demons, driving everyone indoors to hide in screened homes. Large expanses of marsh grasslands in the Florida Everglades fed moisture upward, giving us daily afternoon rainfall-ideal conditions for spreading this pest. The year was 1961, and a fleet of trucks roamed the streets, emitting billowing clouds of DDT. They shaped the pattern of life in South Florida.

The sound of the spray truck approaching sent us dashing into the house if we were near enough. Sometimes, we jogged down a side street or into a neighbor's backyard, holding our breath until the truck passed. Few houses were air-conditioned. People balanced the misery of staying inside the house and enduring the heat against braving the mosquitoes outside in search of a breeze.

My legs were soon covered in welts and scars because, as much as I hated the biting pests, the tropical backyard of Grandma's house enticed me to brave the outside. There were trees with hanging vines to swing on, shrubs to explore, and a clubhouse to build. Walking in the neighborhood, Grandpa would show us banana trees. We collected coconuts and split them to eat when we got home.

Richard, Bob, and I walked or rode our bikes to Oak Grove Elementary. They put me in Bob's classroom. I'd never been a "good" student, but I had trouble adjusting. They had homework, something I'd never experienced before.

"If you don't have your homework, write your name on the board," the teacher would say as we filed in each morning.

So, every day, I'd put my name on the board. It didn't occur to me that I was supposed to do work at home. I wasn't really given a choice of writing my name on the board or *doing* homework. Our teacher also provided a weekly spelling list and asked students to spell words out loud. These verbal spelling tests were humiliating. It was obvious to everyone else that I couldn't spell even the easiest words.

Bob always had his homework. And he could spell words during spelling. He was so good-natured and never kidded me about getting everything wrong. He never gloated about it, and when he saw I didn't want to talk about it, he went along with me and talked about anything and everything else. That year, Bob became my best friend.

Looking back, I think the teacher just wanted to give me some space to adjust to a new school. But it might have helped if she had encouraged me to take part in what we were doing and what I was supposed to be learning.

While Bob, Richard, Jim, and I shared a bedroom, we didn't see Richard during the school day. There was a three-year age separation between us. When he did interact with Bob and me, he picked on us, so we tried to stay out of his way.

Staying with Grandma and Grandpa was always a short-term solution. Eight people in a two-bedroom home was not sustainable, and we needed our own home. So while we were at school, Mom and Dad went through the newspaper looking for jobs and spent the day making phone calls and filling out applications in search of a steady income.

Mom found a job before Dad, as a bookkeeper for a big company, Gulf American Land Corporation. She announced her success over dinner with everyone sitting around the table.

Grandma looked skeptical. "You don't know how to be a book-keeper."

"Well, I had a semester of training in stenography," Mom answered.

"Are they counting that as experience?" Grandpa asked.

"Well, I may have put some things on my resume from New York that weren't exactly true," Mom said.

"What do you know about bookkeeping?" Grandpa asked.

"I've been helping with your store records and took a book out at the library," Mom said, sounding a little annoyed.

"Did you give fake references?" Dad asked. "What if they call them?"

"If they do, they do," Mom said. "But I don't think they will. I met with the office manager during the interview, and he seemed very nice."

I'm sure the interviewer was impressed with Mom's intelligence. I'm also sure that her youth and attractiveness didn't hurt her chances. I suspect he took a chance and hired her because she obviously needed and wanted the job, and he liked her.

Dad bought Mom an old car so she could commute to work. It was so old I could see the road through the rusted floor in the back. A month later, Dad found a job with a small trucking company that used vans to move inventory between garment factory stores.

And just like that, we were on the move again. We'd stayed with Grandma and Grandpa six months, from December to May. I'm sure Mom and Dad were relieved when they had enough money to get a place for us, but the flamingo-pink house and the jungle-like yard are vivid memories that I treasure.

I only found out we were moving when we went on a drive on a Saturday morning, and Dad parked in front of a drab brown house. I wondered what we were doing here. The house looked empty.

"This is going to be our new house," Dad said.

"You're going to love it," Mom added.

We piled out of the car in varying states of excitement. Mom had a big smile on her face, and Richard bounced out, running to the front door. I was more reserved; it had been nice living with Bob, Grandma, and Grandpa. The drive took us across several major intersections that would be difficult to cross.

"You said that when we moved, we'd stay close to Grandma, Grandpa, and Bob."

"It's only two miles," Dad said.

Richard snorted.

"It would take more than an hour to walk," I said.

It didn't matter whether I liked it. Dad had a key. They had rented the house, and we would move again. Two miles is nothing to an adult with a car. But to a ten-year-old, it was like moving to another city. And it was in another school zone. I wouldn't be in a class with Bob. We wouldn't be able to walk to school together. So far, I was unimpressed; this street didn't have the tropical feel of Bob's house. It also meant I would be changing schools, yet again. And there were only ten days left in the school year.

Mom said, "We can get you a bicycle; it won't seem as far on a bike."

Dad opened the front door, and we all went in. The living room had an ugly green carpet on the floor, but the kitchen floor was cool and smooth to the touch. It looked like it had pieces of rock in it. Mom showed us the three bedrooms.

"Can I have my bedroom?" Richard asked.

Dad said, "We can talk about it."

Richard and I walked through the living room, into an enormous family room that extended into the backyard. The room had three walls with jalousie windows and a door to the outside. Mom opened the door, and we all stepped into the backyard.

Richard said, "Wow, look at this yard!"

I looked around at the wide-open space and *knew* he was thinking of baseball. And I could see what he was thinking. We could set up an infield with home plate, first, second, and third base. I could almost see the gears in Richard's brain. If this neighborhood had enough kids, there would be games in our backyard. That pleased me; I liked baseball too.

I was more interested in the dirt path and empty lots behind our backyard. It wasn't tropical with banana trees like Grandma's, but it had a wilderness feel to it. Maybe this wouldn't be too bad.

Mom came out with Jimmy. "It's a nice backyard. It will be perfect for a dog."

"A dog?" I said. "We're getting a dog?"

Mom looked at Dad.

He nodded. "This is the right time and right place. As soon as we settle in, we'll get a dog."

We'd been nagging Mom and Dad for a dog as long as I could remember. If this were a bribe, it was a good one, and I would hold Mom and Dad to it.

I agreed to share a bedroom with Jim so that Richard could have his own room. I didn't want to fight Richard over it, and having my room didn't seem important at the time.

A week after we moved in, we visited the Humane Society and adopted a young female dog. Gigi was tan and white with a cute curly tail and eyes that looked like she was wearing mascara. She was a basenji mix, a breed that doesn't bark. I fell in love with her as soon as I saw her. The rest of the family loved her, too, or at least, they weren't willing to argue with me.

# Chapter 6 ~ Family

The rental house was only two blocks from Sabal Palm Elementary. The school couldn't understand why Mom and Dad moved me to a new school so close to the end of the year. The teacher gave me a desk, introduced me to the class, and left me alone. I didn't even have time to learn where the bathrooms were.

Once school let out, I played with Gigi from early in the morning until bedtime. Together, we explored the empty lots behind our yard. They were a suburban wilderness where small green lizards climbed tree trunks and scores of songbirds hopped between the branches of trees. A distinctive *tok-tok-tok* from woodpeckers tapping on tree trunks filled the air.

Richard, four years older than me, was in junior high and usually hung out with friends. He had pulled apart roller skates and built a skateboard, and he would spend hours practicing tricks outside.

Richard was the oldest, and he would put up with me playing baseball if he needed an extra kid, but other than that, we never really "played" together. There was just too great an age difference for us to be close. And my younger brother, Jim, was only six. He could play Chutes and Ladders and Jax, but that was about it. Jim was good-natured, and unlike Richard, he never hit me or took my allowance.

When I started fourth grade in the fall, Jim should have been in first grade. It would have been fun to walk to school with him. And Mom registered him to start. But it didn't work out. During the first week, he climbed a tree and wouldn't get down. Since he had only just turned six, they decided he needed to wait another year. So Mom enrolled him in a preschool. A van picked him up in the morning and brought him home around five. I missed Bob. So, mostly I hung out with Gigi in the afternoon.

It was lonely, and I wasn't good at making friends. There was one girl on the block that I hung around with. But she usually stayed with her older sister, and I felt like I wasn't really welcome.

Around five-thirty, I walked to where Mom would turn off Sixth Avenue into our neighborhood. She pulled over so I could hop into the passenger seat. I had Mom all to myself for the five minutes it took to get home.

"Hi, sweetie, hop in," she said.

Sometimes, we would just sit and not say anything. It just felt good to be together. More often than not, she asked about school.

"How was school?" she asked.

I always answered, "Okay."

I didn't like talking about school. My handwriting was illegible, and I couldn't pass a spelling test. When they asked me to read out loud, I froze up and couldn't do it at all.

"Mr. Maquire stood on his head and drank water from a straw," I said.

"What?"

"He was showing us you can swallow without gravity."

"I think you have a good teacher," Mom said.

She was right. My fourth-grade teacher was the best teacher I'd ever had. Sometimes, that made it worse. It made me feel like I was disappointing him.

"Anything else good at school?" she asked.

"We did high jump today. I'm good at it. Mr. Small says I can compete in the high jump at the next track meet."

"It sounds like you had a good day."

I thought about it. Yes, today had been better than most days. A lot of days, I just sat in the back of the class and tried not to get noticed.

My classroom was an old wooden portable. Our desks still had inkwells, and the room even had a wood stove, which in North Miami Beach was entirely silly. Somehow, the portable sitting all by itself away from the main part of the school felt safe. But I still waited eagerly for the freedom of weekends. No one liked sitting at a school desk all day.

We went inside, and Mom pulled things out of the fridge to get dinner together. Tonight was pork chops, so Dad would grill them. Mom put the oven on and tossed in potatoes to bake. Then she pulled lettuce, celery, carrots, tomatoes, and cucumbers out to make a salad. She let me peel and cut the carrots.

Over dinner one night, Mom announced, "I got us passes to Monkey Jungle. We can go on Saturday. Who wants to go?"

* * *

We piled into the car and drove to Miami's Intracoastal Waterway, where a jungle-themed boat awaited us. Bob, Grandma, and Grandpa met us there, and we all set off on the "cruise" until we reached a wooden sign that read *World Famous Monkey Jungle*.

A troop of capuchin monkeys watched from above us in the trees, their chattering mingling with calls and songs of the birds. To me, it felt like we were in the heart of an African jungle.

We spent three hours seeing shows, wandering through the park, eating cheeseburgers and fries. Even Richard was in a good mood. He was actually nice to be around.

After a day in the jungle, we took the boat back to our cars and made our way home. Sunday was a chill day. We all needed to recover to be ready for Monday. Mom did laundry and grocery shopping. Richard and I took turns pushing the lawn mower, but Dad finished the job for us. It was a big backyard.

We rotated our weekend outings. We didn't get passes to Monkey Jungle often. More often, we went to the beach or Crandon Park Zoo. Most often we went to the beach. We had a public beach not too far from our house, but more often we went to one of the local motels where Mom would give the pool attendant a modest "tip," and he set up lounge chairs for her. Summer was the off-season, and the motels were never crowded. Our favorite, the Monaco, had a pool with a diving board and a slide.

Mom didn't work when we lived in New York. She came home tired, but I think she really liked the job. She said she had always had a knack for numbers and liked the people she worked with.

I remember one day on a school holiday, I took the city bus and met Mom for lunch. It was a real adventure, and I felt very grown-up. Before we left to eat, Mom introduced me to her boss and the people she worked with. Everyone made a fuss over me.

Her boss was a young man, much younger than Mom. Before we left for lunch, he pulled me over and said, "Your mom is a valuable member of our team."

His words filled me with pride. *That's my Mom he's talking about.*

\* \* \*

Life had settled into a comfortable pattern. Then, Mom announced we were moving again.

"Why?" I asked.

"Well, we want to own a house. This is a rental, and the landlord doesn't want to sell it."

I didn't cry, but I had to work hard not to. While I didn't love school, it sucked to think about changing schools again. And I liked our backyard. I even had some sort of friends on the block. It felt comfortable here.

"We won't move far," Mom said.

"That's what you said last time. Can I help pick the new house out?" I asked.

Mom and Dad looked at each other, and I knew they already had a place in mind. Kids have no rights.

To be fair, the new house was only a few blocks' walk from our rental and was a nicer house. It had a big backyard. It was still an easy walk to Sabal Palm Elementary, and closer for Richard to go to John F. Kennedy Junior High.

Dad figured I was old enough that I was a "young lady" and needed my own bedroom. So, Jim and Richard shared a room. Mom let me pick colors and furniture for my bedroom.

We lived at our house on Eighth Avenue for what felt like a long, long time, five years. It was the longest we had stayed in one place since leaving Hewlett. Dad may have felt I was a "young lady" who needed her own room, but he lost track of the fact that Richard was also growing up.

# Chapter 7 ~ Summer

Summer means freedom: no homework, no tests. No lying about what I was supposed to be reading rather than what I was reading. But the heat was hard to take, even for kids. Well, Florida was known for beautiful beaches and ocean. That was because it was hot so much of the year that it was too hard to do anything but swim. Unfortunately, we couldn't spend all the time at the beach, and we didn't have a pool.

It was Saturday morning, and Richard bounded onto the bed, joining Jimmy and me watching television in the only air-conditioned room in the house, our parents' bedroom. They were having coffee and reading the paper in the family room, with all the windows open and a large fan set up to give a breeze.

"I'm changing the channel," Richard said, glaring at the cartoon show *Jonny Quest*.

"There isn't anything good on," I said.

He flipped through the channels, eventually putting it back where we had it.

"You're right; there really isn't anything on," he said, leaving the room.

I lasted another ten minutes before heading to the kitchen for some cereal. Jimmy followed behind me.

"Can we use the sprinkler?" I asked.

"Sure, it's a good day for it," Mom said. "Make sure you both wear bathing suits."

"Okay," I said.

Jimmy fussed. "This one," he said.

"That's underwear," I said, handing him an actual bathing suit.

Temperatures in Miami could be brutal.

We ran the sprinkler in our backyard and played in our swimsuits. It helped us cool down. It wasn't as good as the beach or a pool. But it was right outside, and sometimes, that was good enough.

Most weekends, we headed to the beach. Mom would sit on her chair, read a book, and dip in the pool to cool down.

There was a city pool not too far from the house, and sometimes Mom would take us there. We would spend the afternoon splashing, swimming, and jumping off the high dive board. When she was too busy, I'd go with friends to an apartment complex a few blocks from our house, walk over, and pretend we lived there. I didn't take Jimmy. They would want an adult to be watching him. We were quiet and polite, careful not to splash or make lots of noise.

No one questioned us, but I figured some adults must have known we didn't live there.

I was so glad I knew how to swim. Lots of kids at my school couldn't do more than a weak dog paddle. They took our class to the pool once a week for lessons. Since I knew all the strokes, they let me work on diving. I couldn't remember not knowing how to swim.

Mom says she took us to a pool near Jones Beach in New York when I was three years old. And I have a memory that I'm sure is from that time. The toddler pool was a large, shallow, circular pool that was deeper in the center. I'd push off the wall and glide over the deeper center until I reached the shallow edge, then stand up. Evidently, I was oblivious to the fact that if I lost speed in the center, I wouldn't be able to stand.

We had swimming lessons at the YMCA in New York when we were fairly young, but by the time we went, I already knew how to float and do the doggy paddle. I wondered why Floridian parents didn't teach their kids to swim. With so much water around, it seemed strange.

During the week, Mom sent Jimmy back to Beacon Hill for a summer camp program, but she figured Richard and I were old enough to be on our own. Sabal Palm had an enrichment program, and sometimes, I went. It was so unlike regular school. It was great. I could spend the whole day working on an art project. They had a room set up with games, and they had basketballs for us to use. But the best thing was that I could go when I wanted and leave when I wanted.

Bob spent a lot of time at our house. Sometimes, Grandma dropped him off. But more often, he rode his bike and we would hang out. We walked to the 163rd Street shopping center, which had air-conditioned shops and a movie theater. On Tuesdays, the theater offered a double feature kids' matinee for $1.25.

But we braved the heat for our favorite places, bicycling to Sky Lake with fishing rods, buckets, and bread to use as bait. We spent the afternoon catching and releasing small fish. Only occasionally did we fall into the cool water, and never on purpose.

"Want to go to Greynolds today?" Bob asked.

"Sure," I said. And just like that, we had a plan for the afternoon.

The park had trails to walk on, a stone "castle" to climb up, and best of all, a lake with rowboats. We pulled cash out of our piggy banks and looked forward to being on the water. For me, being on the water was as good as being in the water.

The lack of structure to our weekends and summer days was an invitation to explore local points of interest and the freedom to find myself, to discover my place in nature, and to learn how to take charge of my happiness.

*Summer, hot and glorious, never lasted long enough.*

# Chapter 8 ~ Fall

I was sitting in my favorite reading corner at the base of a mango tree in our backyard. There was just the right amount of shade. The trunk felt right against my back, and the newly mowed lawn smelled of summer.

Then Mom called from the back door, "You need to come in and get ready. I'm taking you and Richard shopping."

"Mom, can't it wait?"

"No, you need school clothes."

I wanted to stay and read. But I closed my copy of *Gone With the Wind*, braced myself for my loss of freedom, and got up. I didn't care what I wore to school and hated shopping. Mom thought about clothes all the time. Well, she and Dad worked in the garment industry. She brought home samples and enjoyed dressing up. Today, she wore embroidered bell-bottom jeans and a pink shirt. Her hair was fresh from the salon, in a beehive of curls held in place by hairspray.

I was a tomboy. At home, all I wore were shorts, jeans, and T-shirts. Unfortunately, girls had to wear dresses or skirts to school. A fact that made going back to school even worse.

Every year, Mom tried to drum up enthusiasm for the start of the school year. We shopped, then went for ice cream. Every year, I tried to temper her enthusiasm that "this year will be great."

"Mom, no one cares if I wear an outfit that isn't brand new. Why don't we use the money for something important?"

"Like what?" Mom asked, ushering me into the house so we could get ready to go.

"Can I get a kitten?"

"That seems random. We have a dog. You love Gigi, so why would we get a cat?"

"Cats are cool, and if we got a kitten, I bet Gigi would love it."

"Dogs and cats don't get along."

"That's not true. I read that dogs treat kittens like puppies."

I had read the book *It's Like This, Cat.* The idea of adding a cat to our family felt exciting.

"You don't need a cat right now. You need a back-to-school outfit, and so does Richard. Put shoes on."

At least Mom hadn't said no to the idea of a cat.

"Richard, are you ready?" Mom called.

He didn't look happy either. But he was still on good behavior and didn't complain.

Mom took us to Jefferson's; its prices were better than at the mall. It was one of those stores that carried a bit of everything. They had color televisions on display, a jewelry section, and even a food counter that had hot dogs and ice cream. I found an outfit with a black-and-white checkered skirt and a red vest that I liked. Richard got pants and a new shirt. Chore done, Mom treated us to ice cream at the counter, and then we headed home. I tried to get back into reading my book.

I tried not to think about school, but it was hard. Mom's annual "new outfit" shopping had brought the event close and real. My days of summer were almost over. I didn't know that while fourth grade hadn't been too bad, fifth grade would be a nightmare. I didn't know just how bad school could be. But I was about to find out.

# Chapter 9 ~ Meter Stick

Mom said the first day of school was for making good impressions. She made sure we had a nice outfit and were under orders to behave ourselves. We were to be polite and helpful and do what the teachers asked of us. I wanted Mom to be proud of me and tried to be on my best behavior. I smiled, said hello, and tried to be a student that teachers might like to have in the classroom. But I wondered if the same expectation for making a good impression didn't apply to adults, in particular, to teachers.

If it were, Mrs. Maxwell might have greeted us by saying, *"Hello, welcome to fourth grade."*

There was no smile or hello to greet us. Mrs. Maxwell wore glasses and a skirt suit that made her look stern and official. Her brown hair was pulled into a tight bun, showing just a trace of gray. As soon as the bell rang, she held up a binder and said, "You'll need a notebook like this for daily work. It must be on your desk, ready for inspection at all times. Your work must always be neat."

I'd learn later that the students called her the Dragon. She never smiled, and her trademark was a meter stick that she brandished when she felt a student was not working hard enough.

"Hands on your desk," she would say to an unfortunate student. Then she waited while the victim laid hands flat on the desk.

I gave her lots of opportunities to use the device, and I have clear memories of her raising the stick and dramatically whipping it across my hands.

Mondays were risky for me. The day's schedule started with a penmanship lesson. We copied a paragraph from the blackboard onto lined paper. The work needed to be in cursive, and neatness was required. My hand had a mind of its own. The words would not stay on the line unless I stared at my hand as I worked. But if I looked away from the board to watch my hand, I couldn't remember how to spell the words.

It would be years before I was diagnosed with dyslexia, so I didn't know why I couldn't retain the spelling when I looked away from the board. All I knew was that the work was frustrating and that, no matter how hard I tried, my cursive was unacceptable. Even I could see it was hopeless. Some Mondays, she would ignore my sloppy work or even try to offer me some encouragement. It must have been obvious I was trying. Then there were days she lost patience, saying I could do it if I tried.

So I never knew when the smack of the meter stick would crack the room's silence and leave black and blue marks on my hands. Sometimes, penmanship lessons left me exhausted, afraid, in pain, and ashamed. My hands found their way into my pockets to keep others from seeing marks and bruises that seemed to be permanent fixtures.

As bad as Monday penmanship lessons felt, Friday spelling tests were worse. We were given a list of words on Monday. We needed to know how to spell, define, and use each word. I could never sleep on Thursday night and usually had a debilitating headache by the end of the school day on Friday.

The room was silent as Maxwell read from her notebook. "Number one is the word '*block.*'"

I wrote the word on my paper. It looked wrong. I had written the word *block* twenty times the night before, trying to memorize it. I knew it was wrong, but didn't know how to fix it. A knot formed in my stomach, and my hand shook as I wrote a sentence using the word on the line below my misspelled word. We had to write a sentence using the word, and I knew mine had at least two additional misspelled words. My hand was shaking as I imagined the meterstick against my fingers.

Maxwell moved and stood behind my desk, calling, "Number ten is '*Wednesday.*'" She hovered behind me, watching me write.

"Pencils down," she said. "Ann, remain in your seat." She collected our papers and dismissed the rest of the class to recess.

When the last classmate left the room, Mrs. Maxwell returned my paper to my desk and began her work with the red pen. She wielded the pen like a sword. When she was done, the paper was awash in red. It was a pathetic, wounded victim of my inability. I held still and silent, watching my hands, waiting for her to get the meter stick.

Instead, she stepped back and looked at me. Her anger made her larger and more dangerous. I looked out the window as she said, "I don't know why you won't do your work, but you don't belong in this class. Leave. Go to the kindergarten wing. That's where you belong."

As I left the classroom, something in me snapped. I never disobeyed teachers. And I couldn't do what she asked.

I walked away from the class, but turned toward the main office. There was no way I could go to the kindergarten wing, even if it meant disobeying my teacher. I had never been sent to the office, but I knew that teachers sent misbehaving students to the office. So that was where I went.

As I entered, the lady behind the counter motioned to the chairs outside the principal's office, where a dozen kids were already sitting. I waited through lunch and into the afternoon. My head was pounding, and tears threatened to escape and roll down my face. Once, the lady brought me some tissues. I kept replaying the scene in the classroom, feeling the shame over and over again. How would I ever face my class again?

I thought about the many times my hands had felt the blows of the meter stick and realized her words hurt far more. There was no way I could go back to class.

Eventually, it was my turn, and Mr. Keaton's door opened. The kind lady motioned me to go in.

I took a seat in front of Mr. Keaton's desk. He was young and looked less fearful than I expected.

"Ann, I don't have a note from your teacher. Tell me why you are here. What happened?"

I told him about the spelling tests I couldn't pass. I told him about the meterstick. I was crying as I told him about being told to go to the kindergarten room.

He wrote some notes in a book and looked at me. It was obvious he was at a loss for what to do.

"I'll talk with Mrs. Maxwell. She should not have said that to you. You've had a hard day, and I don't want to send you back to class until after I meet with Mrs. Maxwell."

"Thank you," I said, relieved that I wouldn't need to go back to the classroom.

"Is your mom at home? I could call and have you picked up."

"Mom and Dad both work. I'd rather not bother them."

He gave me a pass to the library for the rest of the afternoon.

All afternoon, I sat in the library, with my stomach twisted and hurting. Mr. Keaton would talk to Mrs. Maxwell. But he would also talk to my parents, I was sure of it, and it scared me.

Mom and Dad wanted me to "behave" in class and be respectful to my teacher. They made the message very clear. I'd watched them deal with Richard when they were called to the school when Richard got in trouble. Now they would get a call from the principal about me. Mrs.

Maxwell had been out of line, but I could also be in trouble.

I'd never talked to my parents about Mrs. Maxwell, never told them about being hit with the meterstick. There was too much shame, and I didn't want them to know about it. I felt sick to my stomach, and my head felt like it was splitting.

When the bell rang at three and school ended, I walked home. My head was killing me, and I could only peck at dinner. Mom and Dad left me alone. They knew I got really bad headaches. Mom hadn't said if the school called, and I didn't ask. I went to bed early, glad that tomorrow was Saturday.

In the morning, my headache was so bad that I stayed in my room with the lights out. Mom made me eat, and she was sympathetic about the headache.

"Did Mr. Keaton call you?" I asked.

"He did. He said he would talk with your teacher. We can talk about it when you feel better."

"I can't do what she wants me to do," I said.

"It's not your problem. Mr. Keaton will take care of it. Can I get you some aspirin?"

"Thanks."

I felt a bit better when she left, but it wasn't a great weekend. I braced myself for humiliation walking to school on Monday, but Mrs. Maxwell acted as if nothing had happened. *Did she even remember ordering me to the kindergarten wing?*

She said nothing about it, and soon selected another student to berate.

I wondered why she was a teacher; she didn't seem to like any students.

Everything I did was an effort to avoid attention. We were to put daily work in a basket on her desk. It was easier for me not to turn work in and take an F, rather than hear everything I'd done wrong. On spelling tests, I turned in a blank paper.

"If you don't do your work, you'll need to repeat fifth grade," she said.

I nodded, saying nothing.

Mom asked if things were any better at school.

"She leaves me alone," I said.

*Were things better at school?* I wasn't getting hit anymore. But I suspected that if I turned in messy work, the meterstick would return. It was safer not to turn work in.

I wondered if Mrs. Maxwell had always been like this, or if something had happened that broke her.

Then something happened that changed everything. A tall boy named Urial, who sat in the third row, did something that made Mrs. Maxwell angry enough to raise the meter stick, positioning it to give his hands a smack. Urial stood up, grabbed the stick from her hands, and raised it as if to hit her. The room went silent. He tossed the stick onto the floor, glared at her, and walked out of the room. No one moved. No one said a word.

Mrs. Maxwell broke the silence. "Open your readers to page thirty-five," she said. "Fifteen minutes of silent reading."

We all pulled our readers out and did as we were told. She circulated, checking we were on the right page. The meter stick remained on the floor.

The thing was, Urial didn't look guilty when he took the meter stick; he looked mad. He was mad *because* teachers aren't supposed to be like this. I knew that, but Urial *acted* on his knowledge.

*Why wasn't I able to stand up for myself like Urial?* I suspected he was leaving to go home, not to the principal's office. Why hadn't I just walked home? Urial was confident that he was right. *Why wasn't I so confident?*

At that moment, Urial became my hero. I wanted to be just like him.

His act of defiance felt like permission for my own rebellion. Well, a minor rebellion. It was so small no one noticed; I skipped school on Fridays. I skipped most Fridays and an occasional Monday. Not that I went anywhere or did anything fun. But it was better than being at school. I couldn't go anywhere because I figured people would know I should be in school. The irony was that I spent most of my time reading books. Still, missing school one day out of five meant missing a ton of instruction and set me even further behind.

At first, Mom and Dad didn't know. They left for work early, and my school started at eight. But then the school started calling, and Mom couldn't ignore that I wasn't in school. When the office called in the evening, I'd tell Mom I had a headache. It wasn't always a lie. After a while, Mom stopped asking why I stayed home.

Mom and Dad saw my report card grades. I was in danger of failing fifth grade. They just didn't know what to do about it. Mom stopped asking if things were any better at school. Dad never gave me a hard time about grades. His attitude was that not everyone was good at school, and that was okay. He left school to join the army as soon as he was old enough. Mom had been an excellent student who made grades, had friends, and liked school.

Mom knew I had problems with Mrs. Maxwell, but she never knew about the meter stick. I couldn't tell her. Mom thought teachers were like God. I didn't share her belief, but my own feelings were a mixed-up mess of guilt and fury. I had nightmares of Mrs. Maxwell beating me with her meter stick. I'd wake from the dream shaking, often with my pillow wet from tears.

I don't remember when I stopped dreaming of Maxwell, but some-times, I still dream of being powerless in a classroom. It's the worst feeling in the world.

The school year ended, and slowly, I embraced summer with a vengeance. I was old enough that Mom and Dad didn't insist they needed to know where I was every minute of every day. I rode my bike everywhere. But sometimes, I just stayed home and enjoyed the quiet and tried not to think about school at all. But I couldn't ignore the fact that summer was passing, and soon, I'd be returning to school.

It was fitting that we had a hurricane in following summer. My fifth-grade year had been a metaphorical storm, so why shouldn't nature throw a real one my way?

On August 21, we checked into the Dune Hotel on Miami Beach. Mom and Dad decided we needed a family vacation before school resumed. I think they felt that having us all together for a bonding experience would be a good idea. They had a wing that was "pet friendly," so we even took Gigi with us. Four of us and a dog in one room. We would either bond or kill each other.

Hurricane Cleo was offshore, and the predictions were for it to travel northeast and to miss Florida. With sunny skies, it didn't feel like we were in any danger. Richard was a keen surfer. He had his board with him and was enjoying the unusually big waves.

The storm had moved closer to the Atlantic coast, and Miami was now in a tropical storm watch. The hotel emptied, but Mom and Dad said we would wait longer, since we only lived forty-five minutes from the beach. They wanted to wait and see if the storm would move closer to us or not.

Sunday morning, Gigi escaped the room and went into the ocean after Richard. I ran after her, but I couldn't catch her as she dove into the waves and swam, trying to reach him. I'm not sure whether Richard saw me screaming by the beach or saw Gigi struggling in the water first. But he paddled over and pulled Gigi onto his board. They rode a wave onto shore together.

Sunday afternoon, the hotel staff moved the pool and beach furniture inside. The manager circulated and told guests that the lobby would be open all night for guests who couldn't make it home in time. At that point, the wind had picked up, and Dad decided we were safer staying put. The weather started getting scary around midnight. We could hear branches against the wall, and the windows were rattling. Dad moved a mattress into the closet. Mom, Jimmy, and I stayed in the closet, sitting on the mattress. Dad, Richard, and Gigi stayed in the bathroom. Our room was in an open corridor with the walkway exposed to the thundering rain. We were not tempted to make it to the hotel lobby.

We heard a window blow out, and then the rain and wind were in the room. When we emerged, coconuts littered the room. We gathered our belongings, checked out, and made our way home.

The drive took almost two hours. Trees were down, lights weren't working, and the water was too deep to drive through, which made our way home by taking detour after detour. We pulled into our neighborhood, seeing no evidence of lights. As we feared, our house had also lacked power. We had to empty the freezer and the refrigerator.

Children do not experience hurricanes the same way that adults do. I didn't process the potential loss of property, the impact on employment, and the cost of food replacement. But Hurricane Cleo provided a suitable endpoint to what had been a tremendously stormy and traumatic time in my life.

As summer ended, I hoped for a period of calm because I needed one.

# Chapter 10 ~ End Point: Sixth Grade

Mr. Keaton, the principal, asked me to come in and meet with him a week before school started. I was supposed to start sixth grade, but the school was considering having me repeat fifth grade. Mom reminded me that Bob had stayed back in third grade, and it wouldn't be the end of the world if I repeated fifth grade.

Bob missed school because he was in the hospital having an operation on his eye. I missed school because I didn't want to go and had been skipping. It might have been best to repeat the year; I hadn't learned much. My big concern was not wanting to ever be in Mrs. Maxwell's class again.

We met in Mr. Keaton's office.

"Come in and take a seat," he said, motioning to chairs across from where he sat at his desk. "Thank you both for coming in."

"Are you having a good summer?" he asked me.

I nodded, not knowing what to say. Summer was always good, even with hurricanes.

"I wanted to meet with you and your mom before we assign classes. Obviously, you had a rough time last year."

I nodded again and said, "If I need to do fifth grade again, will I have Mrs. Maxwell as a teacher?"

"You won't be in Mrs. Maxwell's class, but let's not get ahead of ourselves."

He handed me an article about the Everglades. "Take a few minutes and read this. Then we'll talk about it."

I could answer every question he asked. My problem wasn't reading silently. I loved reading. I just couldn't read aloud. I had no idea how to pronounce the words I was reading.

Then Mr. Keaton asked me to work on some arithmetic problems. I wasn't hopeless, but I made mistakes.

"We're going to put you in sixth grade. I think if you come to school regularly, you will do fine."

Mom said, "Thank you."

"Mrs. Rudnick, it will help if you could work with Ann on her multiplication tables. It will also help if you encourage regular attendance."

"I will," Mom said.

A few days later, my class assignment came in. When I saw my sixth-grade class was in a portable classroom again, I took it as an omen. Plus, my new teacher was a man, Mr. Anderson. Remembering how nice my fourth-grade teacher, Mr. Maquire, had been, I felt optimistic.

Mr. Anderson was friends with Mr. Maquire. For once in my life, I hoped my teacher had talked with a previous teacher about me. It would mean I wouldn't have to go through the awkward time when he learned all the things I couldn't do.

Mom really pitched in. She bought flashcards, and we worked on the multiplication tables every night. My memory was awful, but I got better. She also worked on my handwriting. That didn't get better, so she taught me to type.

My difficulty with spelling did not go away, but Mr. Anderson managed to avoid any form of public humiliation. He gave tests back to all students face down, so our grades were private. He didn't make a fuss about my limitations.

In November, they figured out I had dyslexia, and my learning issues became less mysterious. The diagnosis was almost accidental. The school was trying out a reading program where sentences were projected onto a screen. The program allowed the teacher to adjust the speed and determine the speed when student comprehension dropped off. The machine seemed out of place in our primitive portable classroom. Sitting in our seats, we read silently as the sentences crossed the screen. After a passage, the class took a multiple-choice quiz. I never missed a question. It didn't matter how fast a pace they set on the machine. For the first time, I found something academic at school that I excelled at. In fact, I was faster than just about everyone in my class.

That was when the guidance staff decided I had a learning disability and ordered additional testing. It turned out that many people with dyslexia found it easy to read silently and had problems reading aloud.I was something about problems coordinating decoding, pronunciation, and intonation. I didn't understand what they said, but I gathered that people with dyslexia often read quickly, understood what they read, and struggled with reading aloud. Well, that was me. It was nice to know I wasn't alone.

Mr. Anderson started asking for volunteers for class reading rather than randomly calling on students. He said that if I had issues reading aloud, it was likely that other students did too. He also started giving us time for silent reading. He alternated between written and oral book reports. It was fun to talk about books I'd enjoyed in front of the class. It turned out that students wanted to read more if they didn't always have to write a book report.

We visited the library once a month to select a book. But I read really fast and needed to go more often. I tried to figure out how to pick a book and found that paying attention to the author helped. I read all the books the school had by Paul Gallico. Then I came across a book by Hugh Walters called *Mission to Mercury*, about an international team of astronauts: an American, two British, and a Russian. To my delight, the book was part of a series with the same characters. I read through the full series.

When I finished the last book, I returned it to the school library and said I was sad because it was the last one in the series.

"You should try other science fiction authors," the school librarian said.

"Where should I look?" I asked.

"We don't have a separate section here, but I can help you find them."

They didn't have a separate section because they had only a few science fiction books. When I had run through all of them, I rode my bike to the public library to find more.

I was already a huge fan of everything related to the space program. Reading science fiction made me think about the science in the space program. I was hooked. Even at the public library, there weren't many science fiction books in the kids' section. There were more in the adult section.

The librarians wouldn't let me check books out from the adult section. No rules were keeping me from reading them while sitting in the library. It was a bonus that the library was air-conditioned.

* * *

It had been a good year, and for the first time, I was conflicted as summer approached. On the last day of sixth grade, there were cupcakes, punch, and music in the cafeteria. The school gave us an autograph book and time to sign each other's books and say goodbye. We even had time to visit former teachers, say goodbye, and have them write in our books.

I'd only been at Sabal Palm for three years. I visited Mr. Maquire and Mr. Anderson, and they both wrote about how much they enjoyed having me as a student. It made me want to cry about leaving. I went by the library, and the librarian added her good wishes. I didn't have many school friends, but I took the time to connect with the ones I liked. I found Urial Levi, and we had a good time talking about Mrs. Maxwell.

"She's an asshole," he said. "She shouldn't be allowed to teach."

"Yeah, I know."

"Really, I told my folks about what she does, and they filed a complaint. She shouldn't be in the classroom. Did your folks complain?"

"I never told them," I said.

"You should have. She had no reason to hit you." I shrugged.

He looked surprised, but didn't press the point. I think he saw I was embarrassed.

Urial was a good student who usually did well in school. I think that was what gave him the confidence to walk out of the room when Maxwell went to hit him.

I didn't have his confidence, his assurance that he was worthy of better behavior from his teacher. I hadn't had that kind of self-assurance. But maybe I could. Maybe I should.

The school day ended, and I took my time walking home, playing the conversation with Urial over and over in my head. Could I be a good student? Mr. Anderson and Mr. Maquire thought so. Mr. Keaton thought so.

My grades hadn't been bad in sixth grade. Well, spelling was always an F. But mostly, I made average grades. Could I have done better? I hadn't really tried to make good grades. It had been enough not to fail.

Next year, I'd be at a new school. *Could I do well?*

Mostly, what I wanted was the confidence Urial had. To know deep down that a teacher shouldn't ever hit me? And I wondered what it would feel like to earn an A or a B.

That night at dinner, Dad asked me how I felt about starting at the big kids' school after summer.

"I'm nervous," I said.

"Why?"

"I want to make grades. It's a new school, and I want to make As and Bs."

Richard laughed.

Mom glared at Richard, then said, "You did much better this last year. I think it's great you want to continue improving. I'll be happy to help with homework or study."

Dad said, "I like that you want good grades, and I think you can do it. How about I add some incentives? For every report card A, I'll give you a five-dollar bonus. If you make the honor roll, the bonus will be fifteen dollars."

"Thanks," I said. "What's honor roll?"

Richard said, "All As and Bs."

"Okay," I said, thinking if they have spelling tests, I was toast. But it was nice that Dad offered a bonus.

*Only, was he offering an insane amount of money because he knew I couldn't do it?*

# Chapter 11 ~ Becoming A Student

Junior High felt like a series of track sprints. With six classes separated by five minutes to move between classes, it felt like you never got to just take a minute. It wasn't just the rush to get from one part of the school to the next. It was disorienting to be working on math, shutting it down, and jumping into English or History. Well, the same teacher taught History and English, so we didn't need to change classrooms. The downside was that she assigned textbook questions for both subjects, and spelling and handwriting counted for both History and English.

Every night after dinner, I went to my room, sat at my desk, and concentrated on homework. The desk was planks of wood with a contact paper surface, but it was *my desk*. This was the first time I cared about school and was trying to be a good student.

There was always homework because I wanted my work to look normal, neat, and without misspelled words. And I had a plan of action. I'd bought a *Webster's Unabridged Dictionary* from a pawnshop. The book was massive and had a place of honor on my makeshift desk. I did a rough draft of each assignment, underlined each word that I suspected I'd spelled wrong, and spent hours looking them up in my dictionary. News break: it takes a long time to look words up when you don't know how to spell them.

Mrs. Sheffield's Math class was my only relief from dictionary drudgery. She always assigned ten to fifteen problems for homework.

When we entered the classroom, the answers, but not the worked solutions, were neatly listed on the board. We checked that we had the right answers before volunteering to write our solutions, showing all the steps to the class. Most of the students waited, and then just copied the work. I had mine done and would wait for a difficult problem to volunteer.

"Who has the correct answer to number ten?" she asked.

I raised my hand and went to the board.

Mrs. Sheffield didn't always call on me, but I liked it when she did. It was fun to show that I could work the harder problems and fun to explain the steps. It was the first time I got to feel what it was like to be "good" at something at school. It felt even better to know that other students found the work difficult.

My Resource Class was supposed to give me skills to overcome the issue I had with dyslexia and spelling. Mrs. Campbell was kind and made a genuine effort to help me. At the start of the year, we had a conference to identify strategies for my education plan.

"Ann, what words can you spell?" she asked.

I thought hard before answering. "I can spell words like cat, dog, and rat," I said.

"Words with three letters?" she asked.

"I guess so."

Every day, she gave me words to memorize. If I wrote each word ten times, I could hold on to them for the quiz. Unfortunately, a few days later, it was like I'd never seen the words before. We also worked on cursive handwriting. We made some progress, but my efforts were still embarrassing.

"Well, if you become a doctor, you'll fit right in," she said.

Mrs. Campbell might not have helped me learn to spell or improve my handwriting, but it was good to have a teacher acknowledge my difficulty and not attribute failure to laziness. That, even by itself, made a difference.

\* \* \*

The larger school brought together students I hadn't known in elementary school, creating a new social landscape. Among them was Marianne, who shared my passion for science fiction. We bonded over book recommendations and discussions about our favorite authors during Gym class. Another new friend, Phylece, had attended Sabal Palm, but we hadn't shared any classes. She said she was intrigued by the fact I didn't have many friends and didn't seem to care. Her own lack of friends deeply troubled her. Discovering we lived nearby, we quickly became best friends.

It was fun to be back in the same school as Bob again. Grandma used our address to enroll him because JFK Junior High was a good school. He carried his trumpet in a bike basket and played "Reveille" each morning for the hoisting of the flag.

I watched when I could, even though it made me a few minutes late to homeroom.

"That's my uncle Bob," I said to Sharon, the school secretary who brought the flag out in the morning.

She looked confused, then said, "He can't be an uncle. He's a kid."

"He's a kid, and he's my uncle," I said.

Bob and I weren't in classes together, but we met up at lunch and again after school. For twenty-five cents, we could order a Coke float from the counter at Glades Drug Store. Bob was my best friend. I was a tomboy who liked baseball, climbing trees, and fishing. I didn't get along with the girls I went to school with.

Girls were required to wear dresses or skirts. Mom picked mine out, and I didn't care what they were like. Our homeroom teacher would inspect our outfits each day. As we lined up, she would move down the line using a ruler to check our skirts.

"Carol, go to the office, your skirt is almost three inches above the knee!"

"Sally, I'll let you off this time, but it really is a bit more than two inches. Tell your mother to be more careful when hemming your clothes."

She didn't bother to measure mine. She just gave me a quick look before moving on to the next girl. The other girls snickered, and one playfully smacked my shoulder. It wasn't just the clothes, though I couldn't figure out why they were so keen on hemming their skirts. Makeup and boys held no interest for me. Anyway, making new friends wasn't high on my goal list; doing well in school was.

The first report card of the year arrived, and I was thrilled to see my hard work had paid off! I earned As in Math, Art, Chorus, and Gym. History brought a B, and English a C. Overall, I made the honor roll.

I presented the card to Dad. "You don't need to pay for the grades in Art, Chorus, or PE," I said.

He nodded and gave me ten dollars. "I owe you another ten, but it will need to wait until next week."

I was thrilled with the ten dollars. I'd never had so much money all at once.

A week later, my counselor called me to her office, a small room behind the library. Mrs. Smith was a small, older woman with silver hair and glasses.

"It's good to see you doing so well here at JFK. Mrs. Sheffield thinks you have a talent for math."

"It's my favorite class," I said.

"That's why I called you in this morning. We think you should be in a more advanced class, so I've adjusted your schedule."

She handed me a piece of paper with a new schedule. Everything was the same except my Math class.

"Why? I love Mrs. Sheffield's class."

"The class you are in is for students who struggle. Mrs. Sheffield thinks you need a more advanced class."

"Do I have to go? Math's my favorite class." It was also the only academic class in which I earned an A.

"I want you to try the new class. If it doesn't work out, we can move you back."

The first day, I was so lost, I didn't see how both classes could be seventh-grade math. They used a different textbook and were learning topics I'd never heard of. That night, I opened the textbook and worked from the first chapter all the way to where our current assignment was. I didn't work on any other subjects, and it took me all night.

When the teacher asked for volunteers to put a problem on the board, I raised my hand, and I noticed that my hand was one of only three raised.

"You have number six done?" she asked

I nodded.

She seemed surprised. "Put it on the board." She looked at my work. "Good job."

The new class was hard, and I discovered my lack of arithmetic skills held me back. I still didn't know my multiplication tables, so homework took a long time. Even so, when I only made a C in Math on the next grading period, I felt devastated and asked to see my guidance counselor, Mrs. Smith.

"You said I could go back if the new class didn't work out," I said.

"Your new teacher says you are doing well."

"I only made a C."

"Ann, the C in your new class means more than an A in your old, low-level class. Give it another grade period."

It wasn't fair. Why would they put me in a harder class when I was doing well? But the term "low-level class" stung. But she was right.

My A returned the next report period, and I made the honor roll. This time, Dad was ready and had twenty dollars set aside for my reward.

* * *

A lot of the girls at JFK were vicious and targeted me. I didn't dress like them, wear makeup, or talk about boys. They chose the Physical Education class to play cruel jokes and torment me. We had to change into gym clothes at the start of the period, then shower and change before going to our next class.

The "cool" girls delighted in taking my brown-bag lunch from my bag, placing it on a bench, and sitting on it to squash it flat.

It happened repeatedly, and each time my anger increased. It wasn't that I didn't know who was responsible; I just didn't know what to do about it. Then I remembered the time Richard had challenged a bully at Oak Grove Elementary to meet him after school. Richard fought with the boy, and the bullying stopped.

I challenged the group leader, a blond girl who wore makeup, to meet me at the bike rack after school. She came with her friends. Other kids were hanging around, and they quickly formed a ring, giving us space. She seemed confused about why I had asked her to meet me.

"What?" she asked.

"Leave my stuff alone," I said.

Her friends were giggling and having a good time.

"Like what?" she said, rolling her eyes.

My chest hurt, and I felt a warm flush on my face. I hated her and her stupid gallery.

"Leave my bag and my lunch alone at Gym," I said.

She smirked. "Lunch? Do you bring lunch?"

The giggling was louder and blocked everything else out. I don't even remember rushing her, but I must have. My hands were fists, bashing her. I hit her in the face and kept hitting her. Then she was on the ground, and teachers were holding me back. I would have hit her again. I wanted to.

They called Mom and Dad and made them come to the school. I had lunch detention for a week.

Phylece and Maryann couldn't believe what I'd done when they heard about it. Bob remembered Richard's fights and laughed.

Mom was angry, but so was I.

"Why was it okay for Richard to beat up kids and not me?"

"It wasn't okay for Richard, and it was even less appropriate for you."

I was now officially very weird, but no one touched my stuff in Gym class again. They left me alone. Well, almost everyone left me alone, but I was okay with that.

# Chapter 12 ~ Outside Influences

My family was changing. My brothers and I were growing up and spending more time away from the house. I was in junior high, and Richard was in high school. We were spending time with friends. Phylece and I alternated spending time at her house and mine. Her father was a post office manager who loved to garden and seemed to always be building something out of wood. Florence, Phylece's mom, stayed home during the day. I ate dinner at her house often. Florence was a good cook, and Phylece and her sister would set the table and clean up after the meal. I was jealous that Phylece had a sister.

Richard spent time with his friends. They didn't take school seriously. They lived for weekends when they could head to the beach. Sometimes, they didn't wait for the weekend and headed to the beach instead of school. When they came over to the house, they used skateboards or listened to music.

When we moved into our house on Eighth Place, Mom and Dad decided that I needed a room of my own, and Richard and Jim would share.

"You're a young lady now, and you need privacy," Mom said.

They missed the fact that Richard was also growing up. Before we knew it, he was in high school and driving. And he was spending time with girls. Poor Jimmy sometimes ended up on the living room couch.

Mom and Dad also wanted time to themselves and liked to go out on Saturday nights. The problem was Richard was a teen, and so were the friends he invited over. While Mom and Dad were out, Richard and his friends took over the living room and family room of our house, hitting the home bar for drinks, smoking, and playing loud music.

Jim and I hid out in Mom and Dad's bedroom, watching television, although it was hard to hear the show over the music.

One night while the party was raging, I walked into the kitchen to get snacks. Joey, one of Richard's friends, sat at the kitchen table, drinking a bottle of beer and snacking on an open bag of potato chips.

"I like your pj's," Joe said.

I was flustered and embarrassed about wearing pajamas with feet.

"Thanks," I said, taking my cookies and rushing back to Mom's room to join Jim.

Jim helped himself to a cookie. We watched *Gilligan's Island* and *My Favorite Martian*. When I went out for more snacks, some of Richard's friends were cleaning up. They took the empty beer bottles and other trash out of the house.

Mom and Dad had to know about the gatherings. The house smelled of smoke, and I'd seen burns on the carpet. I don't think they ever told Richard he *couldn't* have friends over, but I noticed they were always gone before my parents got home.

Their drinking was a big issue for me. I didn't like it when Mom and Dad drank, which they did often. Mom drank gin, Dad drank scotch. Now I had Richard and his friends to add to my discomfort at home. It bothered me a lot; they were only sixteen, older kids, but still kids.

It infuriated me that Mom and Dad didn't take any action to stop the parties. Richard wasn't great at cleaning up, so I figured they knew about the parties.

*Why didn't they at least tell Richard to leave the booze alone?*

\* \* \*

One Saturday night, the sound of a crash woke me up. There were police sirens. I jumped up to see what was going on.

I walked out of my room and walked to the living room window. Pushing the curtains aside, I could see Richard's car half on the sidewalk. A police car was next to it, and Richard and Dad were talking to an officer. A girl sat on the front passenger seat. She was hunched over and looked really young. I wondered if she was injured or drunk.

The officer wanted to take Richard and the girl to the police station.

"We're done for tonight. We'll do that in the morning," Dad said.

I was standing in the living room when they came into the house. Dad had his hand on Richard's arm and was almost dragging him into the house. It might have been that he wasn't able to walk on his own.

When he saw me, he said, "Go back to bed."

I went to my room, but left the door cracked open to hear.

Dad called the girl's parents, and I guessed they would be coming over to get her. They moved to the kitchen, and I couldn't hear what they were saying.

Eventually, I turned the lights off and went to bed. But not to sleep. I was up most of the night. *Richard had been driving and drinking. Would he end up in jail? I had heard crashes. What did he hit?*

He wasn't the best older brother in the world, but he was my brother. I didn't want him in jail. And then there was a crash. Was anyone hurt?

Slowly, I pieced together the details. After everyone in the house had gone to bed, Richard took his girlfriend for a drive in his car. Only, she took a bottle of liquor from the house before they left. They drove to Sky Lake, an area that had a few upscale houses, but was mostly undeveloped land with lots of undeveloped land covered with Florida scrub. They parked and were drinking when an officer approached them and tried to take Richard's keys.

Richard wouldn't give up the keys. He started the car and raced off. The officer followed him, chasing him through North Miami Beach all the way to our house. Richard crashed through our mailbox and into the neighbor's car. Then, backing up, he hit Mom's car.

The incident left me with an upset stomach. I was intimidated by Richard. But he was my brother, and I hoped he wasn't in too much trouble. There were a lot of angry words and yelling the next day. And for a long time, the Saturday night parties were gone.

Many, many years later, I asked Richard about the incident. He filled me in on most of the details. I asked what consequences he faced. He'd lost his driver's license for six months.

"Did Dad ground you?"

Richard laughed. "Dad never grounded me for anything."

I know my parents weren't good about "consequences." They never punished me for skipping school or making a mess while taking batteries apart. *Should they have?*

I have no memories of spankings, timeouts, or any punishments for me, Richard, or Jim. The only consequences were those imposed by the schools where we spent our days and, for Richard, by the police.

*Did it matter?* I turned out okay. So did Richard and Jim. Maybe it didn't matter, but sometimes the chaos was uncomfortable.

# Chapter 13 ~ Expanding World

Relatives can be important if they are part of your life, or unimportant if they are names you hear about but rarely see. Sometimes, the world shifts, and people take on new levels of importance. The same thing can be true for friends. David had been my best friend in Hewlett. Then, my family moved and we drifted apart I missed David, but gradually, I found new friends.

When we moved, we were close to Mom's family, but farther from Dad's. That changed. When the weather cooled late in October, Grandpa Harry and Grandma Ester arrived as "snowbirds" for two months, escaping the cold of Brooklyn. They were on Dad's side of the family.

Grandpa came into the house carrying their two small suitcases and looked at the large living room.

"What a nice house!" he said.

"Thanks, we like it," Dad said.

One afternoon, I came home and found Grandpa sitting in front of the living room television, watching a newscast. They were showing highlights of the Apollo 11 mission.

"Hi Grandpa, isn't it cool?"

"What kind of show is this?" he asked.

When Grandpa said "show," he was talking about television comedy or drama. He was obviously confused.

"It's not a show. It's news," I said.

He shook his head. "I don't understand what they're doing."

"They sent a rocket into space. The small capsule at the top had three men in it. The rocket took them to the moon."

"They make shows about strange things," he said.

I tried to think about what to say. The best I could do was to repeat that it was the news, and reporters shared what was happening or what had happened. Grandpa just didn't understand television. He was a first-generation American, and his English was limited. He didn't understand technology and thought watching television was like watching a play.

I pointed to the image on the television. "That's Neil Armstrong, the first man to walk on the moon."

Grandpa put his glass of water down on the table. "I don't understand why anyone would make a show like this."

"Grandpa, again, it's not a show; it's news."

He laughed, shaking his head in disbelief, and patted me on my back as if to say he loved me even if I had strange ideas.

I really didn't mind sharing my room or the frustration of dealing with their old-world notions. It was great having them stay with us. And I was a bit sad a few years later when Dad helped them rent an apartment, so they could move to Miami.

We visited every Sunday. Sometimes, Dad brought them to the house. Other times, we went to their apartment complex and swam in the pool. Eventually, Dad opened his own business and was doing very well. He bought them a condominium unit across from a temple where Grandpa could walk to services on Saturdays.

I had a tight group of friends now, and after school, Bob and Phylece often came to the house with me. On weekends, the group expanded to include Maryann, Debbi, Wendy, Mark, and Glen.

Wendy, Bob, Glen, and I had a band. Well, we played music together.

Wendy sang and played guitar. I played guitar and sang backup vocals. Glen was on the drums, and Bob played his trumpet. We had fun and even played at a nursing home. Wendy was Bob's first crush, and Grandma got angry when they disappeared into the bedroom. Glen was a bit older and had a retired mail truck. They only had three wheels, and you could drive them once you were fourteen.

We still rode bikes lots of places. The bus system gave us infinitely more choices for weekends. Phylece and I often went downtown. Taking the bus was an adventure, involving several transfers and landing downtown amid a sea of adults we didn't know. The high-rise buildings and busy streets, and the symphony of city sounds made us feel we had traveled to an exotic, far-off, distant land. We would visit her uncle's jewelry store in the Seybold Building, window shop in the downtown stores, and then go to the enormous downtown library.

Sometimes, we ventured further and visited Vizcaya, a former Italian villa now owned by the city as a museum of Renaissance gardens, architecture, and furnishings. But my favorite by far was our trips to the Miami Seaquarium. Student tickets were just $1.25. Usually, it was Bob, Phylece, my brother Jim, and me. I never tired of looking at the small aquariums filled with tropical fish. We didn't always stick together the whole day. My friends were more interested in dolphin shows than looking at aquariums.

On one visit, I bought a book, *Creatures of the Sea,* from the gift shop. When I was paying, the attendant mentioned that the author, Captain Gray, was in his office down by the collection boats in the marina, and I could stop by to meet him.

I looked and found a door with his name, and after pondering the audacity of my actions, I knocked.

"Come in," the voice answered.

I opened the door and entered. Captain Gray looked just like his picture on the back of my book.

"Could you sign my book?" I asked.

"Sure," he said, reaching for it and signing it with a flourish.

While he was signing, he asked, "What's your favorite part of the aquarium?"

"The small tanks with the tropical fish."

"They're extraordinary. Some of the fish come from here in Florida, and my divers collect them. Others are from Fiji and Hawaii."

We talked about the care and feeding of the marine animals. He was gracious and treated me with respect, making me feel like an important person. Bob and Phylece were suitably impressed with the autographed book and story. I must have read his book cover to cover at least ten times.

I had a Kodak Instamatic film camera and loved capturing a close-up of wildlife at the aquarium. The dolphin shows always arranged a "photo opportunity," and there were iguanas, flamingos, and Galapagos tortoises. I had to be selective because I usually bought the small twelve-shot film canister and had to pay for developing the film.

Aunt Naomi and Uncle Sid lived on our street back in Hewlett. They often came to visit us in Miami, and Uncle Sid looked at my photographs. I hadn't known he was a professional photographer, working for Doubleday Books. He told me that when I was older, he would teach me nature photography with a real camera.

He was good to his word. When I was in high school, I bought a 35-mm Olympus camera, and he took me to the Florida Everglades, giving me tips on working with wildlife. Together, we photographed herons, alligators, and birds of prey soaring through the endless sea of grasses that make up the incredible Florida Everglades.

"Why are we working with black-and-white film?" I asked Uncle Sid.

"Eventually, I expect you will want to work. But starting with black-

and-white will help you concentrate on composition in your pictures."

Today, when I take pictures, I hear Uncle Sid's voice urging me to slow down and compose each shot.

I visited Grandma and Grandpa on my own, first by bus, and then by car when I was old enough to drive. It was part of my growing world, and I loved baking cookies with Grandma. They were observant, conservative Jews, and at first, he didn't understand that in December, near Christmas, they would receive many requests for donations from charities. Once Grandpa understood, he wanted to help all of them.

It became a Christmas-time ritual. I would drive over, and he would have the letters and his checkbook ready.

"This is my balance. We have already paid our bills," he would say.

I opened all the letters and lined them up, then calculated how much he could give each organization. He had me calculate it so that he was left with ten dollars in his account. Everyone received a donation, although sometimes he would write a check for as little as five dollars.

Today, I find it hard to say no when asked for a donation. Grandpa Harry is part of who I am. And for that, I am grateful.

# Chapter 14 ~ Reprieve

As seventh grade ended, it felt like I'd been running a marathon, and now, it was over. No more alarm clock going off at five-thirty, so I could work on math. No more papers, tests, and homework. I'd made honor roll and earned my bonus, and I felt almost giddy about a summer break with freedom to decompress.

They were sending us to Blue Star, a Jewish summer camp in North Carolina. I would have been happy to chill at home, but Dad's new business partner was sending his kids, and encouraged Mom and Dad to send us as well. I understood it was expensive and a privilege to go. Evidently, Dad's business was doing well, and they had money to give us the experience. They weren't sending Richard. He had gone to a summer camp while we lived in Hewlett. They felt it was time for me and Jimmy to go.

So, armed with a list from camp, we shopped for T-shirts, shorts, bathing suits, long pants, and long-sleeved shirts. Mom wrote our names on each tag with a marker, and we packed our summer camp trunks. On Saturday afternoon, we boarded a sleek Greyhound bus along with a full load of other campers heading for Blue Star. Jim and I waved goodbye to Mom and Dad as the bus pulled away from the station.

The ride was twelve hours long, with stops for meals and to stretch our legs. The counselors shared stories about what we would be doing at camp. After a dinner picnic of cold-cut sandwiches and a Kool-Aid drink, we returned to the bus at sunset, spent the next two hours singing songs like "Red Rover," "Bingo," and "One Hundred Bottles of Beer." After a while, they passed out pillows, dimmed the lights, and urged us to relax or sleep.

In the morning, the bus wound its way upward through the mountain roads; from the elevated seat, the view was of the valleys and ridges. I couldn't even see the road, and it felt like we were flying. Jim was equally awestruck. Before long, we came to a private road with a sign saying, *Welcome To Blue Star*, and we pulled up to a flat field by a lake and the dining hall.

We filed off the bus and rushed into the dining hall, taking seats at tables with dishes, silverware, and glasses. Camp staff brought out family-style platters of pancakes, fruit, and pitchers of orange juice.

"Pass the platters to the right. Start with one pancake, and we will refill the platters for seconds."

The platter made its way around the table.

"There's no bacon," Jimmy said.

Some campers at the table grinned, and others giggled.

"This is a Jewish camp," I whispered to Jim. "No bacon or ham."

Jimmy helped himself to a pancake that covered the entire plate and poured maple syrup over it. I did the same. The food was hot and good.

The room was bright and cheery, with large windows allowing sunlight to fill the room. Outside was a lake, with a long wooden platform along the shore, and an area roped off into swim lanes.

I asked one of the older kids at the table. "Do we swim laps?"

She was a returning camper. "Some campers do. We all have swim time. I'm still in lessons, so I don't do laps."

Pointing to the small fleet of tiny sailboats. "Will we get to sail?"

She laughed. "They're going to tell you all about this stuff, just wait. But yes, you can sign up for sailing."

I cleaned the last bite of pancake from my plate and considered taking another since the platter had been refilled and sat near me.

Jim looked at the plate too. "Want to share one?"

I took a pancake, cut it in half, and added it to his plate. We were digging in when a woman walked to the front of the room to address us.

"Welcome to Blue Star," she said. "I'm Cathy, the camp director. I'm excited to share the start of summer with you. How many of you are returning campers?"

I looked around, and there were a few hands in the air, but most of us were new.

"Welcome back," Cathy said. "And to our new campers, a big welcome to our camp family. You're going to have a marvelous summer."

She paused while the staff cleared the last plates and platters from the table.

"This is our dining room, where you will come for all your meals. Each cabin has eight campers, and the tables have settings for eight. We find that campers who share meals tend to make friends quickly. That's our goal, so we ask that you sit with your cabin at meal times."

I looked at Jim, who had edged closer to me.

Cathy continued, "In a few minutes, counselors will be calling you up by name to take you to your cabins."

"What about our trunks?" a girl at my table asked.

"They are being sorted and delivered to your cabin," Cathy said.

Within minutes, the first counselor called from a list of names, and the group followed him out the door.

As they left, Jim said, "Do I have to go?"

"Yes, you need to meet the campers in your group. Don't worry, we'll see each other at meals."

Until that point, I don't think he understood we wouldn't be staying together at the camp. He was in the second group called, and he somewhat reluctantly left the table.

When they called my group, I followed Shelly, a tall girl who sat behind me on the bus. While it felt good to be walking and stretching my legs, by the time we got to our cabin, I was breathing hard. Thank God we didn't have to carry our trunks up. The other six campers were already in the room. Shelly and I were the only campers from Florida.

"Pick a bed," a girl sitting on a bottom bunk said. "They all suck, but it's what they have."

There weren't any bottom bunks left. I took the top one near a window and climbed up to try it out. The bed felt fine. I wondered what she was used to sleeping on.

I learned that Katie complained about everything: the beds were awful, the food inedible. She wasn't the only one. The cabin was nice. It reminded me a bit of the room I'd bunked in with Bob, Richard, and Jimmy back at my grandparents' house. Our bunks were at least as good as the ones I remembered.

And the food was awesome. The first time the camp served fried chicken, I marveled at the wonder of not having an older brother snatch the last piece before I'd eaten my first one. I loved my mom, but she was never a good cook, and she was so overworked that she did what she could to piece our meals together. Camp food was a step up.

When we selected camp activities for two weeks at a time, we would pick different activities for each session. There were limited spots available for each, so if something was closed, we could put our names on a list for the next session. We all had to take swimming; it was a required course.

I was ecstatic that I scored sailing on my first try. The little boats were called prams.

Charlie pointed out the centerboard, the rudder, and the boom.

"Go ahead and sit next to the rudder," he said.

I climbed in and felt the boat rock gently.

"Insert the centerboard into the slot," he said.

We all followed his directions.

We had a lecture in the classroom before going out to the boats, so I knew about holding the mainsail line and the rudder and how to use the sail to figure out the direction of the wind.

Right then, a gust of wind came out of nowhere, and the person next to me forgot to release the rope to the sail. The little boat tipped over.

"Shit," Shelly said, looking like a drowned rat as she pulled herself onto the dock.

Only her pride was hurt, but it took three counselors to get the pram upright and baled out. No one else forgot to release the line when an unexpected gust came out of nowhere. I loved sailing and had fun navigating and exploring every part of that mountain lake. Riflery was almost as much fun.

"Molotov!" my instructor called out when she checked my paper target and found my first bullseye. I loved the feeling of lying on the ground, holding the rifle, and using the sight to line up the target. Her praise filled me with pride.

Over the summer, I rotated through archery, photography, hiking, and "nature", where we cared for small animals. I didn't have to take swim lessons, but I started my morning with ten laps in the lake. The cold water encouraged us to swim fast. You could get out as soon as you finished ten laps; I did so quickly. The best time of the day was the afternoon hikes on the mountain trails, learning the names of plants and picking wild blueberries.

It was my longest time away from home, and like others, I got homesick. We could line up at the phone booth and call once a week. I remember returning to my bunk bed and working hard not to cry in front of the girls in my cabin. Eight weeks was a long time to be away from my home, my dog, and Mom and Dad. But on the whole, I was having a good time and was glad to be at Blue Star.

I looked up at the knock on the door, and a male counselor waited patiently. It was Jimmy's counselor again. Getting up, I walked to the door.

"Does he need me?" I asked.

"Yes. He's having a bad day."

At eight years old, Jim was in the program for the youngest campers. Most of the kids in his group came for two weeks, then went home. Mom and Dad registered us for the full, eight-week program. He cried a lot.

I walked down the mountain path to his cabin. He was sitting outside on a bench.

"Hey, what's up?" I asked.

"I want to go home."

"We'll be going home soon enough. You should try to enjoy stuff here."

"Like what?"

"I don't know. I like sailing. Do you?"

"We don't go sailing."

That was the problem: the youngest kids had limited activities. I guess they were afraid they would get hurt with some things we did. And Jim had to take swimming lessons.

I wished there were more I could do for Jim. He seemed sad all the time.

Then, when we were days away from leaving, he got sick, and we weren't allowed on the Greyhound bus back to Florida. We had to stay a few more days for his fever to break.

Dad had one of his truck driver friends pick us up and take us back to Florida. Jim said he would never go to camp again.

I also missed home and wasn't sure I wanted to spend another summer at Blue Star. Learning new things without papers to write and no tests felt awesome. I was good at lots of things at camp, and it gave me confidence that I hadn't gained at school, where everything was hard. And I loved the North Carolina mountains.

But like Jim, I was homesick, and I felt out of place in a Jewish camp. All the campers had a Jewish education, and I had never learned to read Hebrew. We had sunset Sabbath services on the mountain. The open temple provided spectacular views. I loved the music of the services.

My family wasn't particularly observant. We considered ourselves Jewish and observed the holidays, but we hadn't belonged to a temple since leaving Hewlett to move to Florida. We didn't join another temple until Richard was old enough to study for his bar mitzvah. Mom and Dad didn't maintain the membership or enroll me in religious school, partially because I was a girl, and partially because I was already having so much trouble with school.

The kids and the counselor didn't make a big deal about my lack of Hebrew, but I did feel somewhat out of place. I felt like an outsider, and it wasn't a good feeling.

Summer passed quickly. When Jimmy caught the flu and we had to stay another week, it was hard. All my friends left. Blue Star became the site for Temples across the country to train "youth leaders." I had nothing in common with the newly arriving teens, and I stayed with Jimmy while we waited for Dad's friend to pick us up and drive us home.

It wasn't as cool as going home in a Greyhound, but we were so happy to be going home that we didn't care. Mom made a big fuss when we pulled into the driveway.

"We expected you home almost ten days ago," Mom said.

"I'm sorry I got sick," Jim said.

Dad laughed, ruffled Jim's hair. "We didn't think you did it on purpose. But you're home now!"

Mom said, "My God, do you realize school starts in a week? We need to go shopping."

I groaned, already missing the cool mountain air and trails I'd spent the summer exploring. The best part of Blue Star was stepping away from schoolwork and taking a break from academics, where I had always seemed to struggle to keep my head above water. Summer had been a good reprieve.

But I also realized school didn't scare me anymore. That was big since I often felt sick the week starting a new school year. Last year, I'd shown myself I could handle school and even make good grades. So I considered it a win that I didn't get nervous until the last night before school started, when it hit me that I would have a new schedule, new teachers, and new classmates.

I would miss Blue Star. I realized I would even miss the Friday night services. It was the first time I was sad that I couldn't read Hebrew. I wondered if I would someday be able to learn enough to fit in better.

# Chapter 15 ~ Big Kids

On the first day back at school, I parked my bike and entered the school building. The place felt almost welcoming. I stopped by the library to say hello, and the librarians seemed happy to see me. At homeroom, I picked up my schedule to see which elective class I had and who my teachers would be. I didn't know any of my new teachers. It would take time for me to break them into the fact that my classwork would be a sloppy mess.

I didn't remember asking for home economics, but it was my favorite class. We learned to cook dishes like chili con carne, use a Singer sewing machine, and hand stitch. The room was large, with kitchen sinks, stoves, a large refrigerator, and five tables with chairs instead of student desks. As we walked in, the teacher told us to sit where we liked. There were clusters of kids sitting together, talking excitedly. I didn't know anyone, so I just picked an empty seat. A short girl with curly black hair came and sat beside me. She looked familiar, but I didn't know who she was.

"Did you ask for this class?" she asked.

"Nope," I answered. "I wanted chorus again, but as long as there is no homework, I'm okay with it."

Her name was Phylece. She was named after a relative called "Phil," so her name starts with P instead of F. I didn't know it then, but Phylece and I would remain friends for life. She became the sister I never had. We hung out together after school, sometimes at her house and sometimes at mine.

Phylece had moved to the area from a diverse Latino neighborhood, and was unhappy about her lack of friends. She sat down next to me when she saw me alone and figured I didn't have friends either. Years later, Phylece told me she approached me because I didn't seem to have any friends and didn't seem to care about it. When we talked about it, she said she wanted my secret, how not to care about a lack of friends. Reflecting on it, I wasn't aware of my lack of friends back then. I was a loner trying to catch up after being mentally absent for all of elementary school.

We explored Miami by bike and bus. The 163rd Street Theater was within walking distance, and we would cruise the mall and go to the movie theater. We used the bus system to go to downtown Miami to shop and visit the big library. Parents today would never allow preteens the freedom of movement we enjoyed. I often wonder if the world was safer back then, or if our parents were oblivious to the risks we were taking.

It was 1968, and we were the "big" kids, eighth graders in our last year at junior high. Then, thirty-seven thousand Florida teachers went on strike, and many of our teachers were suddenly gone. School closed for a few days. When it reopened, it did so with less than half the teachers. When my parents heard we might not get credit for the school year, they started looking at private schools. I begged them to wait and see if things would settle down.

We went into each class each day, sat in our normal seats, and waited. Eventually, a parent volunteer came in with worksheets for us to do. Besides lots of worksheets, I don't remember what I learned or did in my English or History classes. I did my best to use good handwriting, but they were never returned. I wonder if anyone looked at them. I have no idea what the school used to determine our grades.

In Math class, I noticed lots of kids found the worksheets difficult. I had been teaching myself math, so it was easy for me to adapt. The current topics included geometric laws and proofs. They were fun. I circulated through the class, helping students. Being seen as an "expert" was tremendously empowering. When the strike ended in March, our teachers returned, and I became just another student in my Math class. But the memory of those five weeks gave me a confidence that has never left me.

By the end of eighth grade, I had read through most of the books in our school library. Somewhere along the line, I discovered science fiction was special. These stories used math and science to explore social issues and wove them into alternative worlds. There were heroes who ignited my imagination and made me think about the meaning of life.

My first forays into science fiction were by accident. I stumbled across Hugh Walters, a British author of young adult books featuring a team of international astronauts who explored the solar system. When I exhausted this series, I drifted into the works of Robert A. Heinlein, Isaac Asimov, and Arthur C. Clark.

After exhausting the school library, I visited a bookmobile that visited shopping center parking lots, the city library, and the big downtown library. Sometimes, I paid ten cents for a book from a thrift shop. A few of us formed an unofficial book club at school and spent our lunchtime discussing books. Reading these books left me with a dichotomy. I couldn't reconcile the excitement of science fiction and the mind-numbing boredom of my science classes. It didn't help that science was taught in an auditorium class with a TV lecture.

As the school year ended, I thought about my last day at elementary school and my determination to do better at junior high. *What would high school bring?* The teachers wouldn't know me and would expect me to be able to spell and use neat handwriting so people could read it.

Would there be bullies? We would be the little kids again. And Richard, my older brother, had been in constant trouble. My parents were called into the office on a regular basis.

What would high school bring for me?

# Chapter 16 ~ Norland

Gigi followed behind me into the dark kitchen. She watched me add Cheerios and milk to a bowl and sit at the kitchen table. Her big, soulful eyes made her look like she was wearing eyeliner. Her expression and pleading whine said, *Where's my breakfast?*

"Don't look at me like that; you have food."

At five-thirty a.m., everyone in the house was still in bed. Even Richard was still asleep. He graduated last year and enjoyed not needing to head off to school. I didn't know what he was going to do next. Mom and Dad were pushing classes at the community college because they didn't want him to be drafted.

The streetlight glowed yellow against the black sky. Walking the two blocks to the bus stop felt like I was walking in the middle of the night. I was a bundle of nerves remembering my first day at JFK Junior High. It turned out okay, but I needed to make sure I didn't walk in any "out only" doors.

One by one, students appeared. Some walked, and parents dropped some off at the stop. Five of us were on the corner by the time the bus came. These were kids I knew, but none were friends.

"Did you pick up your schedule?" Larry asked.

"I didn't know we could," I said.

"Yeah, I wanted Driver's Education, but didn't get it. What elective did you ask for?" he said.

"I don't think my counselor asked me about an elective."

He smirked. "She probably knew it doesn't matter what you ask for. Tenth graders get whatever is left."

I nodded in agreement. We were "little kids" again.

The bus pulled up, and we climbed in. It was mostly empty, so we each took a bench seat. I pulled out my flashlight and book and started reading. I had Heinlein's *The Moon is a Harsh Mistress* to keep me company. It was my favorite of his.

I quickly figured out why we had to be on the bus at six, even though school didn't start until eight. It felt ridiculously early, but we rode that noisy bus through countless neighborhoods in North Miami Beach. At each stop, a handful of students climbed on board. By the time we finished hitting all the stops, three students were packed on each bench. I put my flashlight and book into my bag. It was too crowded and noisy to read. It didn't help that the windows were open, and the air smelled of diesel.

Our bus pulled into the parking lot behind a chain of other buses and stopped. A few students stood up and moved into the central aisle.

"Sit down," the driver yelled.

They sat. We waited. I watched to see what I could of the process and why we had to wait. Three buses unloaded at the curb. When they were empty, they pulled forward, and another three moved to the unloading zone. When it was our turn, we crowded into the center aisle and inched through the door bottleneck. I thought fondly of my days of riding my bike to school. Maybe I could talk Bob into giving me a ride.

Bob was a year older and had his driver's license. He had a Buick Skylark and was able to drive to school. It would take him a while to come to our neighborhood, but I could ask. I hoped we would have a class or two in common this year. We would find out soon.

I walked around the school to the front entrance and followed a stream of students inside. There were no signs reading *out only*. To one side, a life-size Viking in a glass display case seemed to greet us. He didn't look too threatening. I noticed that the inner walls separating the hall from class-way stopped a few feet from the ceiling. I learned later that the design was to maximize airflow. I also learned (much later) that an unintentional consequence was rioters would scale these partial walls, and teachers would stand inside with a broom, beating back the rioters as they tried to scale the wall. High school in the late 1960s and early 1970s was not for the faint of heart.

An assistant in front of the office handed me my schedule. As I looked down the hall, I spotted Phylece in front of the Viking. It was easy to pick her out since most students towered over her. Phylece was five foot two. She had vibrant black hair meticulously straightened to the fashion of the day and wore a skirt with a hem exactly two inches above her knee—the shortest length allowed by school rules. I didn't care enough to hem my own skirts.

"Let's see your schedule," she said as I approached.

We held them together, noting we had the same classes but not the same order: Algebra, Biology, Spanish, History, Typing, Physical Education, and Spanish.

"Did you ask for Spanish and Typing?" she asked.

"No. I think they put everyone in Spanish. I'm guessing my counselor put me in Typing because no one can read my handwriting."

She laughed. "It's probably a good idea. I mean, not that your writing is that bad."

"Yes, it is. Maybe typing will help."

"We don't have any classes together," she said.

"I know. Let's try to meet between classes."

We looked over our schedules and picked a few times we overlapped in hallways for classes, once after Math and once after English. We would try to pause at the stairwell and wait a minute. If we could connect, we would. The school was large enough that I wished we had maps. I hoped we wouldn't spend the whole day lost.

I started down the hall in the direction of my first class, Algebra. I found the classroom and took an empty seat in the front row. It was easier to concentrate in the front. Gradually, students filled the seats. I was dismayed that there wasn't anyone I knew in the class. I didn't see anyone I knew.

Mr. Gilmour, a short man with little hair and a thick waist, stood at a podium and began taking roll. After reading a name, he waited for the student to say "Here" and raise a hand. He fixed his gaze on the student to memorize every detail of their face before calling the next name.

He called, "Rudnick, Ann."

"Here," I said, raising my hand.

He walked closer to my desk, glancing over his reading glasses, "Is Richard Rudnick your brother?" he asked.

"Yes."

"You will not give me any trouble," he said, then turned and returned to the front of the room.

It wasn't a question. It was a statement, and it caused a tightness in my neck and a feeling that would grow into one of my dreaded headaches. This wasn't what I needed on the first day of school.

*What had Richard done?*

\* \* \*

I wanted to ask Richard about Mr. Gilmore, but Richard wasn't living in the house anymore. He'd moved out, although he didn't go far. He was living in a house with two friends who had also graduated high school.

Richard did a term at Dade Community College, but dropped out after failing most of his classes. Now he worked for Dad. He drove a van delivering garments to sellers. He also worked in sales. A few days after school started, I was surprised when I came home from school and Richard was on the phone in the family room.

"Hello, this is Richard Rudnick. Can you connect me with Jerry Chase?"

*Why was he calling from our house? Maybe he doesn't have a phone?*

"Hi, Mr. Chase. This is Richard Rudnick. I'm in town from California, and I'd like to take you to lunch and talk to you about the new line from Judy Ann Dress."

"Great, I'll pick you up at one," Richard said, then he hung up.

"You're in from California?" I asked.

"Hey, it's more impressive."

"If you pick him up for lunch, he's going to see your Florida license tag."

"I'll rent a car, a fancy one."

I shook my head in disbelief. This was what Dad might have done. Looking at him, I saw a youthful version of Dad. Why hadn't I ever noticed before?

# Chapter 17 ~ How to Succeed

The rest of the roll call was a blur. Richard had been my negative role model. He always showed me what not to do, like not drinking alcohol and crashing the car when you were fourteen and you didn't even have a driver's license. It wasn't surprising that he had been in trouble at Norland, but somehow, Mr. Gilmore's challenge seemed personal and targeted. It was hard to regain calm and focus as he closed the roll book to start the class. I almost missed what he said next.

"Welcome to Algebra, a subject used in every branch of science and engineering, business, finance, and many other occupations. I expect many of you will find the class challenging, and I want to assure you that my job is to help you succeed."

The students watched, and I heard a few muffled giggles. I don't think I'd ever heard a teacher start by saying his job was to help me succeed. *Was he serious?* He had my attention, and his remark about Richard faded a bit.

"I teach Algebra, Geometry, Algebra II, and General Math. But Algebra I is the most important class."

"Why?" I asked.

He looked startled. I guess he didn't expect me to speak up.

"Algebra is a gatekeeper class, required before students can continue in higher mathematics. Most students in an academic stream take Algebra in junior high. Students in tenth-grade Algebra are behind in math; you need to catch up. Guidance thinks you have the potential to catch up. They will move you to General Math if they discover they were wrong about your potential."

My guidance counselor made me take a "more demanding" math class in seventh grade. Catching up was incredibly hard, but staying in that class had been the right thing to do. I understood what Mr. Gilmore was saying. But I wondered if I would ever be "caught up."

A girl with blond braided hair raised her hand. "Can we ask to go to a normal class now?"

Mr. Gilmore looked at her and said, "There are no 'normal' classes. If you want to attend college, try your best in this class. Algebra will strengthen your logic, abstract reasoning, and problem-solving. The General Math class extends what you learned in junior high and is an excellent choice if a student will be working after high school without attending college. There is no shame in working straight out of high school, but you're too young to decide you don't need college. I want students to have opportunities."

The answer seemed to satisfy the girl.

He moved closer to where I was sitting. "I'm going to tell you the secret to success. Spend an hour on homework daily, doing your best to solve all the practice problems. Check your work in class if you get something wrong. Do this, and I guarantee you will earn your A."

As he finished, almost on cue, the bell rang, and the students raced out of the class.

That class, that speech, left me feeling confused. I had worked hard in math through all of junior high, and they moved me out of Remedial Math. But now, Mr. Gilmore said even my hard classes in junior high were low-level. *How had I worked so hard in junior high and not caught up? Should I even try to do higher-level math?*

I always had to work on all the practice problems; that was how I did well. Still, having a teacher formalize what I discovered as a "rule" felt good. But I was also afraid. What if higher math was too hard for me? And was I going to college?

My confusion was on multiple levels. Mom and Dad wanted Richard to go to college, but that was because they were afraid he would be drafted and sent to Vietnam. Girls didn't get drafted, and Mom and Dad never talked to me about college. It felt like they expected me to work in Dad's business after high school. Mom had already started teaching me to do some bookkeeping.

Did I want to go to college? I didn't like school; it was hard work. When I worked at Gemini Fashions with Mom, I earned money, even if it was boring. And I had discovered that I enjoyed learning new stuff, particularly in math and science. Making good grades felt like catching a fly ball or making a good hit in baseball.

I didn't have to decide now about college, not while I was in tenth grade. I would work hard in Mr. Gilmore's class.

His remarks stayed with me. Maybe they took a long time to percolate through. Exactly one month before graduating, I applied to college. It was twenty dollars to apply, and I paid for it without telling my parents. Other students had parents who drove them to college and helped "install" them in a dorm. My parents waved goodbye as I drove off.

I was massively underprepared for college and had to self-study trigonometry before they let me take the Calculus class needed for science. But Mr. Gilmore had been correct. I did my work and made an A in every math class.

# Chapter 18 ~ Seacamp

The Greyhound bus flew across the ocean atop the Seven Mile Bridge. We weren't actually "flying," but it felt like it. From my seat, I couldn't even see the railing outside my window—just the blue ocean below. Whenever a truck or bus traveling north passed us, I felt the bus move slightly. It made me wonder how deep the water below was and if vehicles ever ended up in the ocean.

It was a last-minute decision to go to summer camp. I would turn sixteen, and most of my friends were working summer jobs. Instead, I was on a bus heading to Seacamp, a small, little-known environmental/marine biology camp for nerds. I wasn't a nerd, but I wanted scuba certification.

Blame it on my obsession with the space program. My parents took us to Freeport in the Grand Bahamas last year. They went to gamble. I visited the Underwater Explorers Club (UNESCO), where astronauts trained in weightlessness. At fourteen, I was the youngest "diver" in the Introduction to Scuba class.

We worked in a deep swimming pool, learning to use a tank, regulator, mask, and fins. I took a breath in and felt myself rise off the pool floor. The realization was like a brick hitting me. *This was weightlessness.* They taught us safe practices in moving up and down, clearing a mask and regulator, and adjusting ear pressure. When it was over, I couldn't stop talking about how amazing it was to breathe underwater. I wanted to earn my scuba certification more than anything I had ever wanted.

The bus turned off the highway on Newfound Harbor Highway and headed to the island's far end. We pulled up outside a small white administrative building. I exited the air-conditioned bus and into the blistering heat of the mid-afternoon sun. I'd have to change into shorts as soon as I could.

In front of us, a man in a camp T-shirt called for attention and asked us to gather around him. He looked over our group of campers and nodded to a few he recognized. We were a group of forty-five campers. The girls were about my age, but the younger boys outnumbered us. Other campers were walking around the property. We were not the first to arrive. The younger boy campers from our bus were already clowning around and making too much noise.

As our group moved closer, the man said, "Welcome, new and returning campers. Your bus made the trip over the seven-mile bridge without falling off, so congratulations."

There was some nervous laughter. I wasn't the only one feeling a bit nervous during the trip. As soon as the laughter died down, the man continued.

"I'm Dr. Ross. You'll hear more from me at orientation and see lots of me in the labs and on the boat trips. Your counselors will call for you by name and take you to rooms for you to set up your things. I'll see you at orientation in about an hour."

I went with my group to our dorm room, a repurposed old motel room with four bunk beds and a cot for the counselor. We each staked out a bed, made them up, and placed our trunks beneath the lower bunk. My bunkmate was a redhead named Donna, who I later learned was the camp director's niece. She knew all about the camp and had been hanging out with her family, but this was the first year she was old enough to come as a camper.

I liked Donna. All the girls in my room seemed nice. Even Shelly, who was from Canada, brought long pants and long-sleeved shirts. Someone had told her we would have "cool sea breezes." We helped her pick some tee shirts and shorts from the camp store. No one made fun of me for bringing my guitar or paperback books.

They ran the camp like a school. At orientation, we signed up for classes (called activities). At first, this put me off. It was summer. Did I want to take classes? But orientation sold me on the system. There were no tests or grades, and we controlled what we signed up for. If a camper wanted, they could take arts and crafts, sailing, and swimming, and not take anything academic at all. But I loved the Miami Seaquarium and wanted to know more about marine life. With the promise of no tests, I "registered" for Wet lab, Dry lab, boat trips, and shore excursions. I also signed up for sailing. Anything that would have me on the water would be good.

I was excited that my scuba class met every day. We would only have water work every other day, but that was okay. Now, I was getting excited about the rest of the camp. They had a sign at the entrance: *Seacamp ~ For all the sea has to teach us... And all the fun in learning it.* I had a good feeling about being here. It was hard to put into words, but already, this place felt like home.

Boat trips were the best. We snorkeled at Looe Key, an offshore reef with no island, despite its name. We also snorkeled under bridges, over turtle grass flats, and around a patch reef with large coral head formations. On land, we explored the shallows of Coupon Bight, collecting algae and observing fish, lobsters, and an impressive array of invertebrates. We also visited Bahia Honda State Park, the Key Deer Refuge, and the freshwater lake on Big Pine Key.

The wet and dry labs complemented our field experience. We measured oxygen production and worked on guided dissections of fish and sharks. We snorkeled in the shark pit, observing behavior. Each of us set up a small aquarium and cared for the fish or invertebrates we collected.

I spent every minute that I could in the labs. I skipped evening dances to watch sea bioluminescent sea urchins and tiny crustaceans hunting for food. The counselors and lab staff taught us stuff way above our "grade level," and I had a blast. School was never like this.

While all campers visited Looe Key to learn about coral reefs, the scuba class had our open-water dive on the reef. We used a repurposed patrol torpedo boat to travel out to Looe Key with all our gear. There were fifteen of us in the class, but only ten had passed the written portion and had all our water skills checked, so we were cleared for the dive. I don't think I had ever been this excited for anything as we gathered on the dock for roll call.

The camp director, Irene Hooper, came to the dock to say a few words.

"Seacamp is proud of you. I am proud of you. Each of you has demonstrated a seriousness of purpose in your studies and earned the right to participate in your class's open-water dive portion."

She looked up at the blue sky and then back at us. "You have a perfect day to work with and will see Looe Key differently than you did as a snorkeler. Your open-water dive will be your opportunity to be with the fish, unhurried, as you take your time to see the reef in a way few people do."

She looked at the boat captain and nodded.

"Captain Carl will take you to the reef safely. That is his job. Your job is to be serious about boat safety and dive safety. This is not the time for any silliness or horseplay. Stay with your dive partner and in your dive group. Think about safety in everything you do."

Then she smiled and added, "Have fun, have a great dive."

When she smiled, I saw how much Donna looked like her aunt. I wished Donna could have taken scuba, but you had to be fifteen. She said she would be taking it next summer, and I was already plotting how I could come back. It was expensive.

We boarded the large vessel, and the smell of diesel filled the air. I sat on the deck, taking in the sun and watching the islands as we moved through the channel cut into the shallow waters. We passed an island covered in non-native Pacific Island palm trees. It was where they had filmed *PT-109*. I had seen the island many times, but the irony of passing it from the deck of a PT boat almost made me laugh.

As we navigated away from the land, the water became a translucent purple. We were in the Gulf Stream Current, a river of water circulating through the Atlantic Ocean. The sight took my breath away. Sometimes, dolphins swam in the bow wave. It was hard not to feel their exuberance and impossible not to love every minute I spent on the water. Soon, the boat slowed, and I could see the shallow crest of the reef before us. It seemed like fish were lining up to greet us.

I had to ask, "Why are the fish gathering?"

"They think you will be feeding them," Dr. Ross said.

I shook my head. "What?"

"Well, lots of folks get sick and lose their breakfast. The fish know this."

I laughed. "Are you diving with us?" I asked. It was a sure bet that Dr. Ross was certified, but I hadn't seen him with gear.

"Nope. I'm just here for the boat ride and to check each of you on your water entry and how you return to the boat."

We had practiced the entry back at the camp by jumping off the dock. You stand with your gear on, one hand over your mask and one hand on the Scuba valve to keep it from hitting the back of your head. Entering the water was my least favorite part of the dive, but I could do it. This was a big boat, and we were further from the water's surface. But I wasn't too nervous.

We stepped off the transom one at a time, using a scissor kick to keep from going too deep. I managed not to lose my mask, tucked into a surface dive, and swam to the anchor. My dive team assembled on the sand and waited until we were all down. A large barracuda hovered near them as if part of the group. He was at least six feet long, and his teeth made him look fierce. Not for the first time, I wished I had an underwater camera.

The reef teemed with fish of every color, weaving between coral outcrops, over sponges, and up into open water. Sunlight made everything sparkle. My dive partner pointed to a small nurse shark hanging out below a coral ledge. My heart rate accelerated just a bit. Then, I relaxed. A nurse shark was a fish, and the reef was its home.

When I snorkeled, I could hold my breath underwater for over a minute, and snorkeling at Looe Key was amazing. But today, I was on the reef with my air supply. I could watch without feeling the urge to return to the surface. Swimming unhurriedly along with the fish was thrilling. It was true that scuba diving allowed a person to feel "weightless," but that might be the least important part of the experience. Scuba diving allowed a person to experience the serenity of the reef.

Long before I was ready to surface, my dive group headed back to the anchor to return to the boat. The dive leader had a pressure gauge, and when he said we needed to surface, we couldn't argue. One at a time, we worked our way up the anchor line and then up the ladder to the back transom, where we took our fins and had assistance to help us with our tanks.

The dive was over, and I only had one more day at Seacamp before boarding the bus and heading home. Sitting on the deck again, I looked at the majestic crystal blue water. Without knowing how, I knew I would be back.

Everyone at Seacamp shared a love of the surroundings. The water and the life in the water called to us. Stars at night were brighter, and the salt in the air made you feel alive. Everyone felt the pull, and this bound us together. It was as if I found an emotional home where I belonged in a way I'd never experienced.

As the camp session was winding down, my roommates were talking about returning to Seacamp next summer and what science classes they would be taking when school started. They were all interested in science. When I returned to school, I immediately went to guidance and insisted on a change in my class schedule. I wanted science, as much science as I could get.

The following summer, I returned as a counselor in training (CIT), and after graduating high school, I returned to Seacamp and worked as a counselor and laboratory assistant. Over my lifetime, I returned to the Florida Keys again and again. I keep a part of it in my heart wherever I go.

I came to Seacamp for scuba certification and found so much more. My love of the ocean deepened with an understanding of marine life and ecology. By the time I had graduated from high school and spent three summers at the camp, I knew I wanted my life's work to be in science.

# Chapter 19 ~ Making Changes

The week before school started, I visited the guidance department and asked them to add science to my schedule. In 1969, the state only required ninth-grade biology, and the school didn't offer many science electives. So, when I asked for a tenth-grade Science class, they placed me in chemistry.

I felt a little intimidated walking in on that first day. There were only five girls in a class of thirty students. It reminded me of Seacamp, where they reserved twice as many spots for boys as for girls. It seemed unfair. I wondered if Seacamp hadn't expected many girls to apply, or if they simply preferred having more boys. Neither reason was acceptable.

What really bothered me was that I had to *ask* for chemistry. *Was it offered to boys automatically?*

I took an open seat in the first row. There were no desks; instead, there were lab benches with sinks and stools. It looked like a room for doing science, and it made me smile. I'd had some chemistry as part of our scuba instruction.

The teacher came in and took his place at the front of the room. He was an older man, heavyset and balding. Without saying a word, he poured a clear liquid into a large graduated cylinder, and a black, snake-like substance quickly grew, climbing and spilling out the top, tumbling and coiling onto a tray on the lab bench.

"Chemistry means change," he said. "Welcome to Chemistry."

"Wow," the students in the front row said.

I silently agreed; he had my attention.

Mr. Dimartino discussed the rules and expectations, as well as the labs we would complete, and by the end of the class, I added a slide-rule to my list of supplies I needed for school.

My second class of the day was English. When I picked up my schedule, I was thrilled to see that I had Mr. Groff for English again and wondered if he would be giving the same first-day assignment we had last year. Last year, on my first day of school, his assignment triggered my panic reflex. He asked us to write a paragraph about what we liked and hated about English class. I wrote that I like to read, but hated handwriting and spelling. The next day, he returned my paragraph and said we could work this out. From then on, I showed Mr. Groff my sloppy copy at the end of class. He let me take it home, clean it up, and turn it in the next day. Mom was so thrilled with the arrangement that she went out and bought me a typewriter.

The assignment was slightly different, asking about what our favorite subject in school was, and what we liked about it. The intent was the same: provide a writing sample. It was the same assignment, and I wrote my paragraph and showed it to Mr. Groff on the way out.

"Do you want to take it home and work on it?" he asked.

"Yes, if that's okay."

He smiled and nodded.

As I left the English class, it occurred to me I needed to reach out to my other teachers and see if it was okay for me to type my homework. English was no longer a dreaded class.

I remembered from last year walking into the class and finding a record player on a stand at the front of the room.

"We start Shakespeare today," he said, and held up a record album with an elaborate cover with gold lettering saying *Julius Caesar*. "I want you to hear the beauty of the language, so I've brought in recordings by professional readers."

He turned the machine on, placed the tonearm onto the record, and the voices came to life. They were reading, only they weren't just reading words; they were acting. It was like we were at a play and listening to actors we couldn't see.

I opened the book, followed along, and felt transported to Rome, watching the action unfold before me. The readers were so good that I felt I could see the scenes and the action. Class time disappeared, and I was sorry to leave when the bell rang.

This year, the class had new students, and there would be different books and lessons. But my teacher was Mr. Groff; I wasn't worried.

My math class was Geometry. Mrs. Reed seemed nice enough. On the first day, she distributed our textbooks and provided an overview of geometry. As an additional bonus, Phylece was in my class. It looked like geometry was solving proofs, and that looked like fun.

I'd finally found a rhythm to being a student, and no longer felt like I was drowning in work. Chemistry, though, was a different story; it was my toughest class. I was frustrated by how difficult it was.

After returning from Seacamp, I'd specifically asked the counselors to put it in my schedule. I refused to accept that it was beyond me, so I dedicated most of my study time to it. Despite failing a lot of quizzes, I still managed to get a C. What saved my grade in the class were the laboratory activities.

Once a week, we came into the chemistry room and found equipment set up for a lab activity. We used Bunsen burners, balances, and ran chemical reactions in test tubes. They reminded me of my old chemistry sets and the fun I had with them. My lab partner was one of the smartest kids in class and helped me with the write-ups. It was a classic case of the glass being half-full or half-empty. I didn't fail Chemistry, but I didn't exactly excel either.

In spite of difficulties with chemistry and the need to work hard in all my classes, the paralyzing fear of failing that had haunted me in middle school faded. My teachers knew I would do the work and succeed. Their attitude became my attitude. I made the honor roll often enough that my parents seemed to forget that I hadn't always been a good student. Dad stopped giving me bonuses, but that was fine.

Toward the end of the year, we met with our counselor to select a schedule for our senior year. She assumed I wanted science and insisted I take Physics. The school now offered Marine Biology, and that was what I asked for. She said I could do both, but that students interested in science needed the Biology, Chemistry, and Physics. We compromised, and I took both.

The problem was that it didn't leave room for another elective I wanted; Mr. Groff would be teaching an elective in creative writing. My counselor said I could either not take Marine Biology or take an extra class. The school was running a double shift due to severe overcrowding. My shift was from noon to six, but if I arrived at eleven, I could fit in the extra elective.

Mom was surprised I'd chosen an extra English class, but she was happy about it. I ended up as an editor on the creative writing magazine. It was good that they didn't ask me to check spelling.

# Chapter 20 ~ Turmoil

The school library had large tables and a quiet space, perfect for working on math problems and reading in the hours before school started. My schedule had classes starting at eleven a.m., and I tried to be at the library by nine. I had a Toyota Corolla and picked Phylece up on the way to school. We had become inseparable by our senior year at Norland.

"Attention, students and staff: please leave the campus. We are canceling school for today," came the announcement over the public address system.

"Not again," I said.

"Do you think it's safe to go out the back door?" Phylece asked.

"Let's look out the windows. Maybe we can see if it's quiet out there."

We packed up our work and headed toward the library's back door.

"Jesus," Phylece said.

In the parking lot, a school bus sat on its side. Angry students filled the area, yelling, "NO Bussing."

I saw Mr. Foster, our principal, with a megaphone, telling students to leave the area. In the distance, sirens were announcing that police were on their way. *How had we not heard a commotion?*

There was a knot in my stomach. We went to one football game where trouble broke out. By the end of the game, we were hurrying to the car while people threw rocks at us. It terrified me, and I'm still uneasy in crowds.

After my freshman year, Norland adopted a split-shift schedule, and the lunch period and cafeteria disappeared. Half the students attended from six a.m. to noon. The other half of the students attended from noon to six p.m. Those of us with extended days brought a bag lunch and ate in class. The administrators no longer had to deal with fights in the cafeteria.

Most of my friends from junior high were students at Norland now. The exception was Maryann. She lived in a different neighborhood and was zoned for Miami High. It felt like her school was torn apart in the turmoil. She was in the cafeteria when a violent knife fight erupted. The scene turned violent, and students couldn't easily escape the room. She hid under a table and wasn't hurt. But she went home that day and didn't go back. Instead of school, she took a job as a waitress. She was ashamed and didn't tell me for months.

I tried to get Maryann to go back to school, but it was a battle I couldn't win. Neither of her parents had graduated from high school, and they felt she was old enough to go to work now. It filled me with sadness, and I was angry that there were such differences between schools and school experiences.

It was part of a bigger social injustice. The Vietnam War was on everyone's mind. Rich kids got college deferments, and poor kids got sent to war. My parents were terrified that the government would draft Richard. The previous May, in my junior year, four students were killed at Kent State during a protest over the draft and war.

When we moved from New York, Dad's trucking friends helped him pack and move, and he couldn't take them to coffee shops for lunch. The South was segregated, with *Blacks not served here* signs. We were still a racially segregated society. Department stores had bathrooms and water fountains for blacks and whites.

My school, Norland, was all-white until 1969, when schools in Dade

County were court-ordered to desegregate. At that time, there were no vocational education classes available. When students were bused in to satisfy the federal court orders, everyone was unhappy. Black kids were made to ride buses to schools that did not have the classes in auto mechanics or other vocational classes, where they were with white kids who resented them.

Now, in addition, besides tornado drills and bomb shelter drills (the Cold War was still alive and well), we had riot drills and actual riots.

That morning, a group of students tipped a bus over in the parking lot. At the time, we didn't know if it was white kids or black kids who tipped the bus over. All we knew was we needed to get away from a bunch of angry people.

We left the library through the front door and wound through the crowded hallways. Crowds of students packed the halls. No one seemed particularly upset or angry. They were just making their way to an exit, happy to have school dismissed.

We exited the library and navigated the bustling hallways. Students filled the corridors, but no one seemed agitated. They were simply heading for the exits. The school was still "early shift," with classes starting at six in the morning and ending at noon. We were there because we both had extra classes and came early for them.

The school went on a double shift after my tenth-grade year because of overcrowding. They put academic classes in the afternoon. If I wanted Physics and Marine Biology, I had to be there in the afternoon. I wondered if the separation by "academic focus" wasn't another way to maintain segregation.

Some students were speculating on why they canceled school, but most were happy for an unexpected day off school. Everything seemed calm, and we reached the front of the school without incident.

"Want to see if Bob is at IHOP?" Phylece asked.

"Sure, why not? They may not know school is canceled."

Bob didn't have an extra class, so he didn't come to school as early as we did. He picked up a friend he knew from the marching band, and they often stopped for breakfast at the International House of Pancakes up the road. It was highly likely we would find them there. If not, well, we could have breakfast before heading home.

Richard graduated from Norland in 1967, a time with protests against the war and major civil unrest. Richard's classmates were flower children, hippies. But the school hadn't been ordered by the federal government to bus students in and integrate, so his school day was less rocked by chaos.

For the sake of safety, Norland halted any events that would lead to large groups of students in one location, and no sporting events at night. That was when they closed the cafeteria. As students, we lost so much of what should have been our high school experience. There wasn't a choice. The school needed to do what it could to protect students. The effects linger: I still feel uncomfortable in crowds.

Did the government make the right call with forced busing? I believe they did. We are scared of what's different and find security in what we already know. I recall pulling into gas stations when they still offered full service, and an attendant would come to my car. If the attendant was Black, I'd feel a sudden, uneasy jolt of adrenaline. The fear was groundless, stemming from a lack of exposure.

I'd never had a Black classmate or had a real conversation with someone who was African American. The government aimed to integrate schools and help people overcome the fear born of unfamiliarity. Looking back at what we lost and what we gained, I am a firm supporter of integration.

# Chapter 21 ~ It's A Wrap

We sat around the coffee table in my family's living room while Simon and Garfunkel's "Bridge Over Troubled Waters" played in the background. The gathering had a subdued vibe rather than a loud, boisterous party feeling. It had been a day of intense highs and lows, leaving each of us a little dazed. High school was over, and we were graduates.

"What time will you leave tomorrow?" Phylece asked.

"I'm setting the alarm for five. I need to be at Seacamp by nine."

"All packed?"

"Yup. All I need to do is put my bag in the car and leave."

"I'm going to miss you," she said.

"I'll miss you too. I'll miss everyone," I said, looking around the living room.

Rick and Jim were playing chess. Bob and Tom were sitting at the dining table, helping themselves to the spread of snacks we had haphazardly placed for grazing. There were chips, cookies, and a collection of soft drink bottles. Phylece and I were sitting on pillows at the coffee table, along with Debbie. The crowd filled the room with us moving around, talking, refilling plates with snacks, and holding on to our last night together.

There was space to spread out. I think that was why they decided to meet up at my house. Mom's furniture from the modern age seemed appropriate for the occasion—a time to focus on the future waiting for us. The couch was bright white leather in a plexiglass frame with a glass coffee table. The room had an off-white shag rug and looked like it had been inspired by *The Jetsons*, a futuristic cartoon television show.

Someone had turned on the fake fireplace in the corner. It looked like an upside-down funnel with a cutout opening for a fake log with fake flames. The "fire" made popping sounds that were supposed to sound authentic but wouldn't fool anyone.

Mom favored modern artists, and the walls were covered with prints from Miro and Picasso and paintings of less well-known artists with similar styles. One wall had a screen for a projection television set. My folks were early adopters of home theater, a technology that was new in 1971. They even had a VHS player so they could watch movies at home.

Earlier that day, all of us had gathered at the Miami Convention Center with our caps and gowns. We marched across the stage and shook the hand of Mr. Hunter, our school principal. The ceremony took hours and strained the patience of students and parents. There were 991 graduating seniors that year. We were no longer high school students; we were graduates.

After the ceremony, we all went to dinner with our parents. But we agreed to meet at my house after dinner was over.

We had snacks spread across the dining table: chips and dip, cookies, soft drinks, pretzels, and peanuts. Some of the food was from my parents, and it looked like everyone who came brought something for the table. Our gathering wasn't a formal party, just a last night together. The record player constantly provided the soundtrack of our senior year, blasting out songs like "Joy to the World," "It's Too Late," and "One Toke Over the Line." Back then, we had many vinyl records that were "singles," and all of us took turns being the DJ.

We were school friends, and some of us had been part of this group since junior high. We were what people thought of as "good kids." We were respectful and stayed out of trouble. We did our work at school and found ways to be together when school was out. We cruised the malls, went to the beach, played miniature golf, and spent time at each other's houses just to hang out. For much of five years, we had been inseparable.

Rick and I were dive buddies, but not dating. We met in our Marine Biology class, and I convinced our teacher to take our class to Seacamp for a field trip. It was an awesome trip, even if two kids got in a car accident on the way to the camp. Our teacher (Mrs. Metcalf) loved it so much she took up scuba diving. Yeah, I had a convert.

We did everything as a group. We even went to prom as a group: Bob and Bonnie, Rick and me, Phylece and James. The prom was at the Seville, a fancy hotel on Collins Avenue in Miami Beach. We dined and danced and were "seen" at the event. Afterward, we chartered a boat and cruised the Intracoastal Waterway. We walked on the beach, sat, and watched the stars. We ended up at Wolfe's, a favorite breakfast house that opened early. The place was packed with other teenagers ending prom night by eating Danishes, followed by eggs and lots of coffee. Good times.

But tonight, the mood was subdued. We had been friends for most of junior high and high school. This would be the end of our group. Sure, we would get together when we were back in town, but it would never be the same. I think we all realized that tonight was the end of our "pack," and it made us sad.

In the morning, I would leave for Seacamp to start a job as a camp counselor, laboratory aide, and kitchen assistant. Come September, I would start college at the University of South Florida in Tampa. Bob and Phylece would be in Gainesville for college. Tom was heading for Colorado. Rick was joining the Coast Guard. I wondered where he would end up.

But tonight, we were all together. My folks had turned the living room area over to us. We had snacks, soft drinks, and music. The chessboard was in play, but mostly we just enjoyed each other's company and talked about plans for summer and college. Around ten p.m., we said good night and goodbye, and everyone headed home. I cleaned up and set my alarm for five a.m.

In the morning, I put my duffel bag in the car and drove 128 miles to Big Pine Key. It seemed normal, exciting, and sad. By the time I came back to North Miami Beach, many of my friends would have left for college. And I would only be in town to get ready to leave again. I was seventeen years old, and although I didn't know it, I would never again be living in that house for more than a few weeks at a time.

This house would no longer be where I lived; it would have become my parents' house. I was about to step into a larger world where I would be expected to be an adult. It was a little frightening.

# Chapter 22 ~ Working at Seacamp

I left my home and drove 128 miles to Seacamp the day after high school graduation. It was dark when I left my house, but I needed to be there by nine a.m., and traffic would be heavy. The camp administration wanted me to come up earlier, but I was graduating. Training started at nine, and I needed to be there on time. We had a week to train in lifeguarding, motorboat safety, first aid, and CPR.

Once the campers arrived, eight would be assigned to my dorm room. My duties included setting up laboratory equipment for morning and afternoon sessions, as well as helping to prepare meals in the kitchen. I would drive a small boat filled with campers to the open-water snorkeling stations.

Seacamp gave us an incredible amount of responsibility, considering I turned seventeen in July. We handled the eight campers in our room, making sure they kept the room tidy and that no one got hurt or wandered off when they should be in bed. We worked as lifeguards and drove boats loaded with campers to the reefs. Campers registered for activities they would attend during the day, but counselors didn't supervise those. We had other duties.

Two of the activities were science-related: Wet Lab and Dry Lab. My duties included assisting the science staff in setting up lab materials and running the activities. I also had kitchen duty for meal preparation. The job responsibility that scared me the most was using the camp van and driving campers to Key West and back.

"Everyone in the van," I called.

Eight campers filed into the van, each carrying a laundry bag.

The drive to Key West was forty-five minutes, and our first stop was the laundromat. These campers were staying more than a single eighteen-day session, so they needed the opportunity to wash their clothes. That was the main purpose of the trip. But we tried to make it fun. Once the laundry was clean, dried, and back in the van, we spent two hours of "free time" shopping in Old Town, near Duval Street.

The kids loved it, and so did I. Key West had chickens in the street and tie-dye in the shops. We visited the Kino's Sandal Shop and Factory, a local industry founded in 1966 by a Cuban who had fled to the United States in 1960.

"Stay in pairs, and do not go into any bars," I said.

They nodded in agreement and hurried off to spend their money.

We watched the sunset at the pier, then went to dinner at a Sizzler Steakhouse in New Town. While there were more interesting restaurants in the old town, no one wanted to spend a lot of money. The steakhouse was inexpensive. We ended our trip with a movie. The kids had selected *Blue Water White Death*, an appropriate film for Sea-campers. The night drive over the narrow Keys Bridge highways made me shake. I took some NoDoz, caffeine pills, and tried to stay awake and focused on the road.

The summer felt like a roller coaster. I loved being at Seacamp, but I missed home and the close friends from high school. We would be heading off in different directions in the fall, and I worried that I was missing our last summer together. *Had I been right to accept the job at Seacamp?*

Sometimes, I'd walk out to the shark pit late at night after the campers were asleep. I'd sit on the rocks and look at the stars and moon, and imagine swimming out to sea. I'd imagine not coming back.

I came close to quitting and going home. Bob, Phylece, and Rick drove out to see me on my day off. I felt better after that; it seemed to help me over a hump. The rest of the summer was much easier.

It was a summer of firsts; my first real "job" and first boyfriend. I was seventeen, and Gordon was a lot older than I was. He was from New Mexico, and our age difference presented some issues. I didn't know any of the music he liked, and he thought The Beatles and Simon & Garfunkel were new-age crap.

Our age difference also meant we had difficulty going "out." I was too young to get into the bars, and Jimmy Buffett played at the local bar on Tavernier Key. Gordon had me turn my high school ring around so it looked like a wedding ring, and I went in as his wife. They let me get away with it as long as I didn't order a drink.

I was a late starter and hadn't even kissed a boy. So that summer was my first kiss, my first making out, but nothing else. Gordon was mindful of my age, and that he was old enough that it could be considered rape. We kept it light. I hoped and hoped we'd get together the next summer, but neither of us returned the following summer.

My three summers at Seacamp broadened my understanding and love of the ocean and marine life and gave me a reason to take science in school. Even more important, I met serious scientists, and they all had college degrees or were pursuing them. If I wanted to work in science, I'd need to do the same.

# Chapter 23 ~ College: the American Rite of Passage

Two weeks later, I found myself at the Gamma Residence Hall at the University of South Florida. I was alone, along with thousands of students I didn't know. This wasn't my first time away from home. When I was twelve, I went to Blue Star for the summer. Then, I spent three summers at Seacamp. This was different; kids go to camp, adults go to college.

Earlier that day, I'd packed my car with everything I'd take with me and caravaned from North Miami Beach to Tampa with Bob. We carted my stuff up to the dorm room. I hugged Bob, thanked him, walked him to his car, and waved as he drove off. His destination was the University of Florida in Gainesville.

I applied to USF back in May, and they accepted me. They were the only school I applied to, and I hadn't thought about it other than in abstract ways. Now it was real. The dorm room was clean and air-conditioned, but sterile, a symmetric rectangle with two twin beds and a long double desk, which I would share with a roommate when she arrived. The gray cement walls gave way to one narrow floor-to-ceiling window. I could see the library a short distance across a green, empty lawn, and off to the left was a building boasting the sign, *University Center.*

The room felt empty, even after unpacking and arranging my clothes, books, record player, and kitchen supplies. I'd left the door to the hall open, hoping to meet some students, but few were around. Today was Saturday, and none of the administrative offices were open. I needed to register on Monday and wanted to be settled in before then, but it appeared I might be in a minority of early arrivals. It felt like the walls were closing in on me. Feeling an urgent need to escape the gray institutional room, I took the elevator down to the lobby and headed to the University Center.

My room was on the east fifth floor in Gamma, a dorm set aside for freshman girls. The floor had twenty rooms, each of which would hold two students. We had an enormous bathroom with multiple stalls and showers, as well as a community phone in the hall. The dorm had kitchen facilities on the first floor, where we could cook meals, but most students had a meal plan. I did not, and I would have to figure out how to manage food on a budget.

I headed across the field. The afternoon rain shower was over, and the air smelled of rain. But the sky had cleared. I walked across the empty field and opened the glass door. It felt like I was walking into a shopping mall, but it was quite empty. *Where were all the students?*

I walked through the hall to the information counter.

"Welcome to USF. What can I help you with?" the attendant said.

"Thanks. Do you have a campus map?"

"New student?" he asked, handing me a map and a package of handouts for student clubs and organizations.

"Yes. Where is everyone? I didn't expect the school to be so empty."

"Classes end at noon on Friday, and since most of the students are commuters, the campus is fairly deserted by this time. It will be like this until Monday morning."

"Does the University Center close for the weekend?" I asked.

"No, we stay open for students in the dorms. Downstairs, there is a cafeteria and an activity room. You should go check them out."

"Thanks," I said, taking the map and handouts.

I went downstairs. The student activity room wasn't quite empty. Four guys were playing cards at a table. They looked older than me, and I assumed they were students. Two others were intently playing chess. So far, the only girls had been back in my dorm. Where were they? The billiard and ping-pong tables were empty. I hadn't expected how empty it would feel when classes weren't in session. The emptiness could make me miss my friends even more than I expected.

I knew almost nothing about the campus. Well, I knew Tampa was near the coast and that the school had a marine biology program. I'd been to the campus for a brief visit with my parents, but we came on a weekend, and tours weren't available. But now, I was "free" to do what I wanted until Monday morning. So, I left the Student Union determined to use my map to do my own tour and learn my way around.

I stepped out onto the walkway in front of the University Center. It was warm, but not unbearably so. The walkways crisscrossed the campus, lined by seedling trees. None were big enough to provide shade for the walkways. I located the Administration Building on the map and, sure enough, I could see it across from where I stood in front of the Student Union. I needed to pay fees on Monday before I could register, so this would be my first stop.

My self-guided walking tour was brief. The school was larger than a high school but still small, and none of the buildings were open. It was 1971, and USF was in its infancy. The buildings included Administration, Fine Arts, Chemistry, Biology, Physical Education, Science, Business, a library, and two theaters.

There was also the University Center that I had already visited. That was it. I took under forty-five minutes to look at each building. The air was still warm and humid, so I was a hot mess when I returned to the dorm. I took a shower to clean up.

When I applied to USF, I was aware that the school was small. I hadn't realized that almost 80 percent of the students were commuters. Even the dorms emptied on weekends. The students went home for the weekend. For most of them, home wasn't very far away. My home was a six-hour drive away, and I was never fond of driving. My trips home were infrequent.

In retrospect, USF's small size made it a safer emotional and academic environment for an underprepared freshman. However, the downside was that I found weekends to be lonely and boring.

Linda, my roommate, arrived Sunday morning. She had a part-time job in a flower shop and brought a few arrangements to brighten the place. I had a small refrigerator covered with a tablecloth. Linda arranged a vase of flowers and disguised it as a table. Refrigerators were not allowed, but I doubt our RA was fooled. We went shopping for posters to put on the wall. Linda had a boyfriend from high school, another freshman living in a nearby dorm. After a while, it felt like I had two roommates.

Most dorm students were on a food plan and ate meals in one of the included food service cafeterias. The cost was high. The refrigerator allowed us to have cereal and sandwiches. We each had a popcorn popper to heat soup or make boxed macaroni and cheese. The University Center had a cafeteria where we could buy occasional meals, and we both had cars to drive off campus. But back then, there weren't many restaurants near USF.

And then it was Monday. My to-do list was overflowing: pay fees at the administration building, take a swimming test, and register for classes. Fees were $125 a term and covered full-time registration. Taking twelve credits satisfied full-time status, but it cost no more to take up to eighteen credits. The line to pay fees snaked around the administration building. The process took roughly an hour. It was the first check I ever wrote; I felt so grown up.

I had to take the swim test before registering, because if you failed the test, you were required to register for a swim class. They used an indoor pool in the Physical Education Building. It wasn't hard; you had to swim two hundred yards by swimming laps in a twenty-five-yard pool. That was laughably easy for me, as I had been swimming a fitness open-water half mile twice a week at Seacamp.

We crowded around the pool deck, waiting for our turn. The coach called eight swimmers to the lanes at a time.

"Next," he called as a group of swimmers completed the task.

I followed a group of swimmers to the lanes, taking one in the middle of the pool. At the sound of the whistle, we dove in and swam. I kept pace with the swimmers. After my lap, I climbed out, walked to the wall, and retrieved my towel. The boys had pulled themselves out of the pool and sat on the cement, trying to catch their breath. I hadn't realized they were trying to keep up with me. It helped that I was fresh from Seacamp and had been in the water every day that summer.

I dried off and lined up at the table to get the card showing I'd passed. The coach handed me my card and asked if I was interested in joining the swim team. My high school had a swim team, so I was familiar with it. But in high school, no girls were allowed. His comment was my first clue that college might be a really different experience. It was nice to be asked.

"Not this term. I'm a new freshman, and I want to put my focus on classes," I said.

"See me when you're ready; I'm Coach Prather."

"I will, thank you," I said.

I never joined the swim team, but Coach Prather was also the gymnastics coach. I was fascinated with gymnastics and took it as an elective repeatedly. My high school had excluded girls from gymnastics, but I enjoyed watching it. At USF, I wasn't on a team, and there was no pressure to be "good." It was nice to have a non-academic class on my schedule.

It was now ten-thirty a.m. I'd completed two of my tasks. I headed back to the gym for registration. It was a madhouse of confusion. Stressed-out students stood in lines at registration tables or stared at chalkboards with lists of classes, many sections had already been crossed out, showing they were full. A few sat on the gym floor crying. I heard more than one lamenting, "I need the class to graduate."

I stepped into line for Biology, my first choice of course. Reaching the table, I selected a section that met on Monday, Wednesday, and Friday at eight a.m. and an evening lab. Registering for my first class took ninety minutes, but I was glad it was still early. Freshman composition was next. It was a required class for freshmen, one that you were to take in your first semester. By the time I reached the front of the line, only one section was available. And, it conflicted with my Biology class. I registered for English and got back in line to get a different section of Biology. Nothing was available.

It was now three-thirty p.m. I hadn't had lunch and was afraid to leave. By the end of the day, I needed to have a schedule for a full-time student. I went to an advisement table.

"If no Biology is available, register for Chemistry. You're going to need it anyway," the adviser said.

It wasn't what I wanted to hear. Chemistry was insanely difficult in high school, and I earned nothing above a C. But I wanted a science major, and the adviser was right, I should be taking a science class. So I went through the line and registered for Chemistry.

I was moderately terrified about flunking out. With Chemistry on my schedule, I decided that twelve academic credits, the minimum full-time schedule, would do for my first term. Math would do it. I registered for a class in Finite Mathematics. Then, on a whim, I added gymnastics, figuring a non-academic class would give me something interesting to do and not add to my studying or homework load. Chemistry, English, Math, and Gymnastics. With twelve credits on my schedule, I had completed my tasks for the day. It was after five, and I was starving. I left the gym in search of food.

Feeling better after a dinner at the student cafeteria, I returned to my dorm room.

"Let me see your schedule," Linda said.

I pulled out my worksheet and showed her.

"Chemistry! On your first term, are you crazy?" she said.

"It was the only science I could get into. How did you do?" I asked.

"I registered months ago," she said and showed me her schedule.

"Too bad we don't have the same sections of math and English," I said.

"Yeah, it's best to register early; by this time, lots of classes are closed."

"I didn't know you could register early. I was working down in the Keys over the summer, so I wouldn't have been able to drive up."

Linda nodded sympathetically. "Well, Chemistry looks like your only hard class. You should be okay."

I didn't tell her that English was likely to be just as hard as Chemistry for me. *How did I end up with English and Chemistry in my first term?* High school Chemistry was hard, and English was always difficult. These were college classes. *Was I going to wash out of college in my first term?*

Terrified of failure, I went to the library every morning and set up a study carrel, where I spent my day reading textbooks and reviewing notes. The only times I left the library were to attend class or go to the Chemistry Department for extra help. I left materials in my study carrel and returned to do more work, only leaving at dinnertime. It was easier to work in the library than in my dorm room.

There were two reasons I didn't like to study in my dorm room. First, Linda often had her boyfriend in the room, and she really didn't want me hanging around. But also, the dorm was all freshmen. A ton of students at school were there to party and find a husband. I found the atmosphere distracting. When exams came around, the atmosphere turned desperate. That bothered me even more. By the end of the first semester, many had dropped out, and almost half the rooms were empty. That gave me an idea.

I knocked on my RA's door.

"Come in."

I opened the door, and she looked up from the desk. "What's up, Ann?"

"I see we have a ton of empty and half-empty rooms on the floor. Could I move to another room? Maybe get one by myself?"

"Are you and Linda having problems?"

"No, but she's really social, she has lots of friends over, and I can't really study in the room."

She laughed. "Linda doesn't have lots of friends over. She has *a friend* over a lot."

I blushed. I really didn't want to get Linda in trouble about her boyfriend.

Then she said, "I get your drift. I'll see what I can do."

Two weeks later, I had a room to myself. Still, I continued using the library for study, even when I had a room to myself. It was closer to the classrooms and made it easy to go back to studying between classes. Besides, it had worked well for me the first semester. Why change it?

My grade report for the first semester bothered me, which was ridiculous. I expected the A in Gymnastics and math. I was hoping for a B in Chemistry and English. When grades were posted, mine were all As. That was crazy wrong. Chemistry had weekly quizzes and three exams. I hadn't failed anything, but I sure hadn't made an A on any of the exams. *What kind of a curve was he using?*

English, I could sort of understand. We turned in a paper every week. She gave feedback and allowed resubmission, and I really didn't understand how she would assign a grade. *But all As? A GPA of 4.0?*

I couldn't get rid of the feeling that USF wasn't a "real" university, and that made my grades less impressive. Bob and Phylece were at UF, which was massive. They were in very large classes. How would I have fared in grades at UF?

I would never know for sure. Still, I didn't regret choosing USF, and was happy with the small university atmosphere.

Shortly after the first term ended, I was in the game room at the Student Union. My former teaching assistant from math invited me to join his table for a bridge game. One of their regulars was out, and they needed a fourth. They were older than me, but didn't seem surprised that I knew the game and had a head for cards. I felt like I fit in and had a good time. I felt like I was an adult. It was a good feeling.

# Chapter 24 ~ Brave New World

I walked across campus to the Chemistry building, a short, two-story building next to the Chemistry lecture hall. I'd been to the first two lectures; they met three days a week in the morning. This was my first evening class, a lab that met once a week for three hours.

I enjoyed Chemistry lab in high school and was optimistic that I would continue to enjoy it in college. I'd been to the lecture section already—it met three times a week and held 150 students, which intimidated me. But they capped the lab at twenty. When I arrived fifteen minutes before class, students were waiting outside the locked room. Most of them were a lot older than me; USF was a commuter school, and the evening classes were often attended by working adults taking night classes. It felt like déjà vu—being the little kid again.

A few minutes before seven, a young man wearing a lab coat opened the door and let us in. "Pick a lab station; it will be your lab station for the term," he said.

The room contained long rows of black benches, each with a sink and a Bunsen burner. I picked the first open station, opened the top drawer, and found an impressive collection of glassware, clamps, and equipment. A few minutes later, everyone had settled in, and I had a lab partner. He was male, and I guessed, in his late twenties.

While Chemistry in high school was hard, the lab part of it had been cool, and from the look of this room and the equipment on the bench and in the drawer, it looked like college Chemistry labs were going to be good. And I was right; they were a lot better than high school.

We had instructions for the activity before we came to class and three whole hours to work at the bench. While we had lab partners, each of us set up our own experiments. That was great because in high school, my partner, who was a better student, did the fun parts. Here, partners shared some equipment and assisted each other, but I got to run my own experiments.

Steve was diligent and pleasant to work with. He had been in the Army and was using his benefits to return to school. He was a good partner, and while we each did our own formal write-up and wrote to our own conclusions, it was good to talk about our work before we left the lab at night. We both took work notebooks home to type up the formal lab report. When the instructor said we had to type up lab reports, I was thrilled.

The Chemistry lecture class was another story, and I was apprehensive. Chemistry had been a challenge in high school. And I was right. It was difficult in college, but not as bad as I'd feared. Oh, lots of students flunked, but I didn't.

I might have found the subject easier because I was older now, or more motivated. However, I suspect that technology played a significant role in it. Inexpensive calculators were now available and were much easier to use than slide rules. And my professor, Dr. Davis, was an early adopter of video lectures. He put them in the learning lab, and we could access them whenever we wanted.

During the scheduled lecture periods, which were optional, Dr. Davis talked about chemistry research. These sessions were sometimes dull, but I always went. They made me feel like a scientist—or someone who could one day be one. Between recorded lectures and a calculator, I had more resources and a determination to use them.

And last of all, I remembered a ton of what I'd learned in high school.

Mr. Dimartino had been an excellent teacher. I might have only earned mediocre grades, but I learned a lot of chemistry. While I spent a ton of time reading, studying, and working chemistry problems, the class was manageable.

* * *

There were no students in line outside Freshman Composition on the first day of class. Instead, the door was open, and students sat waiting for the teacher, who had not arrived. I took a seat near the front of the room.

Just as I took out a notebook and pen, a woman came into the room, followed by an angry man. He seemed upset about a grade. Her voice was low, and I couldn't hear what she said to him.

"Bitch," he yelled and stormed out of the room, slamming the door closed.

The woman walked to the board and said, "Welcome to Freshman Composition. I'm your instructor, Elizabeth Rose."

She wrote her name and the room number on the whiteboard. We all took it down.

"Please take out a sheet of paper and write at least one hundred words detailing your observations from the start of class."

It was only then I realized the scene with the angry student was a setup for our benefit.

She looked up and called on a student with his hand in the air. "Yes?"

"I'm not sure I can fill one hundred words," he said.

"Try. The only rule is that you write observations, not analysis."

That made me smile. She reminded me of Mr. Groff. I got to work. I described the man, what he looked like, how he entered the room, what he said, how she looked and responded, and her instructions to us. It didn't take one hundred words, but it came close. I worked as neatly as I could and tried to use words I knew how to spell.

The next class period, she asked me to stay after class.

"Ann, I liked your paper. You did a good job with the observations. But do you have dyslexia?" she asked.

I nodded. "I was going to talk to you about it. When I write at home, I look up words in a dictionary to make sure they're spelled right. Am I going to pass this class?"

She smiled. "I'm sure you'll do fine."

"Can I use a dictionary in class?" I asked.

She pulled out what looked like a tiny dictionary. "You might do better with this," she said.

I opened the book. It had columns of words in alphabetical order, but no definitions.

"What is it?"

"It's called a *Word Book.* Secretaries use them to check spelling. They don't need definitions, and I suspect you don't either."

"Where can I get one?"

"You can keep that one. You'll find them in office supply shops."

"Thanks, this should help a lot."

"When we write in class, underline words you suspect are wrong, then use the word book to check them. You can have extra class time to make a clean copy."

"Really?"

"Yes, really. Ann, you have a specific learning disability identified in your academic file. You're entitled to extra time on in-class assignments and tests. Didn't you know?"

"No."

"Well, you do now."

Whoever came up with the idea of a "word book" was a genius; it was fast to use and made such a big difference. It became my constant companion in all my classes. We needed to write one paper a week.

Between my word book and electric typewriter, I did fine. Mrs. Rose was what the university called a teaching assistant, a graduate student who taught freshman classes. She was fantastic, and I hoped they paid her well.

* * *

I accidentally registered for the wrong math class and only discovered the fact when it was too late to drop, so I had an "elective" math class. It's a good thing I liked math, or I would have been upset. The class was called Finite Mathematics and had set theory and logic -topics I'd never had in high school and found interesting and easy. In retrospect, the class actually was a nice elective for a nervous freshman, and it gave me confidence to take other math classes as electives.

My other elective was Gymnastics. I registered for it because my high school hadn't allowed girls on the gymnastics team. I loved watching their competitions, and the sport looked very cool.

Coach Prather explained the class was for fun and exercise, and that all of us were too old to be competitive. And it was fun. We learned movements on the balance beam, flew on the uneven bars, and practiced handstands and back walkovers. It turned out I had little talent for gymnastics, but that didn't keep me from loving the class. By the end of the term, I had an impressive collection of black and blue bruises. And I still signed up for a second term.

* * *

The sixteen-week term passed quickly. And when grades were posted, I'd earned a 4.0 grade point average. When I opened the letter and saw the results, I was stunned. *Straight As?* Part of me felt vindicated;

I'd worked incredibly hard for those grades. But I couldn't shake a nagging feeling that the grades weren't real.

*Was USF not a real university? It was a small school, was that why I made all As?* I tried to shake it off; I knew lots of kids were struggling, but I had a sense of letdown I couldn't shake. In the end, I had to accept that I was odd enough to be depressed by making a 4.0 for my first grade report.

# Chapter 25 ~ Money and the Unintended Curriculum

Without a doubt, attending college exposed me to an unintended curriculum that one could call "Adulthood 101." This curriculum was more than academics at its core.

I graduated high school in 1971 and turned eighteen the summer before starting college. Boys my age had to register for the draft. They were old enough to be sent to Vietnam, and many were on campus because attending college provided deferment from the draft. The legal drinking age at the time was eighteen. We could order alcohol at the University Rathskeller.

But there was a fairly obvious contradiction. Our dorm had a ten p.m. curfew. If we came back to our dorm after that time, we had to call security to let us in. They reported our transgression to the resident aide. The policy confused me. Were college students adults or minors? My parents had never imposed a curfew, so why should the dorm?

The policy directly resulted from the public outcry the previous year. A lawyer on the Florida Board of Regents called Florida college dormitories "taxpayers' whorehouses." The outcry caused the university to place all first-year students in one dorm complex with the ten p.m. curfew. I found the mixed messages confusing. Was I an adult or not?

I had other things to worry about, and sex wasn't even on my radar. I'd never really had to think about money before. Mom always had food in the refrigerator and in the pantry. Instead, I now had a check for one hundred dollars in hand. As soon as I was registered, I walked into the bank with a check for one hundred dollars from Dad, and a promise that they would send this amount each month.

I walked up to a teller at the bank and said, "I need to open an account."

The young man took the check. "Can I see your ID, please?"

I handed him my driver's license, and he entered the information on a computer. A few minutes later, he gave me a checkbook.

I was grateful for their generosity, but it was a challenge to stretch the money in a way that allowed me to eat. I'm not sure what they had in mind for a budget. One hundred dollars a month came to $3.30 a day. And I also needed to pay for school supplies, gasoline, and toiletries. I had some money from my summer job, but not much. Textbooks had been expensive.

*Should I look for a job?* I decided not to. It was more important not to flunk out than to eat. After all, Richard flunked out in his first term, and he didn't have dyslexia. Maybe in the future, I'd look for a job, but for now, I thought it best to make sure I could pass college classes before dividing my time and efforts.

It was a challenge. I kept cans of soup and tuna, boxes of macaroni and cheese, bread, peanut butter, and jelly in the dorm. A family friend, Pat, worked in the campus bookstore. Pat was a junior majoring in foreign languages. Our dads were business partners, and Pat's Mom, Maryln, often had us over for dinner. She was a great cook. Her folks asked her to look in on me. Pat was horrified that I was trying to stretch one hundred dollars to last a month.

"Take these coupons," she said, discreetly handing me a stack of glossy cards, each with a picture of a hamburger.

I put them in my bag, saying, "Thanks."

I could exchange each card for a "Whopper" at a new fast-food restaurant just off campus.

For the next few months, I made a weekly pilgrimage to Burger King. At first, they expected me to buy a drink and fries, but after a while, they recognized me and took the coupon without question. Pat's generosity went a long way to feeding me that first year.

I bought a meal ticket book for eighteen dollars that contained twenty-five one-dollar tickets. It was a great deal. I exchanged one-dollar tickets for an apple and a chunk of cheddar cheese for lunch most days. But, even watching every penny, by the end of the month, I was out of food and eating popcorn for meals.

I wondered how other students managed, but most of them were on scholarships or other forms of financial aid and had meal plans. I had no idea how they got. Mom and Dad hadn't been to college; they didn't know anything about college or financial aid applications. I was on my own.

Sometimes, particularly when I ran out of food, I envied the dorm students on the "meal plan" who could just show up and eat. One day at the start of a month, I paid $2.50 to try out a lunch. The food wasn't bad, but the cost of the plan was far more than I could afford.

There were students in the dorm who had families in Lakeland or other nearby areas. Sometimes, they would go home for a weekend and return with home-cooked food to make the week easier. My drive home was almost six hours. I didn't do it often. But I kept my envy in check, realizing it was hard to be on my own, but there was also a satisfaction to being able to work it out on my own. I could do this.

I rarely spent money on entertainment. First, I was studying so much that I rarely had downtime. Second, living on campus, there were plenty of things to do for free. The theater department and music department didn't charge students for productions, and the campus movie theater only charged one dollar. There were pools to swim in, and the gymnastics room was available for me to practice. The university even had a waterfront park on the Hillsborough River with canoes available. That was great when I could find someone to join me.

Then there was the card room at the University Center. The first friends I made were bridge players looking to fill a fourth slot for weekend games. My math instructor called me over for a game during my first term on campus. Most of the players were graduate students in math, but they were friendly and seemed happy to see me. I'd learned the game at Seacamp and was glad that they didn't play for money.

I didn't include any money in my budget for alcohol. I never drank. The decision was a deliberate one, not made solely for financial reasons. Growing up, I'd seen too much of my parents' drinking. My mom became a sloppy drunk. We often needed to help her to the car. Dad could hold his liquor better, but he got obnoxious. Bob's parents, my grandparents, also had a drinking problem.

At USF, an academic year consisted of four terms. Students attended three of the four, taking fifteen credits a term. You needed to earn forty-five credits over the year to maintain full-time status. By the end of my first year, I looked like a successful science major. I had completed forty-five credits, with a grade point average of 3.3 out of 4, and had fulfilled my requirements in chemistry, biology, English, math, and electives.

But I was riddled with doubts about my academic abilities. It had taken Herculean effort to excel in my classes. I was in the library studying for at least six hours a day. *Could I sustain this level of commitment?* I feared there wasn't a middle course. If I didn't study from morning to late at night, I'd surely flunk out. I'd watched hordes of students waiting for grades to post outside the Chemistry Office, desperately looking for their student numbers and praying for a passing grade. I'd seen the empty rooms in my dorm, a testament to how easy it was for students to fail.

Mom and Dad were generous enough to pay my tuition and housing, but I felt guilty about taking money for college if I ultimately wouldn't be able to complete a degree. But what were my choices? Return to North Miami Beach and ask Dad for a job at his business? I wasn't ready for that.

Mom wanted me to train as a bookkeeper and trained me to help in the office. She loved the work, but I didn't. *Did I want to continue as a zoology major at USF?* I had a passion for marine biology, but with the difficulty I experienced in lower-division biology classes, I was concerned about what upper-division work would be like. I made an appointment with an academic counselor. Perhaps it was time to reconsider zoology as a major.

"I don't see what you're worried about. Your grades are very good," he said.

"I love science and biology, but I studied nonstop as a freshman. Half the students in my dorm have already dropped out. How much harder are the upper-division classes?"

"They expect you to be serious in your studies, and they expect students will have an aptitude for the subject. Are you having second thoughts about a biology major? Why did you select biology? Are you thinking of pre-med?"

"I want to work in marine biology. I'm not interested in medical school."

He nodded sympathetically. "It's unfortunate that most students in your classes are looking to go to medical school. That fact dials up the pressure. Just remember, they need to keep a 4.0 grade point average. You do not."

"I have dyslexia, so memorization is harder for me. I'm not sure I can keep studying twenty hours a day."

He nodded sympathetically. "Have you considered joining the co-op program?"

"What is it?"

"The office finds jobs that are in your field. Once you're placed, you alternate full-time study with working. It could help you avoid burnout."

I was more than just interested. A work-study could be an answer to burnout, as well as to being financially strapped.

"Do they have jobs in marine biology?"

He hesitated.

"They have science placements. Why not meet with them? "

I headed directly to the co-op office. After talking for just five minutes, I filled out the application, excited about a program that might lead to a job in biology. Most of their placements were in business, but they said they would work on finding me something and promised to contact me when they had a placement.

My time at Seacamp had filled me with excitement. The thought of working in biology, now, before I needed to complete my degree, was intoxicating.

I had to temper the excitement. They had warned it could take a while to find a placement. The next day, I packed my car for the summer and headed to my parents' house, figuring I could find work to build a buffer in my savings account.

I could feel the surge of optimism. I had a plan, and I felt hopeful. Even if the placement office took some time to find something, knowing they were trying would help. I wouldn't give up. Leaving campus, I was committed to returning for another year.

# Chapter 26 ~ Dream Job

After saying hello to Mom, Dad, Jim, and Gigi, I unpacked my car and opened the paper to look for a job. The savings from last summer were long since gone, and to return to USF in the fall, I wanted to put some money away. Dad helped by making some phone calls, and I soon found factory work at American Hospital Supply.

The work was dull, but it paid a lot more than Seacamp (where the pay was next to nothing). Phylece, Bob, Debbie, and Rick were in town. It was fun to reconnect with my old friends and revisit old haunts.

It was odd being back in my old bedroom. Mom and Dad left for work early in the morning, and my shift at American Hospital Supply ran from three p.m. to eleven p.m. On weekends, I got together with friends, so I didn't see my family all that much.

It was fun to reconnect with Jim. My younger brother was now in high school, with a group of friends who came and went from the house. He would be heading off to college himself in another year.

"What are you up to this weekend?" I asked.

"Not much. We're going water skiing," he said.

He'd traded our Boston Whaler for a boat that was better for skiing almost as soon as I'd left for college. I liked water skiing, but not as much as diving and snorkeling.

"Thanks, I'm good."

The out-of-sync schedules worked well. Like most teens, I found being with my parents stressful. They drank from the time they came home until they stumbled into bed. They talked about business all the time.

Summer passed quickly, and I was pleased to have bolstered my savings account, providing a nice buffer for my junior year. The first Sunday morning in August, I was preparing to leave for registration at USF, when Dad asked what I was studying in college.

"Zoology," I said.

"What are you going to do? Work in a zoo?" he asked.

"Maybe," I said.

He looked at me, confused. We had been to zoos, and maybe it didn't occur to him that people working at zoos would need a college degree. Not that I had ever thought about working in a zoo. I didn't know what I wanted to do.

I was driving to Tampa for early registration, so I'd spend a couple of nights in a dorm. That way, I could hit early registration in the morning. The memory of the chaos of "regular" registration, with closed classes and panicked students from a year ago, remained strong. It turned out that early registration was easy and uneventful. The process took under two hours, and I got every class I wanted. I finished before noon, so I headed to the co-op office to check in and let them know I was still interested.

"A spot just opened at NOAA in St. Pete Beach," William said. "Your file was on top because your Seacamp experience makes you the perfect fit. Can you head over there for an interview?"

"Now?"

"Yes, it is an opening for a biological assistant in marine biology. A student had to pull out, and we need a replacement."

"I can go."

"Good. Here's the address. I'll call and tell them you're on your way."

"Thanks," I said, taking a slip of paper.

I was dumbfounded. It was almost too good to be true. He was talking about my dream job. Then, I realized I didn't have anything suitable to wear for an interview.

I went to the campus bookstore and selected a school T-shirt. It was new, clean, and had an official-looking logo. And, it didn't cost too much money. I bought it.

The drive took ninety minutes. *That was a long commute to do every day! Could I rent an* apartment? Not only would it be expensive, but I was not sure Mom and Dad would let me. Dad was uneasy about my even being in a dorm. In his view, girls lived at home until they got married.

Well, I'd worry about that if I got the job. I didn't want to count on a job offer. *But, NOAA!* I was excited. I'd really like to work for NOAA.

I pulled into the driveway at the office, a small tan building next to a huge, pink, derelict hotel that looked like a castle. I pulled into the parking lot and walked in.

"Hi, I'm here for an interview. I'm from the USF co-op office."

She smiled. "We've been expecting you. Carl said You would be coming. This building is the office, not the lab."

She pulled out a paper map and drew on it. "Take Gulf Boulevard for half a mile. The field station is on the left. It's a large steel building. You can't miss it."

The building looked like a run-down warehouse, and I wondered how it could be a lab. But the address matched, and it was indeed a large steel building on the water. So I tentatively walked inside. The building didn't have interior walls. It was literally a large shell of a building. Metal shelf units filled with specimen jars were everywhere. I looked closer and saw there were tiny fish in some jars, and invertebrates like starfish in others. The shelving units were arranged to create distinct work areas, each with a desk and a lab bench. The metal building really was a working lab environment, even if the place was shabby and primitive.

"Hello," I called out.

A middle-aged man, balding and wearing jeans and a short-sleeved khaki shirt, looked up from a microscope.

"Can I help you?" he asked.

"I'm looking for a Mr. Solomon," I said.

"That's me. Are you Ann?" he asked as he stood up, walked over, and extended a hand to greet me.

"I am. Thank you for fitting me in for an interview on short notice. Can you tell me about the position?"

He motioned to a seat across from his desk, and I took it.

"We're a field station for the National Oceanic and Atmospheric Administration. We have funding for two student research assistants. The program has been going on for the past three years, and we've had students who alternated terms until graduation. It works for us because we aren't constantly training new students."

"Can you tell me what I'd be doing?

"Part of the job is taking measurements of tide levels, water and air temperature, and collecting water samples to send out for lab analysis of oxygen levels. I'll show you the equipment out on the dock so you get a sense of how that works."

I nodded. "I've done some of that working down in the Keys," I said.

"That's excellent," Carl said. "Some of the work is off the boats. We collect fish and crustaceans from traps up and down the bay and shallow parts of the gulf. We cut samples up and test for heavy metal concentrations. That part can get smelly and messy."

"I'm not afraid of smelly and messy," I said. And now, I was glad I hadn't dressed up for the interview.

"Good," he said. "Let's take a walk, and I'll show you around."

He led me through the old building. The room was large, and there seemed to be no pattern to the placement of tables set up as working desks and research stations. We stopped at each station, and Mr. Solomon introduced me to three other researchers. They were all middle-aged, casually dressed men.

Carl led me out onto the working pier and showed me the equipment for collecting tide and water quality data. Then he took me to see the boats. One was a large cabin cruiser. The other was a small boat with an outboard motor. It was similar to the one I used at Seacamp to run kids out to the reef for snorkeling. It looked like an old friend.

"I'm going to be honest. Ann, we've never interviewed a woman for this student position. As I said, the work is smelly, and often the men shower out on the dock when they finish. We would have to figure something out for privacy."

I didn't say anything. I wasn't sure what I could say. Finally, I broke the silence. "I'm not afraid to get my hands dirty," I said. "I'm sure you can figure out a way for the men to clean up, even if it's just me leaving the area to give them time to shower."

I didn't address my need to shower. In the Keys, we cleaned up using a hose while sitting on the lawn. There wasn't much water pressure, so we all just kept our bathing suits on and sat on the ground. But I didn't think it was appropriate to bring that up.

He didn't look convinced, but nodded. We walked back into the building, and Carl pointed to the jars of specimens on the shelves.

"You'll spend about a third of your time working with preserved samples of sand and mud collected from around one hundred meters off St. Pete Beach. It's part of a study to measure the impact of beach replenishment on animals that live in the sand."

"You're talking about diversity?" I asked.

Carl gave me a strange look. Maybe I had surprised him by knowing about diversity. He nodded in agreement.

"We separate invertebrates by phylum. Then, each researcher

identifies and counts the number of individuals per species. We have a computer specialist who analyses the data."

I understood only about half of what he said, but it sounded very neat.

"It sounds exciting," I said.

"Well, it takes patience and a good eye. The person we hire will work with marine worms. They're called polychaetes. Do you know what they are?"

"I do. I've had my first zoology class, and we examined preserved specimens in the lab. I've also looked at living ones in the ocean."

"Good," he said. Then he paused, looking embarrassed. "I mentioned that we had never had a woman apply for one of the co-op positions. Really, other than administration in the other building, we just don't have any women working here. You sure you don't mind the idea of working with fish guts?"

"I don't mind at all, and I'm very excited about working here."

"Good. I'm going to need to work out some practical details. There are a few details I'll need to see to. We can solve the privacy for showers, but, I don't think we can include you in overnight boat work, given that there is only one cabin for sleep quarters. Let me talk to the men and figure it out. You'll hear from me soon."

"Thank you. When you talk to the other researchers, please tell them how excited I am about the job, and that I can be very flexible about privacy and any other issues they may see as a problem."

"I will," he said. "Thanks for driving out to meet with me. I have your contact information. You should hear from me in a few days.

We shook hands, and I walked out to my car. It took me a few minutes to turn the car on and navigate out of the parking lot. I wanted this job. I didn't know how I would take it if they didn't offer it to me. Suddenly, the thought of going back to campus and starting a new set of classes seemed unattractive. I wanted to work at the lab, on the water, working in marine science!

I could not help that I was female, but I could just go inside and leave them to their showers. The boat was another story. And Carl was right to have concerns. I wasn't just female; I was an underage girl. There would be legal concerns about having me on a boat overnight with a bunch of guys.

What I couldn't figure out was why there were so few women interested in working in marine science. It seemed unimaginable that I was the only female to apply. *What was I missing?* Science was obviously a male-dominated domain. My question was: why? And how does one overcome the issues of being the minority sex?

# Chapter 27 ~ Change of Plans

The six-hour drive back to my parents' house tempered my excitement. When I pulled into the driveway, I decided not to say anything to my friends or Mom and Dad. Dr. Solomon had been upfront with me. His team didn't want to hire a girl. They had other applicants to interview, so I would only get this job if no one else applied. When Friday rolled around without a call from the co-op office, I figured they had found someone else.

With my folks still at work, the house was quiet. I sat at the kitchen table and stared at the printout with my schedule: Calculus, Chemistry, Biology, Humanities, and Gymnastics. I would have been excited if I hadn't gone to the interview. But now, all I could think of was how hard classes were and how I always felt on the verge of failure.

For the next week, my job kept me busy. Then it was over, and I had a week to do whatever I wanted. *What did I want?* The job interview intensified my feeling of loss for not working at Seacamp over the summer. Working at American Hospital Supply was a means of earning money to go back to school, but it hurt that I couldn't spend the summer in the Keys. I had a week. I would drive down to Big Pine Key for a visit.

The road trip helped. They offered lodging for a few days, and I helped around the grounds. I talked about college, and they reassured me that academic life would get easier. It might not have been true, but hearing it made me feel better as I left and drove back to spend the last two days of my summer with my folks.

As I walked into the house, the phone was ringing. Dad picked it up.

"Hello," he said.

I listened, waiting quietly. Dad got business calls all the time. He would have told me if it were for me.

"She's starting classes in a few days, so I think you have the wrong person." He hung up.

"Dad, was that for me?" I asked.

"It was someone in St. Pete Beach calling about a job. You're not looking for a job, are you?"

"Dad!" I said. "How could you do that?"

I raced back to my room and got the phone number for NOAA. I was shaking as I dialed and tried not to get too excited. They might have been calling to let me know they hired someone else.

"Hello, is Dr. Solomon in? I may have missed a call from him. I'm Ann Rudnick."

"Hold for a minute while I connect you," the woman said.

That minute felt like an hour.

"Hi Ann, this is Carl. I was calling to offer you the job. Would you like to work with us?"

"Yes, I would. I'm very excited."

"Great. We will expect you on Monday, August 28, at seven-thirty a.m. Do you have questions?"

"No, I'll call if I think of something. Thank you."

I hung up, feeling stunned. Dad was staring at me.

"What is this about?" he asked.

"I just accepted a job working for the National Oceanographic and Atmospheric Administration. I start in a week."

"Where?" he asked.

"St. Pete Beach."

"Sit down. We need to talk," he said. "What about college?"

I sat down. It hadn't occurred to me I should have talked to Mom and Dad before applying for jobs. *Why would they care?*

"Dad, I'm sorry I didn't tell you about applying for a job. When I registered, they sent me for an interview. I didn't expect to be offered the job."

"They sent you during registration? Is the job for the college?"

"Not exactly. It's part of a work-study program where you alternate a term at college with a term of work in your field."

"That's going to slow college down, isn't it?"

"Yes, but not too much. I can take extra classes on campus, and one of the work sessions will replace the summer quarter. So it means attending two quarters instead of three each year."

"Where will you live if the job is in St. Pete Beach? That's a long way from USF."

"It took me ninety minutes to drive from campus. I need to look for a short-term rental."

Dad looked unhappy, but he wasn't saying anything.

"You don't want me driving that much every day. Do you?"

"No, I don't. I don't think it's a good idea for a young, unmarried woman to take an apartment alone."

"I don't see I have a choice," I said.

"Is the job that important to you?" he asked.

"Yes."

"Let me talk to Mom about it."

They took the weekend to decide. The logistics caused problems. Dad's view was not uncommon. Many apartment complexes would not rent to an unmarried young woman. While I looked, I was staying in one of the university's "guest" dorm rooms. They let me out of my dorm contract because I was now officially a co-op student. So, I had all my belongings in my Toyota trunk while I looked.

It took a few days, but I eventually rented an efficiency apartment. It was a converted motel that would let me rent month to month. They made me sign a contract that I would not have male visitors. The small room had a pull-out sofa, kitchenette, small fridge, stove, and sink. The other renters were largely divorced women raising kids. I wondered how they fit more than one person in the unit. But it was on the intracoastal Waterway and only five minutes from work. For me, it was perfect.

I adjusted my registration and signed up for Co-op and Calculus. Twice a week, I would drive to campus for the evening class.

I would still drive to and from campus only twice a week. When I started work, I was settled in and felt like a local.

By Wednesday, I had unpacked and settled into my first apartment. I had the rest of the week to explore St. Pete Beach, my new town. The Pass-a-Grille Beach was right down the street, and it was stunning. Wood walkways rose over the sea oat-covered dunes to the white sand beach. The water glistened in the sunlight, with gentle waves lapping at the shore. Just offshore, several dolphins swam, rolling their fins and disappearing into the water. I bought a beach chair and a towel and spent the four days before Monday on the beach.

# Chapter 28 ~ NOAA

My apartment was so tiny that I had to close the sleeper couch before opening the refrigerator. I rushed through a bowl of Cheerios and a cup of coffee before heading to the lab. When I pulled in, the parking lot was empty, and I wondered if I had misunderstood the work hours. *Didn't work start at seven-thirty?* I sat on the dock, waiting, and watched the fish swim around the pilings. The water was clear, and the early morning sun cast a pastel glow over everything. At exactly seven twenty-eight, six cars pulled into the parking lot. It was an impressive display of punctuality, or perhaps they had all had breakfast together.

Carl unlocked the building and waited for everyone to enter, then reached out to me, saying, "Glad to have you on board. Have you met Lee?"

"No," I said.

A tall, good-looking young man stepped forward and took my hand.

He said, "You must be the other USF student. I looked for you at orientation."

"They hired me after orientation. I think they were holding out, hoping a guy would apply."

Lee flashed a big smile and shook his head. "That sounds about right. I'm on my third rotation, and I haven't seen any women working here. Anyway, welcome to the team."

There were so many things I wanted to ask Lee, but Carl was hovering and signaling for me to follow.

"Thanks," I said. "We'll catch up later."

I followed Carl through the building until we stopped at an empty table between rows of industrial shelves, each filled with hundreds of mason jars.

"Here is your workstation. It's where you'll work on taxonomy," he said. "Think of it as a combined desk and lab bench."

The bench held a dissecting microscope, an adding machine, and a large magnifying lens mounted in a circular light fixture.

"You'll spend mornings recording tides and taking samples for water quality testing. Some mornings, we'll be out on the boat. Other mornings, we'll all work on preparing the fish samples to send for mercury testing. We spend the afternoons working on core samples."

Carl pointed to the jars. "These are sediment samples taken from testing sites off St. Pete Beach. We identify and count the invertebrates, then analyze to see if diversity recovers after beach replenishment."

I looked closer at the jar. "The label has the collection site, water depth, and date. Is the liquid above the sample seawater?" I asked.

"No. We store samples in formaldehyde solution."

He opened the sample and showed me how to waft the air toward my nose to smell it. I learned to "waft" in chemistry. It was a way to detect the presence of odor when the gas might be hazardous.

"Wow, that is strong," I said.

"Yeah, it's a great preservative, but you'll need to wash samples before you work on them. And you'll wear gloves while you drain and rinse them."

He showed pouring a jar over a mesh sieve, collecting the formaldehyde, then running water over the sand and debris, and then taping it into a shallow dish of water.

"We collect the formaldehyde for disposal; we don't want it going down the drain. Remember to wear gloves and avoid breathing the fumes."

"Got it," I said.

He pointed to the chair in front of the lab bench. "Have a seat."

I sat down, and Carl moved the viewing magnifying lens/lamp into position to direct the light onto the sample. Looking through the lens, I saw tiny crabs, worms, and even a few brittle stars—tiny starfish.

Carl opened a box of small jars and set them on my desk.

"Most invertebrates in the samples will be crustaceans, mollusks, echinoderms, and polychaetes."

Carl reached for a textbook, *Barnes Invertebrate Zoology.* "Have you had a class in invertebrate zoology?" he asked.

"No, but I had a biology class at USF that introduced the major groups, and my marine biology class in high school used *Barnes* as a textbook."

"Great."

Carl picked up a pair of tweezers and started sorting the invertebrates into groups. He picked up the crabs, dropping them one by one into a small jar. He filled it with 70 percent alcohol and labeled it *Crustaceans.*

"You use the viewer to sort the invertebrates into crustaceans, mollusks, echinoderms, and polychaetes and store them in the smaller jars. Label each jar with the sample number, today's date, the name of the invertebrate group, and the number of specimens in it."

I wrote my notes, then looked up and said, "Got it."

"You keep a tally of the numbers of each group from a sample. We will analyze diversity at the class level. You take the sorted jars to the researcher working on each class. Bill does crustaceans, Lee does mollusks, I get the echinoderms, and you keep the polychaetes."

My position was to identify the marine worms to genus and species. My desk had an up-to-date copy of *Barnes Invertebrate Zoology* for me to consult for the initial sorting and classification keys to marine worms. It might sound dull, but I found it was fun identifying the worms. The marine worms were varied; some looked like dragons. Most looked like nothing I had ever seen. And it was fun telling people my job was to "count worms."

In 1972, electronic calculators and adding machines were making their appearance, but the lab was "old school." My desk had an old-fashioned mechanical adding machine to keep a tally of specimens. I knew how to use the adding machine because Mom trained me on it when she hoped I'd go into bookkeeping.

Each of us gave John Blake our initial numbers for each sample. He used the lab computer to analyze the data at the species level. Back at USF, there was a building with a huge mainframe computer. I had friends who took Introduction to Computer Science. They wrote programs and then used a device to punch them onto cards, which they fed into the mainframe.

Our lab computer was not a mainframe. It was the smallest computer available at the time, taking up an entire six-foot by four-foot table, and it could accept a program of up to seven cards. John used a hand punch to set up each card. No one else knew how to make the magical device do its "thing." Everyone was terrified that we would have to handle all the data using our mechanical adding machines if John were to leave the program. We would be doomed.

When we took a break for lunch, my head was spinning. I was suffering from information overload, but I was thrilled to be in a place where I could apply what I'd been learning. To be honest, my first year at USF had been brutal, and I wasn't ready to go back to classes.

*By the end of my first day, I knew I had made the right decision in taking the placement. Maybe, just maybe, I'd find motivation to stick with the classes back at USF.*

# Chapter 29 ~ On the Water

The researchers stopped for lunch at noon. Carl asked me if I'd like to go, but I brought lunch and said I'd join them another day. I took my lunch out to the dock and settled in to watch the fish. Lee, the other USF student, joined me with his lunch bag. We were trying to save money for when we would be back at school.

"Is this your first co-op placement?" Lee asked.

"It is."

"This is my third. It's a great place to work, but the commute kills me."

"Yeah, I'm driving to USF twice a week for calculus. So you're staying on campus?" I asked.

"I have an apartment in Temple Terrace with a year-long lease, so yeah, I'm commuting."

"I was in the dorm last year, and they let me out of my contract because of the co-op placement. Of course, it means a dorm room may not be available for next term."

"I stayed in a dorm my first year. I'm finishing my junior year and will be a senior when I go back."

"Are you a zoology major?" I asked.

"I was, but I switched to natural science interdisciplinary. It gives more flexibility in selecting classes," he said. "So, where are you living now?"

"I have an efficiency about a mile from here. It's a converted motel room, but it's cheap."

"This is my third placement. I started right after my freshman year. I'll be a senior after this placement. I'm unsure if I'll do another quarter here; I need to graduate already. "

"That's why I'm taking Calculus at night. And I'm going to max out classes when I go back; I understand we can take up to eighteen credits without breaking any rules."

"I failed Calculus twice, which is one of the reasons I switched my major. Natural science doesn't require Calculus."

I didn't know what to say to that. This would be my second class in calculus, and the first term wasn't particularly hard. Just then, the cars started pulling back into the parking lot. Lunchtime was over.

Lee was cute and smart. We took our bag lunches to the pier almost every day. It was great to have someone to talk to about classes and being a college student. John and Steve, one of the researchers Lee worked with, teased and nagged Lee to ask me for a date.

The teasing was because, in all the time Lee worked at NOAA, he never mentioned a girlfriend. They were clueless, and Lee was my first gay friend. He told me he was gay in the second week of the term, while we had lunch together on the pier. He didn't want the researchers to know his orientation. We went out for dinner a few times, and I kept it to myself that Lee wasn't interested in girls.

There was a rhythm to working at the lab. I pulled into the NOAA parking lot at sunrise. It was my responsibility to record the seven a.m. tide levels. It was a nice routine: do tide levels, collect samples to send out for testing of oxygen, phosphate, and nitrate levels. Then I went out on the pier and measured turbidity, and how the visibility of the water was. I lowered a Secchi disk into the water, measuring the depth where I couldn't see the patterns on the surface. The mornings were magical, with the sun painting pastels over the water. I felt like I was in a fairy tale.

Around eight, Carl came out to the dock, and we took the boat out to check the fish traps. We used a sixteen-foot open craft with an outboard motor. It reminded me of the boats I used to ferry campers to snorkel sites at Seacamp. This one had a large outboard motor, and Carl kept a spare, smaller motor in the boat for emergencies. He said that because the Gulf of Mexico was so shallow, storms could cause rapid changes to waves, and being caught in a storm could be deadly if the engine cut out.

We traveled along the coastline, past the natural sandbar that forms off St. Pete Beach. We visited a series of ten fish traps marked with buoys. At each trap, Lee and I pulled the large wire basket close to the boat, and Carl reached in to collect the fish. We had ten buckets set aside, one for each fish trap. Back at the NOAA dock, we took tissue samples to send for mercury testing.

Spanish mackerel were small enough that the testing never showed any mercury levels. So Carl let us take as much home as we wanted once the samples were packed to send for testing. I learned many ways to cook the fish. And there was a place nearby that would smoke fish for a very reasonable price. I ate very well that term.

While we were collecting from the traps, we saw dolphins, manatees, and sharks. Most of the sharks were a short distance from the sandbar. At low tide, the top of the sandbar was so shallow that people swam out from shore and waded on it, collecting sand dollars and shells. They were oblivious to the sharks swimming a very short distance from them.

These were big, fat bull sharks that looked dangerous. Carl said shark attacks were rare, but he also told us that when NOAA sent divers down, they got hazard duty pay. He said that was because great white sharks were also known to frequent the area. I decided that when I was at the beach, I would stay well in from the sandbar.

The beach was gorgeous, a wide expanse of white sand with gentle dunes covered with sea oats. The Gulf of Mexico was often so still in the mornings, it resembled a pond. Brown pelicans would dive into the water with a splash. The first time I saw a seagull perched on a pelican's head, I thought I was imagining things. Lee teased me, saying it couldn't be. But I kept seeing it. Eventually, Carl explained that seagulls do that, eating scraps from the pelicans.

On collection days, we finished the water work and packaged samples by noon. Then we cleaned up for lunch. We were glad to spend the afternoon processing benthic samples, identifying the invertebrates, and making tallies for analysis. It made for a pleasant flow to the day. At four-thirty, we closed up the lab, and everyone went home.

I knew I'd love the boat work. *Who wouldn't love being out on a boat?* However, I didn't know how much I'd enjoy working with the microscope and using dichotomous keys to identify marine worms. It was like working on a challenging puzzle, and I looked forward to every day. I told my friends I counted worms for a living.

My coworkers were amazing people: smart, funny, and kind. Every day, their actions toward me expressed the attitude that they expected me to one day make a life for myself in science. It was a revelation. Although I didn't enjoy *taking* biology classes, I loved *working* in biological science. Working was so much fun that I felt guilty cashing my paychecks.

What I did not know was that the government was closing this branch. Shortly after I left to return to school, the scientists were transferred to Panama City. Unfortunately, they could not offer co-op positions at the new location. I was heartbroken when I found out.

The sixteen-week fall term ended all too soon. Lee and I said goodbye to friends and coworkers at NOAA, knowing that the research station was closing and we would not be returning. The sadness we both felt was palpable, leaving us feeling empty inside. We would miss morning trips out to the fish traps, as well as Carl Solomon and all the researchers. We would miss working together. Oh, we would cross paths back at USF and would get together for lunch dates, but it wouldn't be the same.

# Chapter 30 ~ Balancing Act

Co-op students could take up to six credits while on a work placement without incurring additional tuition fees. While I wanted a break from classes, the temptation of free tuition was too strong for me to pass up. So, even though it meant driving forty miles from St. Pete Beach to Tampa twice a week, I signed up for an evening Calculus class.

My coworkers at NOAA thought I was crazy for taking Calculus. "Take something easy," they said.

But math had always been predictable, and I knew I could handle the subject. I'd taken the first term of Calculus last spring and made an A, so a second semester of the class seemed like a good choice. Like most college professors, mine assigned homework, but didn't collect it. I always did my work and checked my answers. He would work any problem on the board if a student asked for it. What amazed me was that most students didn't do the homework, even after failing the first test. Despite hating the drive home at night, I never skipped class and maintained my A in my third math class at USF.

The drive took ninety minutes. If there were a lot of traffic, I would be late for the six p.m. class. However, I never missed a class and always completed my work on time, so the professor never complained when I arrived a few minutes late. By the time I drove home, it was nearly ten p.m. With my seven-thirty a.m. start time, I went straight to bed.

Taking a night class gave me insight into the world of commuting students at USF. I gained comfort in my role as an independent human being in the larger world. I was, indeed, growing up.

There were some positives about being forced to do the drive. With no highways, my route took me through the cities of St. Petersburg and Tampa. Early in my commute, I discovered Haslam's, a store with signage proclaiming it was *Florida's Largest New and Used Bookstore*. I didn't doubt the sign; it occupied an entire city block.

The shop was huge, and it was organized like a library, making it easy to find a favorite author or topic. My discovery was dangerous because I had "disposable income." Even paying for an apartment and saving for my next term, I had money for used books and the occasional new one. On my first visit, I scored two used hardback books by a favorite author, Robert A. Heinlein. I became a regular and devoted customer from that day forward.

While driving through Tampa, I discovered that there was a downtown area at that time, almost like a miniature Miami. In the area near campus, I found shops with signs boasting Cuban sandwiches and black beans and rice.

\* \* \*

USF used to operate on a quarter system. Full-time students took fifteen credits per term, totaling forty-five credits annually. To graduate in four years, 160 credits were needed. Working at NOAA put me behind. It somehow seemed more important now that the NOAA position was gone, and I might be back to just doing classes.

It was insane, but I registered for twenty-two credits to try partially catch up. It was a delusional mistake. What *was I thinking?* Organic Chemistry, Calculus, Botany, and Expository Writing made for an insane load.

That term was my first experience with organic chemistry, and it was insanely difficult. The lectures seemed more like a foreign language than chemistry. There were impossible quantities of unrelated content to memorize. I didn't expect chemistry to be like this. General chemistry was problem-solving, and I was good at problem-solving. Organic chemistry was memorization. The labs were fine. In fact, they were fun, but they did take a lot of time at the lab bench.

Years later, with a greater understanding of how to study, I found patterns and rules that made naming organic compounds easy. I don't know how I missed the importance of recognizing and understanding functional groups back then. But in the winter term of 1972, it felt like I was drowning in an ocean of academic trivia.

That semester was a blur of studying. I'd cram for one exam, then dive straight into preparing for the next in a different class. By the middle of it, I was a mental mess. Twenty-two credits were way too much, and honestly, it was a miracle I passed anything at all.

Midterms were brutal. I had a Calculus exam on Tuesday evening. As soon as that was over, I tried to cram as much organic chemistry as possible in the forty-eight hours before the Thursday exam. The subject felt impossible, like it was magic or some kind of voodoo. The carbon, oxygen, and hydrogen structures made no sense, and distinguishing between ketones, esters, and ethers seemed like a monumental challenge. Thankfully, I passed the test the next day, which was a huge relief.

Two hours after the Organic Chemistry exam, I walked back into my Calculus class again and nearly lost my mind when the professor passed out blank exam papers to us.

"We took this on Tuesday," I said.

"There was a problem with the exam. We're giving an alternative one," he said.

I stared at the exam paper, knowing that I was so exhausted, working through the problems would be difficult. When the professor finished passing papers out, he sat at his desk.

I walked to his desk and asked, "What was wrong with the last one we took?"

"The scores were very low. Almost everyone failed. I may have misjudged the difficulty. You should find this test more reasonable."

"I know I didn't fail the test. I'm taking a heavy course load, and I'm exhausted. This isn't fair."

He looked embarrassed, something I'd never seen in a professor. "You made 86 percent, but the next highest score was 62 percent."

"Can I just take my 86 percent? I'm really exhausted."

"I'll take your highest score," he said. "I'd like a comparison between the test, so I'd like to know how you do on this one."

I sighed, returned to my seat, and took the test. No, I didn't beat my 86 percent.

* * *

The term ended, and I resolved never to take that kind of overload again. Not wanting to stay another term, I hounded the co-op office for another placement. It was a long shot. Most placements were business-related, and I had told them repeatedly that I wasn't interested. I registered for classes, sure that it wouldn't happen for the next term, when the phone rang. The number on display was the co-op office, and I answered as calmly as I could.

"Hello."

"Hi, Ann, we may have something for you. Are you available for an out-of-state placement?"

"Where?"

"It's in Bethesda, Maryland, working at the National Institutes of Health."

I paused. It was science, but not marine science. *Did I want to work in the medical field?*

"Can I get more information on the placement?" I asked.

"Come over, and I'll give you the file. If you're interested, the director will interview you on the phone. They don't expect students to fly in."

"Okay, I'm on campus. I'll be over in ten to fifteen minutes."

"I'll see you then."

The position was working with neurological slow viruses. It was a placement that had nothing to do with marine science. *Was I interested?* I wasn't sure, but I thought it might be good to broaden my work experience. Maybe I would enjoy working in medical research.

Then I noticed a statement on the information sheet: *Male applicants preferred.* I groaned to myself, thinking, not again.

And the location was Maryland. That was near Washington, DC, but that was all I knew. But I figured it wouldn't hurt to have the interview.

Two days later, I sat in the co-op office. Dr. Gibbs would interview me by phone. If I took the job, he would be my supervisor for the placement. They had faxed him a copy of my resume.

The co-op office initiated the call, and Dr. Gibbs answered on the second ring.

"Joe Gibbs here, is this USF?"

"Yes, this is Terry here. I have Ann with us. I'm going to step out of the office so you two can talk."

"Thank you," he said.

"Thank you for taking the time to interview me," I said.

"Hello, Ann, I'm glad you could get us your paperwork and be available for an interview on short notice."

"I'd be eager to hear about the position."

"I see your experience has been working for NOAA and for a camp in the Florida Keys. This position is with the National Institutes of Health. Are you interested in medical research?"

"I'm from Florida, and most of the science available has been in marine science. But I'm only a sophomore, and I'd like to explore other areas of research. Can you tell me about the placement?"

"We work with slow viruses in animal models and in cell culture. The position involves working with our veterinarian and learning to culture cells."

"Cell culture is growing cells in dishes?" I asked.

"Some people use plates. We grow cells in flasks and roller bottles."

"It also sounds interesting. Is there a reason your information sheet says you are looking for male applicants? And is this likely to be a problem?"

"The work with animals can be smelly, and there is some heavy lifting involved. Would you be able to carry fifty-pound loads for short distances?"

"The lifting shouldn't be a problem, and lots of the work at NOAA was smelly. I can't see animal work being a problem," I answered.

After a minute, I asked, "Do you have any questions for me?"

"I'm looking at your grades and recommendations. If you want the position, I think you'll do fine."

I said, "Thank you, sir."

"Is that yes?" he asked.

"Yes, sir, I would like the job."

"Good, we'll get the paperwork set up."

As I hung up, my hand started shaking. I'd just accepted a job in another state. I hadn't asked my mom and dad. What would they think about my moving all the way to Maryland? And what was I doing? Accepting a job in virology? It wasn't something I knew anything at all about.

Mom and Dad went ballistic when I told them that night. I agreed to come home for a weekend and talk about it.

"Where will you live?" Dad asked.

"I took an apartment for the job at NOAA. I guess I'll need to find another one."

"You could stay at the dorms while you looked. If you didn't find something, you had a backup plan to commute."

"Sid lives in Silver Springs," Mom said.

"Who is Sid?" I asked.

"Grandma Jean's youngest brother. That makes him your great uncle."

"Have I met him?"

"No, but family is family. When you get into town, go directly to his place. I'll let him know you're coming."

Well, they were letting me go; that was a positive thing. I looked up as much information about Washington, DC and its surrounding areas as I could. I would be living and working right outside a large city. It should be an interesting term.

I wouldn't need to be on my own; The Co-op office placed two of us at NIH, the other student was Phyllis McDonald, an Anthropology student at USF. We didn't know each other but met up for lunch after I'd accepted the placement. I mentioned to Phyllis that the lab had hired two women after advertising that they were looking for male applicants. We had a good laugh over that. I asked why someone with a major in Anthropology wanted to work in a medical research lab. She said jobs in Anthropology weren't easy to find, and she was hoping to expand her interests. So, we had something in common.

During the interview, I had told Dr. Gibbs I wanted to explore a larger world of science. Mostly, I said it because I desperately wanted a job offer. However, there was truth in the statement as well. I wanted to work in science; it was time for me to explore possibilities. Maybe I would love virology.

# Chapter 31 ~ Washington DC

Mom and Dad were nervous about my second placement. Not only would I be off campus (again), but I would also be in a big city, in another state. They weren't thrilled that I needed to drive over a thousand miles to get there. This was before GPS was a thing and long before cell phones. The drive took me two days. After the first day, I checked into a motel and made a long-distance collect phone call to let them know I was safe. Phyllis was driving up on her own. We had plans to meet up as soon as we were both in town so we could look for an apartment.

After a second day of driving, I pulled into the driveway in front of a brick house in Silver Springs, Maryland. It was the address my mother gave me for her uncle Sid. I'd never met Uncle Sid, and I wasn't great at using maps while driving. I checked the house number to make sure I was at the right place, walked up to the door, and knocked.

An older man opened the door, looked at me, and said, "Renee?"

"No, but Renee's my mother."

He opened the door wide with a big smile on his face. "Come in, come in. My god, you look like your mom." He called into the house, "Sue, Renee's daughter is here! Come meet her."

They made a big fuss over my arrival. Sid was the same age as my mom, and they had grown up together but had drifted apart as adults. Sid and Sue offered to put me up in their spare room while I looked for an apartment, and when they found there was another student from USF, they invited Phyllis as well.

We stayed at the house for two weeks. When we found a sublease nearby, they loaned us a few pieces of furniture, including a bridge table, chairs, and an old rug. We each bought an inexpensive foam mattresses to sleep on.

Our apartment was right off the Beltway, a massive highway that circled around the district. I soon learned that the National Institutes of Health had branches in the suburbs surrounding the district. Phyllis and I were scheduled for the branch in Patuxent. We unpacked and then drove out to the lab to make sure we would be able to find it on Monday.

Driving to Patuxent felt like a scenic drive through a national park. I was surprised by how much forest there was. The lab itself was located in a wing of the Wildlife Research Center. And, the wildlife researchers weren't thrilled at giving us space. They protected animals, and we used them for experiments. I understood why they were concerned. This work was important, but I had no experience using animals as test subjects. The practice made me feel uncomfortable, too.

Our work involved fatal, slow neurological viruses, "wasting" diseases, where viruses ate away at brain tissue. Our big three were Creutzfeldt-Jakob (C.J.), Kuru, and scrapie, viruses now called "prion" viruses, but this was 1972, before Mad Cow disease and before everyone was talking about prions.

With all these diseases, the first sign is a loss of memory. In humans, they call this dementia. As the disease progresses, subjects shake, lose control of voluntary motion, and eventually die. In all cases, an autopsy will show the brain with areas where the tissue has been eaten away, leaving a "sponge-like" texture.

But in 1972, while I worked at NIH, no one had heard of these viruses. It was difficult for me to tell people what I did for a living. During our second week, Phyllis and I were asked to help the vet with an autopsy. On a 250-pound chimpanzee named Bill.

Phyllis and I never dealt directly with the primates. They were kept in a self-contained building and cared for by animal technicians. The technicians warned us that the chimps would spit on us if we got close and could break bones if they were able to reach us through the bars. So we kept our distance. Bill had been infected with Kuru almost ten years earlier, and was showing advanced signs of the disease. He had been huddling in a corner of his cage, unable to walk even a short distance to get food.

That morning, Bill was sedated and moved by gurney into the autopsy room. He was sedated, with needles in his veins and tubes attached to a pump. The procedure would "bleed" the animal out. Our vet assured me the process was humane and Bill wouldn't be in pain. But I still found the process disturbing. The goal was to replace the chimp blood with a powerful preservative so pathologists could examine the organs and look for structural changes from the disease.

By ten AM, the chimp had passed away, and the official autopsy commenced. I observed as the vet cut open Bill's chest and took out large pink mass that he put on a glass tray I was holding.

"Bag this and label it for shipping," he said.

"What is it?" I asked.

He looked at me, unbelieving. "You don't know what it is?"

"No."

"Lungs," he said, shaking his head in disbelief.

It was embarrassing. Well, with only one year of college, there hadn't been time for me to take Vertebrate Zoology yet. In high school, the only animal we dissected was a frog. Maybe I should have recognized the lungs, but I didn't. And I wasn't sure I wanted to do more dissections. Was I in the right major in college?

I remember how much I loved the work from my first week at NOAA.

This wasn't NOAA. I was determined to keep an open mind. The job paid well and was certainly better than being back at school in classes. But this work wasn't something I loved. It made it worse that our lab was in the middle of the Wildlife Research Center. Why wasn't I working with them?

Well, I had three months on this placement and would make the best of it, especially since I am in Washington, DC If I didn't warm up to the job, maybe the co-op office could find another placement.

# Chapter 32 ~ Out On the Town

We were in the rotunda at the National Museum of History, in front of a display that looked like a large and fierce elephant.

"What is that?" Phyllis asked.

"An African Elephant," I said.

I was a bit startled. What did she think it was? I mean, it couldn't be anything else. A five-year-old girl standing beside the display looked up at the tusks in awe. Her petite presence accentuated just how large these animals are. I'd seen elephants at the zoo, but none as large as this one or in such a fierce stance.

The life-size replica of an African Elephant held a place of honor on a raised rotunda inside the grand entrance. Visitors walked up the stairs to the granite and sandstone building. This was my first time here, and walking through the large columns into a hallway with impossibly high ceilings took my breath away. The elephant had his trunk raised toward the domed ceiling and set the stage and expectations for a memorable visit.

Phyllis grabbed a museum map. It was immediately clear we couldn't see everything in a single day, so we spent a few minutes studying the map to strategize. We were both museum enthusiasts, practically giddy with excitement. Growing up, I'd visited the Miami Museum of Space, which you could breeze through in a couple of hours. This museum, however, would require days, not hours. The building was enormous, with wings extending from a central rotunda like the spokes of a wheel, each wing housing exhibits on a specific theme.

"Let's do the exhibit on early humans first," Phyllis said.

Her choice didn't surprise me. On our first day, Dr. Gibbs, the lab director, stopped by to introduce himself. He asked about our backgrounds. I said zoology, and Phyllis mentioned anthropology and archaeology, with a focus on human evolution. Dr. Gibbs didn't react. We later learned he was a staunch creationist. It made sense that she'd want to start with the *Emergence of Man* exhibit.

"Sounds good. I want to see the full evolution display, including the geological time *Deep Space* exhibit. Are you good with it?"

She agreed, and just like that, we had our plan for at least the morning.

When the Smithsonian first opened, it featured an exhibit on Charles Darwin and his fossil evidence. Years later, the museum expanded the exhibit to include primate and early humanoid replicas, like a Neanderthal, as well as dioramas depicting prehistoric life. This expansion sparked controversy regarding the use of museum resources to promote evolutionary theory. Regardless, the exhibit drew large crowds. A few years afterward, the Smithsonian was sued, though unsuccessfully.

Back at school, I rarely went out. All I did was study. Honestly, that was a lot of what I did in high school. I wanted to take advantage of being in the nation's capital. Granted, visiting museums was a bit nerdy, but baby steps. I was optimistic that my new roommate, Phyllis, would be a good influence on me. While I was shy, Phyllis was a gregarious extrovert.

\*\*\*

Phyllis and I were great roommates. We weren't super close or have much in common, which actually worked out well. It meant we were both careful to respect each other's space and be considerate. I remembered the first time we met, almost three months earlier. The co-op office had arranged a meeting for the two of us a month before the end of the term, suggesting we look for housing together. We went for lunch, and while we had little in common, she seemed nice enough. The idea of sharing housing appealed to me, remembering the difficulty of finding an apartment for one person in St. Pete Beach.

I was an introvert who wore jeans and a plain (cheap) T-shirt everywhere. At five foot five, I was plump and plain and didn't much care about how I came across to members of the opposite sex. It was a point of pride that I didn't own makeup or a dress. My friends often asked me if something was wrong because my natural expression was a frown. Not that I was always sad. But when I was preoccupied, my face relaxed into a frown. And I spent an awful lot of my life preoccupied.

Phyllis was a tall, slender woman with light brown hair and blue eyes. We met for lunch back at USF to talk about our placements. She arrived at the cafeteria in a dress and wearing makeup. But what really caught my eye was her smile; it gave her a carefree appearance. Over the next three years, I realized that smile was always there. Phyllis rarely seemed troubled by anything. She was, without a doubt, the most genuinely happy person I'd ever known.

A few months into our placement, I joined Phyllis for a family gathering in North Carolina. Like Phyllis, her family had fair skin, light brown hair, and many had her blue eyes. When we first arrived, they seemed to stare at me a great deal. Later, Phyllis admitted I was the first Jewish person they had ever met. They were Southerners, and they showered me with Southern hospitality.

They shared that Phyllis was born with a hole in her heart, and the doctors said her chance of survival was low. They flew her to Johns Hopkins and performed surgery to repair the heart wall. This reconstructive heart surgery is done almost routinely today, but in 1952, it was experimental and almost unheard of.

Phyllis's parents felt the surgery was a miracle and that each day was a gift from science and God. When Phyllis was little, her mom packed her days by taking her to the circus, amusement parks, and horseback riding. The family behaved like each day might be her last. The panic eased up as she got older and seemed healthy.

But when we talked, Phyllis expressed her belief that she was unlikely to live past thirty. She believed this and was determined to live with gusto, embracing every opportunity to experience something new.

Over the next three months, I would accompany Phyllis on many adventures: hiking in the Shenandoah Valley (Old Rag Mountain), rock climbing, and going to parties and bars to listen to bluegrass. She also introduced me to Jerry, my first boyfriend since my Seacamp days.

***

But today was our first weekend outing and my first time at the Smithsonian. Neither of us knew our way around the District; we started planning with maps days before we ventured out. We were out the door at seven a.m., navigating the Beltway with cars all traveling at an insane speed. We parked easily, but the street parking would be gone in another hour.

I needed a break once we exhausted the exhibit on man and the geological periods. I was getting hungry.

"Are you hungry?" I asked.

"Yeah. Want to go to the museum cafeteria?"

"We could, but Uncle Sid said the Mall has inexpensive food trucks. And, it would be nice to get out of the air-conditioning."

"Good idea. We could use a break. There's no way we can see everything in one day," she said.

"You're right, and there are eleven museums on the Mall."

We walked out the main entrance and down the stairs back to the National Mall. There were indeed food trucks. We found one with hot dogs and soda.

Near where we sat, people were playing guitar and singing on a small stage. We settled down to enjoy the music and rest our feet. They were outrageously good and very different from anything I had heard before. Sometimes it was one artist, but most of the time, they sang in small groups of two, three, or four. The harmonies were hauntingly evocative, and each song was new to me.

"I wonder if they work for the Smithsonian," Phyllis said.

"Could be. They are good enough to be professionals."

I had played enough guitar to recognize the mastery in front of me. They were finger-picking instead of strumming, and their left-hand work was all over the fretboard. None of them seemed to strain at all. But it was the singing that captivated me. Sometimes, they sang without instruments.

"This is great, but don't you want to see more of the Mall?"

Phyllis was a good sport; we'd been outside on the Mall for over an hour.

I pointed to a table close to the stage. "I'll pick up handouts. Be right back."

A glance at the handout told me they weren't professionals; they were from the Washington, DC Folk Society. I had information on meetings and about a local bar that hosted an open mic on Mondays. It was my introduction to a music scene that would shape my life for the next three years and, indeed, for many, many years afterward.

Deciding we would explore other areas today, we walked over to the Arts and Industries Building to see an outdoor exhibit of missiles and rockets known as "Rocket Row." I was thrilled to see the Atlas rocket that had launched the Mercury capsules into space. Inside, they had the Freedom 7, John Glenn's capsule, on exhibit. I watched that launch when I was nine years old, and seeing the capsule close-up filled me with excitement and awe.

We finished our first visit to the Mall by walking to the Washington and Lincoln memorials, with a side wander through some of George-town, where we stopped for a mid-afternoon snack. By the time we were back in the car, I was exhausted.

Over the next three months, we did a lot of exploring together, and our friendship lasted for years after we were no longer roommates. But our interests weren't perfectly aligned. We didn't always hang out together.

I explored the rich folk music scene, became obsessive over the guitar, and even started performing at the Red Fox. Phyllis liked to party and seemed to have no difficulty finding parties and getting invitations. She started dating an animal caretaker from work. He was a Pennsylvania Dutch Mennonite who rode a motorcycle. He had been excused from military service because he was a conscientious objector. It was a good thing we had a two-bedroom apartment, and I had some privacy.

# Chapter 33 ~ Upper Division

I returned to USF in June and registered for the summer term. The campus felt like a ghost town, or like a scene in one of those movies where everyone has mysteriously disappeared. On the positive side, I had no difficulty getting a dorm room. On the negative side, I was, again, without a kitchen. By this time, I was an expert at preparing meals in a popcorn popper.

Phyllis would be with her family in Lakeland for the summer.Bob and Phylece weren't taking classes over the summer. Bob was working for his mom at the dry cleaning shop, and Phylece had gotten a job with the post office. Granted, they weren't students at USF anyway, but I wouldn't be able to take a break on weekends by driving up to UF for a visit.

I needed to attend because of co-op. Even using the summers, it will take me five years to complete my bachelor's degree. At any rate, without friends around, weekends were going to drag. I promised myself that Saturdays would be spent at Pass-a-Grille Beach, with a stop at my favorite bookstore, Haslam's.

I was now officially a junior taking upper-division classes. These were restricted to students who had passed all the prerequisites and who were officially majoring in zoology. Most of these students were pre-med and were intent on graduating with top grades to get into the highly competitive medical schools. The expectation was that we had mastered the introductory-level classes and study skills.

I made friends with another student in my dorm, Her name was Jan Endsly, and we were taking a lot of the same classes. She was pre-med, and was very high strung about grades, be we got along well and it was good to have someone to study with, and to hang out with.

For the first time since starting at USF, I took the minimum number of classes to maintain full-time student status. I had a realistic understanding of my abilities and understood that difficulties with memory-rich tasks needed to be considered as I balanced my course load. My selection of Physics, Expository Writing, and Cell Biology was enough for a summer term.

Physics and Cell Biology had lectures on Monday, Wednesday, and Friday; Expository Writing was on Tuesday and Wednesday. My lectures were ninety-minute morning classes. Physics lab was Tuesday afternoon, and Cell biology lab was Thursday afternoon. Most science labs were scheduled for three hours, but Cell Biology had an "open lab," meaning that besides your scheduled lab time, the room was staffed with a teaching assistant from five p.m. to ten p.m. to allow students additional study time.

College science labs were usually run by graduate students, who were enthusiastic, knowledgeable, and approachable. I liked labs. Even the Organic Chemistry lab was fun. Lab classes, even Physics, boosted my self-esteem and my grade point average.

But the Cell Biology lab was neither fun nor easy. All we did was look at slides under a microscope. The intent was for students to relate each slide to "slices" of embryos at specific stages of development. There were cast models of the chicken embryos with arrows identifying where each slide section would be found. No matter how long I stared at a slide, I couldn't identify the section location or tissue. Drawing the slides, which seemed to help, most students did nothing for me.

I spent countless hours in the lab working on the damn slides. By the end of the term, the professor shared that she had never had a student work as hard and do as poorly.

After the midterm, the professor handed me my exam paper. She said, "Really, I feel bad about how hard you're working. Is there anything I can do to help?

"I think I need a new brain."

She looked confused, and I felt bad for her.

"I have dyslexia. I'm finding the slides hard to learn."

"How does dyslexia make it hard to work with the slides?" she asked.

"I can look at the slides and draw what I see. But when I'm not looking at the slide or drawing, I can't recall the details. It's a problem with visual memory."

She tried to help, explaining that I should think of the slides as sets, showing me the cast models of embryos at different stages of development, and explaining how slides of different stages would have tissues characteristic of the stage. Her explanation helped a little and showed that she cared. I still didn't do well, but at least I passed the final exam.

Shortly after the midterm, a set of slides disappeared. Someone wanted to have them at home to study, and it must have been someone failing the class. That would be me, except who had a microscope at home?

The professor said no grades would be released until she had her slides back. The threat panicked the pre-med students, who needed scores released in time for their applications.

I was in the lab wasting my time staring at meaningless slides when one of the morons approached me.

"I know it was you. Bring the slides back if you know what is good for you," he said.

At first, I thought he was kidding. "Steve, I could study these slides twenty-four hours a day, seven days a week. It wouldn't help."

He didn't seem convinced. Like the other students, Steve couldn't imagine that anyone had plans other than medical school. Really, I tried hard in that class. While it wasn't relevant to my previous work at NOAA, it was relevant to my work at NIH. But, unlike the other students, I just needed to pass the class.

My other classes were fine. Physics was easy for me, and I made my usual A. Expository Writing was not easy, but I was keenly interested in developing skills in writing, and I did fine. Cell Biology was my Waterloo. I stopped going to the lab for extra study time in the evenings. I wasn't convinced the students were capable of physical intimidation, but I wasn't sure they were not. I took the exam and immediately left town to drive to my parents' house in Miami. I had a one-week break before the fall term.

I earned a D in the lecture and the lab. The grade was a conceded pass and would not be considered passing for a prerequisite, but a D was good enough since I never intended to take more advanced classes in cell biology or developmental biology.

A week later, I returned for the fall semester. My upper-division biology class was Genetics. To my great relief, it was very mathematical, and I did fine. By the time I completed the fall semester, I had transitioned to taking all upper-division science classes and electives in English to satisfy my general education requirements. As I headed back to NIH for another co-op education term, I was confident I would graduate, something I had not been confident about.

Jan had been struggling as a pre-med enough that she decided to explore other options. To my delight, she applied for the co-op placement at NIH. We would be traveling to the big city together.

# Chapter 34 ~ Oil Embargo

We sat in my car in a line that didn't seem to move. At least twenty cars were in front of us, and I thought hard about leaving. I still had a half tank of fuel, almost five gallons.

"What do you think?" I asked Jan. "Should we go or stay?"

She looked at the fuel gauge.

"Stay. We have five gallons, so while it could get us to Sanford, we would be on empty."

It was October 1973, and the United States was in an oil embargo. Sometimes, the station ran out and closed before you had your turn. That might happen today. They would often sell only five gallons per car to serve as many customers as possible. You didn't look at the price of fuel. You didn't care.

Each pump had two workers. One handled the sale, taking cash or credit cards. One pumped gas. One time, while I waited, a man pulled up in a Volkswagen.

He pulled up next to the front of the line, opened the door, and yelled, "It's an emergency."

The manager talked to him. He must have made a good case because they sent an attendant inside for a one-gallon container of gas and added it to his tank.

There was a constant threat of violence breaking out. I tried not to go to the station alone and used the car as little as possible. The oil embargo had minimal effect when I lived on campus at USF. I focused on my classes and ignored the world of campus.

As January neared, I panicked. It was time for my work-study program. Driving across country was daunting, but I'd need my car to get to work. We were driving to Sanford to take the auto train. That was why we were in my car today, attempting to fill the gas tank.

Finally, we reached the front of the line.

"Only five gallons," the attendant said. "You need to pay in advance."

My car took less than four gallons to fill the tank. The attendant seemed surprised when he had to give me change for a five-dollar bill.

He looked appreciatively at my small Toyota Corolla and said, "I guess the five-gallon limit doesn't affect you."

"Well, the lines do," I replied.

We drove to Sanford, loaded the car onto the auto train, and settled in for the trip.

Dr. Gibbs normally hired two co-op students from USF. This was the first time I had encouraged a friend to apply for the second spot. I was excited. Jan was my first friend at USF. The two of us stood out on the dorm floor as the quirky students with an interest in science. Like me, Jan was the first in her family to go to college. She invited me to go home with her for the weekend, and I fell in love with Crystal River.

Jan's mom was a former mechanic from Detroit who owned and operated a boat mechanic shop. When her husband died from cancer, she moved her kids to an empty block of land her father had left her in Crystal River. She built a roughly finished house on her own. The block of land was still wild and wonderful. They had banty hens that would jump up to be petted and an almost domesticated bobcat named *Buzzard.* Sometimes, they lost a banty hen. Jan shrugged and said, "That's nature."

The marina was on the bank of Crystal River. I relished the visits because we took a small John boat and explored the backwaters near the marina. One day, we went all the way to Three Sisters, an amazing, large spring filled with manatees. The water was so clear it felt like nothing was holding me up.

We didn't go to Crystal River every weekend, but we went often. Jan and I became best friends, so I was thrilled when she decided to try out a co-op semester and applied to NIH.

I'd talked to Jan about my experiences at NIH, and she asked me to arrange an application. I understood her motivation and thought it was a good idea. When Jan started at USF, she was on a full scholarship, but lost it after she made low grades in Chemistry and Calculus. She took out loans for tuition, but really needed money. It was more than just money. She worried that she wouldn't get into medical school without a 4.0 grade point average, and didn't know if she should continue at USF. Working at NIH might help her decide if working in science could be an alternative to being a doctor.

I hoped it would be a good experience. And introducing Jan to the Smithsonian and to the exciting city would be an additional bonus.

My Uncle Sid was expecting us and had again offered temporary accommodation. With the oil embargo, we took a short-term rental in Bethesda, only a mile from the NIH campus. It was expensive, and we would be sharing a one-bedroom apartment. We hadn't realized that most people would assume we were gay, a fact that we didn't understand until gay couples struck up conversations.

The complex at Pooks Hill specialized in short-term rentals. Once we signed the paperwork and selected rental furniture, they assured us we could move in on Sunday. It was all so incredibly easy that we could go to work from our own place on Monday.

# Chapter 35 ~ National Institute of Health

"Jan, that's the third outfit you've tried on. It's time to go. We don't want to be late."

"I want to make a good impression. What should I wear?"

When I shrugged and didn't answer.

"What do Dr. Gibbs and the other researchers wear?" she asked.

"Dr. Gibbs wears a dress shirt, tie, and slacks. Mike, the technician who works full-time for him, wears a collared shirt and slacks."

"What do girls wear?"

"There weren't any working out at Patuxent. Phyllis liked dresses, and sometimes, she wore one. Other times, she wore jeans. I don't do dresses."

I was wearing black jeans and a light blue turtleneck sweater. For me, this was dressy, but I figured it would do for the first day. She looked at me and ducked back into the bedroom. When she came out, she had black slacks and a light tan button-down shirt. We left the apartment and took my car, all of one mile to the NIH campus.

"We could walk," Jan said.

"We may need to if gas is too hard to get, but this is our first day. Let's not walk in all hot and sweaty, and I want to get a parking sticker for the car."

We pulled into the parking garage next to Building 35, where our lab was located. The first floor of the garage was filled with small cars that looked like a fleet of mail carts. There were lots of colors, but they were obviously all the same make and were plugged into boxes on poles next to each parking spot.

"OMG, these are electric cars. How cool is this?" I said.

Jan pointed to the *Electric Cars Only on First Floor* sign. We navigated to the second floor and parked. That year, electric cars were definitely the thing to own in DC. They were ahead of their time, but could only travel fifty miles before needing a charge. So people who used them all had other "real" cars. But the doctors who had them didn't have to wait in line for gas as often as the rest of us. I'll admit, I was jealous.

Walking up to the large building seemed weird. It was hard to believe I was returning for a second work placement with the same research team I had left only six months earlier. While I was back at USF, NIH closed the lab back at the Patuxent Wildlife Preserve and moved the researchers to Bethesda. This was going to be different, for sure. This campus was a sleek and modern forest of concrete and glass buildings separated by roads and parking garages. I would miss the serenity of the old place.

We stepped through the sliding glass door into building 35. We were greeted by an officer at the information counter. He was large, bald, and heavyset. His uniform was tan, and I could see he had a gun.

"Can I help you?" he asked.

"We're starting a college work-study semester in Dr. Gibb's lab. Today's our first day."

"Welcome to NIH," he said.

He picked up a phone and made a phone call.

"I have two students at the desk. They said they're here to work for you."

He was silent for a minute. Then I heard him say, "I'll send them up."

When he hung up, he pulled out a map and used a highlighter to mark a path.

"They're expecting you in room 11 C. Before you report to your lab, you'll join a group of new hires for orientation. The process takes about an hour, then you'll report to your lab. Your boss knows you need to go through orientation."

The "orientation" was unexpectedly intense. There were ten of us seated around a conference desk. The first order of business was to distribute a document for us to sign.

*I will support and defend the Constitution of the United States against all enemies, foreign and domestic; that I will bear true faith and allegiance to the same; that I take this obligation freely, without any mental reservation or purpose of evasion; and that I will well and faithfully discharge the duties of the office on which I am about to enter. So help me God.*

The lady in charge of orientation told us that every employee who worked for the federal government had to take the oath. Once she distributed the document, we raised our hands and repeated after her to take our "oath," then signed and returned the document. After that, we were all fingerprinted.

I couldn't help but wonder about two things. Why hadn't I had to sign this when working at NOAA or at the Patuxent facility, and how was I supposed to preserve, protect, and defend the Constitution of the United States as a lab technician?

At this point, I felt guilty about bringing Jan along, but she didn't seem bothered by the document or about being told we were not to wear any political buttons or garments to work.

The rest of the orientation was important, normal stuff: where to park, how to sign in if we needed to enter the building after working hours, and familiarizing ourselves with the campus map. The orientation finished in just under an hour, and we made our way up to the fifth floor to our research lab.

It wasn't until months later, when former teachers, employers, and friends asked me what I was doing and why the FBI was asking about me, that I realized our "orientation" started a background check.

# Chapter 36 ~ Blue Thumb

When I worked for NOAA, my lab was in an old marina, and my desk could have been from the Civil War. In my last session at NIH, our facilities at Patuxent were on the rustic side. There was nothing rustic about the Bethesda laboratory; everything looked new and space-age.

I recognized microscopes, glassware, and balances. But the room was awash with centrifuges, hot water baths, filtration units, and countless devices of unknown uses. Jan was just as intimidated. Dr. Gibbs's assistant, Monica Lewis, showed us around the lab and her tissue culture room. Then, she demonstrated "explanting," taking a sample of tissue from a mouse and preparing it for culture.

She had a section of skin in a sterile beaker in the biological isolation hood, a countertop metal and glass chamber with an air system that isolates the space inside. Monica explained that the chamber protected the samples from her germs and us from any viruses that were in the tissue. That was important because the mouse had been sick. It had been given a disease called scrapie.

We watched Monica dice the tissue into pieces and transfer it from the beaker to a flask with red media. Once she was done, she pushed away from the hood, removed her gloves, and brought the flask to a microscope. There were cells floating around in the media. She placed the flask in an incubator and explained that in time, the cells would attach to the plastic and start to grow. This was the coolest thing I'd seen in a long time. The idea that you could grow cells outside of an animal seemed straight out of science fiction.

"Are we going to learn to do this?" I asked.

Monica smiled. "By the time you leave to go back to school, Dr. Gibbs wants you to be experts. So, yes, you are going to learn tissue culture."

It turned out I had a gift for this type of work. First, I found it fascinating. Second, it was hands-on science, which I loved. I learned how to make the media, how to sterilize glassware, maintain the incubators and hot water baths, and most of all, I learned tissue culture.

Explanting was just the first stage. Every day, we would pour the old media off and re-feed the flask with fresh media. When the cells completely covered the plastic, I would place the enzyme Trypsin into the flask and cause the cells to float off the plastic. We would collect the floating cells, centrifuge, wash with fresh media, then split them into two or more flasks. Each time we "split" the cells, we labeled the flasks with a passage number. When we had ten flasks, we would collect them and store them in ampoules with dimethyl sulfoxide (DMSO), which would keep the cells from bursting when we stored the ampoules in a liquid nitrogen freezer.

One day, when I was taking a glass ampoule from the freezer, it exploded. I had a gash on my thumb and was bleeding. I immediately shoved my hand into a bucket of bleach we kept by the hood for disinfecting.

Dr. Gibbs noticed and asked, "What was in the ampoule?"

"Crutchfelt Jacob, passage 2," I said.

He looked at his watch and said, "Keep your hand in for five minutes."

I kept it in for ten. Crutchfelt Jacob is a neurological slow virus. I wouldn't know for years if I was infected, and it is a terminal and terrible disease. I kept my hand in the jar of bleach for ten minutes. That was fifty-two years ago. I still have a scar on my hand, but I don't have CJ. I figure that was a win.

Over my co-op period, I did indeed "learn tissue culture." I gained a reputation for having a "blue thumb" and could explant and grow cells with proficiency. My sterile technique was excellent, and I rarely had any contamination. Monica, impressed with my work, gave me literature to read and encouraged me to think about a graduate degree in cell biology. Dr. Gibbs was enthusiastic and offered to write a letter of recommendation.

I knew that cell culture was an emerging industry and that there were real possibilities for working in the field. Even as a co-op student, I was being asked to meet with start-up companies that were interested in recruiting me. It was a strange time for me, and I knew I had an important decision to make. I loved working in the lab, being around exceptionally brilliant people, and hearing them talk about cutting-edge research. But the literature scared me to death. It was so technical and detailed that I was afraid if I took classes in this field, I would be overwhelmed and would flunk out.

The one class in cell biology back at USF had put a terror of the subject in me, and for better or worse, gave me a reality check on my capabilities. I told Dr. Gibbs I would look into the program at George Washington, and the tuition was thirty-seven thousand dollars for out-of-state students. That was not a good option for me.

# Chapter 37 ~ Light at the End of the Tunnel

Two weeks into the summer term, as we sat with coffee, Jan was leaving college at the end of the term to join the military. I didn't know what to say. I knew the work at NIH hadn't been as thrilling for her as it was for me. But this felt extreme.

"You're doing *what*?" I said.

"I'm going to complete this term, but after that, I'm taking a break from school. I visited the recruitment office, and I'm signing up. I thought you should know I won't be going back to NIH with you."

I was stunned and felt as guilty as a person could feel. My last placement at NIH had worked great for me. But I knew Jan was less thrilled with our time in Washington, DC. The oil embargo and gas shortages kept us from doing much exploring. We spent hours sitting in line at the gas station. As long as we only used the car to go to work and get groceries, we only had to fill my Toyota once every two weeks.

I was shocked by her announcement. It also made me feel guilty. I'd encouraged Jan to apply for the NIH placement. I loved it, but Jan hadn't taken to working in the lab like I had. The oil embargo and gas shortages made it difficult to explore the city. It had been a dull time for her.

I had explored most of the city and sights on my previous placement, and I tried to make sure Jan got to see the sights. We made our way to the Smithsonian a few times. But we couldn't go often. We stayed local and spent way too much time in the apartment. It was a one-bedroom apartment, and I knew she was restless and bored.

I couldn't feel guilty about the real issue. Science research didn't have the same appeal for Jan as it did for me.

"I know how you feel," Jan said. "But I'm thrilled they are taking me. I don't know what I want to do with my life. But I don't want to be buried in debt. The military actually seems like a great idea."

"Why?"

"It will give me time to figure out what I want to do. And I can use my pay to help Jeff go to school."

"I'm going to miss you," I said.

"Same. You know, I enjoyed the time in Washington, and I'm glad I went. I discovered something important. I don't want to work in science research."

"Do you know what you'll be doing in the military?"

Her smile was genuine, and she was excited. "After basic, they want me to train to be a translator."

"Really? That's cool."

"They gave me a bunch of aptitude tests and found that I have a gift for languages. Which I knew."

"It does sound cool. I'm still going to miss you."

"I'll miss the folk music scene in Washington, which was actually cool and a lot of fun."

I left the dorm feeling washed out. Joining the military seemed like a drastic step, but it was good to see Jan happy again. She had been having a rough time of it. I'd hoped that the co-op placement would do the trick. Well, maybe it had clarified for her. She seemed to think it had.

I had enjoyed introducing Jan to the Folklore Society of Greater Washington, DC, and I was glad that she said she would miss it. While Jan didn't play an instrument before our placement, she enjoyed attending the monthly meetings at the society. We sat in a circle, taking turns performing folk songs. The informal, friendly nature of the gatherings made it perfect for a novice to play or sing in public for the first time. I found the adrenaline rush of playing in front of people addictive and spent a lot of time looking for songs that fit each month's theme. Jan liked the fact that people sang without playing an instrument, and she joined in, too. She even picked up a penny whistle and learned to play.

Our apartment was close to both NIH for work and the Red Fox, home to a Monday open mic frequented by folk artists. The absence of a cover charge was a big bonus for impoverished co-op students.

Like the open sing, the music was traditional American or English folk music. But performers were on stage singing into a microphone. Most of them were accomplished musicians. I wasn't ready to be on stage, but both Jan and I found it fun to watch. And for me, it gave me a glimpse of what I wanted: to be good enough. So my evenings were filled with working on my guitar skills and practicing singing; ultimately, I wanted to be good enough to be on that stage.

I felt guilty despite Jan's comment that she had enjoyed the folk scene. My evening obsession with guitar and folk songs had been hard on her. We did live in a one-bedroom apartment. We should have gone out more often, despite the gas shortage. Now that opportunity was gone.

We would be parting ways at the end of the term. It made me sad, but my time as a college student was also coming to an end. I would complete my coursework in the spring. By not applying for graduation, I was eligible for one more placement at NIH. I would graduate in December 1976, having spent five and a half years earning a bachelor's degree. But I would also have two years of full-time work experience.

After the summer, Jan left for boot camp. I bought a twelve-string guitar, and when I wasn't studying, I practiced. I didn't want to look for new friends.

My classes were all senior-level or graduate-level classes. There was a light at the end of the tunnel; I took an animal behavior class and elected a senior project working with tropical reef fish. And I was able to sign up for marine botany, a graduate-level class. Both of these brought me back to my love of marine studies. The animal behavior class even included a field trip to the Keys.

The university required 160 credits for graduation. I worked the numbers and realized I had eight more elective credits available. Non-Euclidean Geometry and Advanced Expository Writing found their way into my schedule. I'd be graduating with the minimum number of credits required in Zoology. I wasn't proud of that fact, but didn't care enough to take more.

I couldn't attend my graduation. I'd be in Washington, DC when I officially graduated. It was still surreal that I was actually graduating. Being the first in my family to go to college, I'd been navigating unfamiliar waters since high school. My initial goal was just to try college for a year. And now, I was graduating. The uncertainty of what came next bothered me. This feeling gave me a better understanding of Jan's choice to join the military.

I hoped to figure out my future before completing my last placement at NIH. At the end of the summer term, I left for DC without a roommate. It was fine. I was ready to be on my own.

# Chapter 38 ~ School's Out

I drove my car out of the USF parking lot after my last exam. The class was Organic Evolution, and I enjoyed the class and felt I did well on the exam. Everything I owned was in the back of my car. I'd spend a week at my parents' house, then drive to Washington, DC, for my last cooperative education placement.

USF was the center of my universe for over five years. I knew lots of people felt that college was the best years of their life, but it was hard for me to feel affection for the place. Too much of my time had been spent studying for exams and feeling the constant fear of flunking out.

School was out, but I didn't know what was next. I deliberately hadn't applied for graduation so that I could remain eligible for a final work-study placement at NIH. Dr. Gibbs agreed to hire me for a six-month placement. So I'd graduate in December with my bachelor's degree in zoology. Hopefully by then, I'd figure out what comes next.

My boss, Dr. Gibbs, wanted me to apply to graduate school in Washington, DC. It wasn't a suggestion that I could take seriously. I lacked confidence and financial resources. Gibbs was pushing George Washington, where Monica studied. It was very expensive. I couldn't qualify for a scholarship, and my family wasn't rich. Even if I could afford to go, I didn't think I would pass classes in cellular biology.

I wanted to work in marine biology. I'd hoped that medical research would appeal to me as well, and to be honest, I liked my job. But I just couldn't see doing a graduate degree in the field. My job was restricted to undergraduate students, but maybe I could find something like it while I was in Washington.

Once again, Sid invited me to stay at his house in Silver Springs while I looked for a place. There was a bulletin board in the NIH cafeteria with notices of room for rent. I found a room in a small two-bedroom cottage in Tacoma Park, near the University of Maryland.

It was a thirty-minute commute on the Beltway. But the gas shortage was over, so the location worked. I liked Tacoma Park a lot more than where I stayed with Jan in Bethesda. Returning to the lab felt like coming home. I fit in with Monica, Rand, Dr. Nemo, and Dr. White. And my boss, Dr. Gibbs, was wonderful to work for. I wished I could just stay and work in the lab, but everyone had graduate degrees. My position really was just for students.

A visiting researcher from the University of Queensland, Dr. Kitson, was in the lab. We talked about Australia and the Great Barrier Reef. He had a research assistant traveling with him, and when the subject of graduate school came up, they were horrified to hear that Monica was paying over twenty-five thousand a year in tuition. Dr. Kitson was outraged and suggested I apply to the University of Queensland.

I wasn't sold on graduate school, but Dr. Kitson's remark hit home. Seeing the Great Barrier Reef would make graduate school bearable and almost worthwhile. It took me a while to realize he was serious.

It was the summer of 1976, and living in Takoma Park, I was close to the House of Musical Traditions, an incredible music store with a miniature concert hall. They had "house concerts," intimate gatherings with a singer/songwriter on a small stage, and fifteen to twenty of us in the audience.

I went to concert after concert at the House of Musical Traditions, and soon started taking guitar lessons from Bruce Hutton, a regular who worked in the shop and played a unique style of *Old-Time Music.*

My own music skills were advancing, and I was now a regular performer at the Red Fox.

It was the summer of 1976, and the entire region was bursting with musicians. The Smithsonian hosted a twelve-week Festival of American Folklife in honor of the bicentennial. Musicians from all regions of the world and thirty countries came. They performed in theaters within the Smithsonian and on the outdoor stages at the Smithsonian Mall. But they were in town, and musicians played in restaurants, bars, and house concerts everywhere you went. And of course, at the Red Fox.

My brother Jim visited that term. He crashed on the couch in the cottage where I had rented a room.

"I'm not going to tell Mom and Dad what you're living in."

I laughed. "It's not that bad."

"What are you going to do when you leave here?" he asked.

"I'm not sure. I'm thinking about applying to do a graduate program in Australia."

"Really? Haven't you had enough of school?"

"Probably, but if I can go to the Great Barrier Reef, it might be worth it."

"Okay, what are you really going to do?"

Look for a job.

My other visitor was Phylece. We had a blast with the music concerts on the Mall, and I promised that when I could, I would visit her in San Francisco.

# Chapter 39 ~ Crossroads

My time at NIH and in Washington, DC, was passing too quickly. I was beginning to be uneasy at my lack of a plan for what would come next. In December, I'd graduate from USF, and my job would come to an end.

For the past five years, I'd taken one semester at a time. *What classes would I take? Where will I live during my work* placement? I didn't even plan the work placements—the cooperative education department placed me.

Now, I faced a turning point: should I apply for a technician job or pursue graduate school?

I was tempted to look for a job. Tissue culture fascinated me. That a piece of muscle, diced into small pieces and incubated in media, yielded millions of cells to harvest was straight out of science fiction. And I had a reputation for being able to grow just about any kind of cell. They called it my "blue thumb."

The field of study was experiencing exponential growth. Start-up companies had popped up all over the place. These companies produced cell lines and biological compounds used in medical research, labs like my own at NIH, and in clinical settings with patients. Once I graduated, I could remain in Washington and find a job. The question was, *is that what I wanted?* I suspected the work would be mundane without the excitement of research at NIH.

My lab really was working on cutting-edge science. While I was there, the foundation gave Dr. Gajdusek the Nobel Prize in medicine. We threw a party to celebrate.

Gibbs and Gajdusek were a team. They had collaborated for fifteen years, studying neurological slow viruses like Kuru, Creutzfeldt-Jakob, and scrapie. Gibbs always wore a suit and rarely smiled. He was a religious man, known for his kindness. Gajdusek, in contrast, was flamboyant and larger-than-life, often wearing a flannel shirt and jeans. He had a colorful way of speaking and rarely seemed serious.

Gibbs wasn't impressed when he wasn't part of the award, and the Nobel Prize committee asked him to pick out a suit, but he took it reasonably well.

Their work proved that Kuru was a transmissible disease, not a genetic disorder. It was a disease that ravaged the population of New Guinea. Our lab received a large number of cards and letters stating that they knew it was a team effort and that the prize should have been shared among the team.

My inner voice resisted the path to finding a job. Washington was landlocked. Staying here meant giving up my dream of working in marine science.

At Dr. Kitson's urging, I wrote to the University of Queensland and requested an application form. They responded with a letter. They asked for my background and intended field of study. I replied with a summary of my academic background, work experience, and intention to study coral reef biology.

To my amazement, the next letter came from Dr. Endean, a faculty member in the Department of Zoology, who worked on crown-of-thorns reef infestations. He wanted more details on my interests. I wrote back saying I admired his work and that I wanted to work on coral reef ecology with a focus on invertebrate associates.

We exchanged three more letters over the next six weeks. I answered questions and asked some of my own. My interest grew, and I wrote again to the admission office, requesting an official application and information on student fees. They responded that there wasn't an application form, that Dr. Endean was expecting me in February. The only fee was the $125 student activities fee. They asked me to confirm whether I would be attending. Once I agreed, the Zoology Department head would send a package of information.

I was stunned. *Dr. Endean was expecting me? Didn't they need to see an official transcript or letters of recommendation?*

I replied, and two weeks later, I had the package from the Zoology Department with directions. They were sorry they could not offer financial support as a "tutor" position until I passed my qualifying exam at the end of my first year.

Dr. Kitson said he wasn't surprised by the casual attitude. He noted that things were "casual" in Queensland. He pointed out the clause about paperwork for a student visa. He warned me I needed to show I had financial support.

That made me wonder, if there was no tuition, how much financial support would I need? It turned out to be ten thousand dollars for the first year. I had three thousand dollars in the bank and could sell my car. But as much as I hated to, it was time to talk to Mom and Dad.

Mom was upset at the idea of Australia. Jim had already let her know that I was looking into it, so she wasn't too overwhelmed. Dad said he could obtain a letter from his business bank associate, showing that I had the means to support myself. He also said he would set up a bank account for me to draw on.

Having made my decision, it was easier to focus on making the most of the time I had left in Washington. My job would end in December, and I'd be bound for Australia come February.

The thought was exciting and terrifying. I called Phylece and said I would drop by in San Francisco on the way out. She suggested that since I had the time, I should plan an extended visit. It felt satisfying to have a plan.

"Hey, you're graduating!" she said. "We need to celebrate."

"Yes, we do."

That was when it became real. In December, I'd be awarded my degree. Not only that, I'd be heading to Australia to continue my studies on the Great Barrier Reef. The thought was unbelievably exciting.

# Chapter 40 ~ Folk Getaway

I woke up in the cold and dark and snuggled into my sleeping bag, tucking my head inside. Even my toes were like icicles. A glance at my watch told me it was only four a.m., way too early to get up. I might be living in the Washington DC area, but in my heart, I was a Florida girl, and anything below 60 degrees Fahrenheit was just too cold.

The annual FSGW getaway weekend was late October, and the campground at Prince William Forest was downright cold. The temperature outside registered at 12 degrees Fahrenheit, and the camp cabins lacked insulation and heating. Even in my sleeping bag with my head tucked inside, I was freezing.

As soon as I detected light out the window, a hint that morning was approaching, I crawled out of my bunk, bundled up in all my clothes, and went over to where a few brave folks were sitting by a fire. The smell of coffee was heavenly.

"Can I pour you some coffee?" the older blond woman asked.

It took me a minute to recognize her as Helen Schneyer, a fantastic vocalist and performer of gospel music, who had joined us the night before, singing by the campfire.

"Thank you, I would love some," I said, picked up a mug, and held it for her.

Helen used a pole to snag the coffee pot, carefully lowering it to the ground. With a heavy glove, she handled the pot, pouring the hot liquid into the metal mug. I wrapped my hands around the mug, reveling in the warmth that seeped into my fingers. I sat on a log beside the fire. Despite wearing long underwear, jeans, wool socks, and boots, as well as a long-sleeved shirt, sweatshirt, and coat, I was still cold.

Last night, I sat by this fire singing Christmas carols with a group of fifteen. Yes, it was only October, and most of us were Jewish, but the choice of songs somehow drifted in that direction. The drift might have been because carols are lovely songs with great harmonies, and we all knew them. We sang late into the night, warmed by the fire, as budding friendships and wonderful music filled the air. It was a great way to cap the first night at a folk music weekend festival.

Hillary and Joan, the students working in Dr. Gajdusek's lab, invited me to ride there with them after work on Friday. They were active in the folk society, and Joan would be presenting a session on "rounds." Joan brought lyrics for us to practice on the car trip to Prince William Forest, and the hour-long drive was so much fun. I was looking forward to her session.

I'd been regularly attending concerts, open mics, and folk society open-sings, and had performed at each of the venues. But this weekend-long folk getaway was an order of magnitude above anything I'd experienced. It was immersive. From Friday to Sunday afternoon, there was music, dancing, storytelling, and most of all, singing.

By the end of the weekend, I had lost all hesitancy and was willing to perform in front of rooms filled with polished, amazing performers. I performed two songs at the Saturday night concert, working with a cellist on songs we had polished over the afternoon. I was terrified, but the adrenaline rush was incredible, and we did an amazing set. I knew I'd never sung better. I returned to DC with a renewed resolve to continue immersing myself in music and improving my guitar playing.

A feeling of impending loss settled over me. My time in DC was drawing to a close, and I knew I'd be saying goodbye to the people I loved from work, the smart, fascinating individuals I looked forward to seeing daily. I'd also be leaving behind the community I'd found in the folk music scene.

As December approached, I felt increasingly lost and began to question my decision to move to Australia. Why hadn't I searched for a job in DC? Why was I leaving everything behind?

But Australia and the Great Barrier Reef beckoned. In my heart, I knew that if I didn't go now, I never would. This was the time for me to travel and to go to graduate school. If it didn't work out, I would come back. But I had to try. And it was time to make arrangements.

I would be going for at least a year, and the airlines limited your luggage. I bought an enormous steamer trunk and shipped my dive gear and personal items, which I'd been packing and unpacking as I moved from Tampa to Washington. Bob bought my car, and the money would cover shipping and give me funds for the trip. I wouldn't touch Mom and Dad's account until I was in Australia.

I would be spending the holidays in South Florida and then flying to San Francisco for most of January, taking Phylece up on her offer for an extended stay. I would also stop in Hawaii to see Richard and Debbie on my way between San Francisco and Australia.

The travel would be exciting, and I tried to hold onto that thought and push down the feelings of loss for what I'd be leaving behind.

# Chapter 41 ~ California

Thick fog blanketed the water. Even with layers of clothing, I shivered and hoped the sun would be high enough for additional warmth and better visibility. It would be nice to see where we were heading.

"Ray, can you see where you're going?" I called to the back of the canoe.

Ray laughed and said, "Honestly? No, but I have a compass. This is San Francisco; there's always fog."

Ray was a whitewater canoe guide who had invited Phylece and I to canoe across to Alcatraz for a picnic. Three people heading out to sea in San Francisco Bay. What could go wrong?

Phylece and I grew up in Florida and had dressed in layers to keep warm. We had a T-shirt under a long-sleeved shirt and both of us wore an outer coat. Ray wore a T-shirt. He laughed at our outfits, saying Floridians must have thin blood.

"We'll lose some layers when we reach Alcatraz," Phylece said.

Two hours later, as we approached Alcatraz, the fog thinned, but visibility was poor enough we couldn't read the *No Trespassing* sign until we were almost on shore.

Phylece all but lost it. "Ray, for God's sake, haven't you done this before?"

Ray, red-faced and scowling, said, "Sorry, I'm trying this for the first time. Let's check the other side."

*No Trespassing* signs were everywhere. I groaned, thinking about another two hours of paddling to get back to the shore, with no way to stretch our legs. Then I realized Ray had the canoe pointed at another island.

"Let's move our picnic to Angel Island," he said.

I stared at the island in the distance. The fog made it difficult to judge distance. *Was it closer than San Francisco?*

"How far is it?" I asked.

"About the same. It's still early, and we can still have a picnic," he said.

We started paddling toward Angel Island. I didn't say anything. My faith in our guide had been shaken when he didn't know we couldn't land on Alcatraz.

So, we paddled. Well, Phylece sat while Ray and I paddled.

In a way, heading into fog toward an island an unknown distance matched my emotional state. Here I was in California on my way to Australia – a country I knew little about. In a bit over a month, I'd be starting a graduate program at the University of Queensland.

Warmed by the exercise and sun, I peeled off my jacket and thought about my friends and all the people I'd left behind in Washington, DC. It had only been three weeks since I said a tearful goodby at NIH, stopped briefly for a visit with my parents in Miami, and then boarded a plane for California.

When Phylece suggested I crash at her place and explore the San Francisco bay area on my way to Australia, I jumped at the chance. That was how we ended up in the bay on a foggy morning late in December.

Angel Island loomed in the distance. I didn't want to complain, but I was cold and tired. I tried to be careful, but the occasional splashing sent water onto my arms. The cold water reminded me this wasn't the Florida Keys; prisoners from Alcatraz had died of hypothermia, trying to swim to freedom.

"Are we there yet?" I called out playfully. "When are we going to be there?"

"We should be about halfway," Ray said. "But it's hard to judge on open water, especially in the fog."

"Are you hungry?" Phylece asked. "It's almost one o'clock. I have snacks I can pass around."

I was hungry but didn't want to stop paddling to eat. "I'm okay."

The sun was up, although you could barely see it in the fog. After three hours of paddling, I'd worked up a sweat and peeled off another layer for Phylece to stash in the dry bag. I noticed she still had a coat on, but then, she hadn't been paddling.

I was looking at the chop on the water when I noticed that in the distance, there was a red and blue cargo vessel making its way across the bay.

"Ray, should we be worried about that?" I asked, pointing to the large, ghostly ship.

For the next hour, as we paddled, the ship grew larger. As the fog lifted, we saw other boats and realized we were in a shipping channel, and the cargo ship was on a path that could indeed result in a collision. If that happened, there would be nothing left of our canoe. *Would anyone on the cargo ship even notice?*

"Paddle faster," Phylece said.

We paddled as fast as we could. Angel Island was closer, but so was the cargo ship. The fog lifted, and we could make out the details on the ship. *Should we turn around?* Ray thought we were more than halfway through the shipping channel.

The banter from earlier was gone. We paddled so hard my arms ached. Then, suddenly, the cargo ship was on the right.

We had crossed far enough to be out of danger. I pulled my paddle up to take a breather. Ray kept his stroke constant. In the silence, I heard a familiar *click*. Glancing back, I saw that Phylece had her camera out and was taking pictures. Well, at least we would have great pictures of the cargo ship that almost hit us.

"We're out of the shipping lane," Phylece said.

"How do you know?" I asked.

Phylece pointed to the left. "Rocks with sea lions. This water isn't deep enough for big ships."

"She's right," Ray said. "We can take it easy now."

The muscles in my back and shoulders ached. "Thank God."

"Can we get closer to the sea lions?" Phylece asked. "I'd love to get some close-up shots."

We were about three hundred yards off Angel Island, close enough to hear the sounds of seagulls mixed with the barking of sea lions. Like Phylece, I wanted to get closer, but worried about the time. The sun was low in the sky. *How were we going to get back to San Francisco before sunset? Did Ray have a plan?*

When we were less than thirty yards from the impressive mammals, Ray told me to stop paddling, and we drifted with the current toward the colony. The barking was almost deafening.

Phylece pulled the camera out and took pictures.

I felt the canoe jiggle as Phylece stood to snap a picture. I was about to yell, "Don't do that," but it was too late. Phylece tumbled out of the canoe, making an impressive splash.

The canoe rocked like crazy, and the sea lions erupted into intense barking, and many dove into the water. I wondered, *Are sea lions dangerous?*

We hadn't flipped the canoe. But Phylece wasn't a good swimmer and would be weighed down by many layers of clothing. *Would I need to go in after her? I hope not.*

She floated with her face out of the water, and her arm holding the camera above her head. Thank God, we were wearing life vests! Phylece was cursing, and Ray's face was white. He was equally freaked out.

"Goddamn it, this water is fucking cold," she said.

Ray said, "Phylece, we need to get you back in the canoe."

"No kidding," she said, swimming to us.

I could just about hear her teeth chattering. She reached us and handed me her camera.

I said, "When we lean to the left, kick hard and pull yourself in on the opposite side."

Her first attempt rocked the boat, and she fell back in, but we didn't capsize. She got closer with the second attempt, but again, landed back in the water. For the third attempt, we grabbed her and pulled her in.

She was shivering, and her lips were blue. Phylece and I had done some seriously crazy stuff growing up, but nothing like this. We needed to get onto the island and get her dry.

We paddled onto Angel Island as the sun reached the horizon. As Ray jumped out and pulled us onto the shore, a park ranger jogged over to us.

"Are you okay?" he asked Phylece and tossed her a blanket. She wrapped it around her shoulders, not even saying thank you.

He looked up at the setting sun. "Crossing San Francisco Bay in a canoe isn't a great idea, and spending the night on Angel Island is illegal. I'm going to have to send you on your way."

The three of us just stared at him. *Was he serious? It would be pitch black in less than an hour.*

The ranger said, "We're about a mile from Tiburon Point. If you hurry, you can make it before it gets too dark. It takes thirty to forty minutes."

Ray nodded. "We can do that."

Phylece peeled off layers of wet clothing. The ranger turned away, and Ray stood there looking embarrassed. I handed her a pair of Ray's pants from the dry bag and a sweatshirt from me. Both were way too big, and she looked absurd.

Ray pushed the canoe off the shore. "Phylece, Ann, hop in."

We got in, and he pushed us out into the water. I wondered if Ray had lights. Probably not, he had to be the most underprepared canoe guide in the world.

The last of the daylight disappeared, and we paddled in the dark. We were in a small boat at night without lights, halfway between Angel Island and Tiburon. We could see lights onshore. It wasn't far away.

As I watched, I saw something that made my heart race. It was a boat light coming straight toward us.

"That's the ferry!" Phylece said.

*Oh my God,* I thought as we paddled. *It was dark, and we had no lights. Were we visible?*

After a minute of panic, I realized this was a small ferry, not a gigantic cargo ship. It was scary, not terrifying. They were close to the water and would see us. Well, I hoped they'd see us. But if they didn't and hit us, at least they would notice. The ferry horn blasted at us, so they saw us. *Thank God.*

When we reached the shore, the last traces of light were gone, and the moonless night was so black I felt blind. But I could tell there was something in front of us. I reached out and felt it, an honest-to-God solid rock cliff.

I could feel the cliff features with my hands. I'd done some rock climbing along the Potomac, but that was with safety equipment and not at night. These cliffs were so smooth I wouldn't try it even in daylight with equipment.

I'm from Florida; we don't have cliffs in Florida. I didn't know what to make of this thing. *All I could think of* was, *where was the beach? We needed a beach.*

"What do we do?" Phylece asked.

Ray turned the canoe to the left. "We'll work our way around the island and find a place to land."

Even in the black of night, the glowing features of my diver watch were visible; it was six-fifteen p.m. Ray had told us the last ferry would leave at seven. We were running out of time.

We came to a rope ladder hanging down the side of the cliff.

"Stop paddling," Ray said and took hold of the ladder. Then he handed it to Phylece.

"I need to stay with the canoe. Phylece, do you think you can climb up?"

Phylece said, "Yeah, I'll go."

Ray said, "Ask where we can go to pull the canoe out."

"I got this," she said, taking hold of the rope ladder.

I said, "Don't push off with your feet; use both hands and pull yourself out of the canoe."

"I know. Don't tip us over. I got it," she said.

We watched her go up and disappear into the night. Ray and I sat in silence. I think he was embarrassed about his poor planning.

Ten minutes later, she called, "Coming down."

She lowered herself into the canoe. "We're about six hundred yards from the Yacht Club."

"Shouldn't we be able to see it?" I asked.

"If we keep paddling in this direction, we go around a bend in the cliff, the Yacht Club is right there."

We paddled hard. Sure enough, the welcome sight of boats and docks came into view. We maneuvered to a low dock, and Ray held the canoe in place so Phylece and I could climb out. We helped him pull the canoe out of the water.

Ray looked at his watch and said, "If you run, you too can catch the 7:00 pm ferry back to San Francisco. It will take you close to where we are parked. I'll call my girl friend to come pick me up with the truck. She isn't going to be happy."

"Where do we go?" I asked.

Ray gave us directions, and we raced. As we turned onto the last street, we saw the ferry pulling away. We ran, screaming at them to stop. The ferry reversed the engine and backed up to the dock. We jumped onto the deck and collapsed onto the seats.

"You're the guys we saw in a canoe, aren't you?" the attendant asked.

"Yup," I said.

"You need lights at night," he said. "We could have hit you."

We both laughed, saying we knew that, and we told the crew the story of our day on the waters of San Francisco. One attendant brought us hot chocolate, which we gratefully accepted.

Our ill-advised canoe trip matched the mood I'd been in for the last few months. Here I was spending time with Phylece before starting grad school on the other side of the globe. Had I lost my mind? I was no "good" student; college was a struggle. I knew I might not finish the degree. The canoe trip might not have been the only bad idea.

# Chapter 42 ~ The Land Down Under

The customs officials in Brisbane unrolled my socks and squeezed my toothpaste, examining the contents. Evidently, my appearance caused them to suspect me of transporting and using drugs.

After two weeks hiking and visiting family in Hawaii and Phylece, I picked up a serious cold. Even after pushing my flight back five days and resting, the cold just wouldn't leave, and I was already late reporting to the University of Queensland. So, gulping cough syrup and loading up on Tylenol, I suffered through the fourteen-hour flight. By the time the plane landed, my hacking and shaking had persuaded everyone next to me to move.

Customs grilled me hard enough to make me wonder how bad I looked. When they let me enter the main terminal, a tall, thin man with red hair held a sign with my name. He must have been wondering what was taking me so long because he looked flustered. I walked over to him, trying to smile despite how crappy I felt.

When he noticed me, his look of frustration shifted to that of alarm.

"Hi, I'm Tim Hanley. The Zoo Department sent me to take you to International House. Are you okay?"

I nodded. "I'm okay, it's just a bug I caught in Hawaii."

"You look terrible," he said, and he reached over and put his palm on my forehead.

"Yeah, I'm holding myself together with cough medicine and

Tylenol."

He put my bag in the trunk of his car and gestured for me to get into his car, a cream-colored Holden. The passenger seat was on the left, which felt wrong, but I was happy I wasn't driving. We passed through suburbs, traveling on a busy road that wasn't quite a highway. Time pointed out landmarks, but I wasn't taking much in or up to small talk. We pulled onto campus and parked at the Student Center.

"This isn't International House," I said.

"We're not far from it, but I'm taking you to the student infirmary. You're boiling, and I think a doctor needs to check you out before we expose students to whatever you have."

"Should I take my bag?" I asked.

"Leave it for now. If they are going to keep you here, I'll bring it in."

I followed Tim inside. We took the elevator to the third floor and into a door marked *Student Infirmary.* A young woman looked up as we walked in.

"Can I help you?" she said.

"Ann's a new graduate student. She'll be staying at International House. I'm supposed to take her there, but I think she's running a high fever. Thought I should bring her by first."

She nodded and walked over to us. "Let me have a look."

The next thing I knew, I had a thermometer under my tongue. She took my blood pressure, then pulled a stethoscope out and listened to my breathing.

"I'll call the doctor in. It sounds like you have an infection in your lungs. I suspect he'll send you for an X-ray. Your fever is quite high."

"I have travelers' insurance," I said, worrying about starting my stay in Australia with a big doctor bill.

She smiled and winked at Tim, who was suppressing a laugh. "This isn't America. Don't worry about it."

Honestly, I was too sick to worry about it. I sat back in the chair and closed my eyes.

Tim retrieved my bag from the car and left it next to me. He handed me a card with his name and a phone number. "I need to go by the department. You're on campus and close to International House. If you want me to walk over with you, call me when you're ready."

"Thanks," I said. "I'm sure I'll be fine, but I'll call if I run into problems."

"I'll let the department know you may be late checking in."

I nodded, feeling miserable. What a way to start graduate school.

"Follow me," the nurse said and picked up my duffel bag.

We walked down a hall, and she showed me to a room with two hospital beds, separated by a curtain. The room was clean and sterile. No television, but I was too sick to care.

"Get comfortable, the doctor will be in soon."

I lay down on the white sheets and must have dozed off. When I woke up, a doctor was by the bed.

He listened to my breathing and said, "It sounds like it's in your lungs. How long have you been sick?"

"About a week."

"We're going to start you on antibiotics and keep you for a few days for observation. Sally, our nurse, will take a culture to test for sensitivity. I could send you for X-rays, but that would mean a trip to the hospital. I'd rather watch you for a few days."

For a doctor, he wasn't bad. As a kid, the only time I saw a doctor was when I needed stitches and Mom dragged me to the local hospital. As a teen, they took me to a doctor for migraine headaches. I'd always associated doctors with pain, but so far, this one seemed okay.

It was an amazingly informal system. They hadn't even asked for my ID, much less a credit card. The doctor recorded my name and birth date on an index card! He listed my vitals and what drugs he prescribed. Then he filed in a card box. Evidently, that was the way they kept track of patients.

The doctor ordered a broad-spectrum antibiotic. Three days later, they had confirmation my bug was susceptible to the antibiotic they had prescribed. The nurse gave me a university map highlighting the way to International House and sent me out into the world. My fever was gone, and I felt human again. Slinging my duffel bag over my shoulder, I headed across campus.

This part of the campus felt like a botanical garden. The path curved and wound through huge ferns and tropical plants. The birds' chatter reminded me of my visits to Parrot Jungle. Soon, I looked up and saw a sign marked *International House College*. Behind the sign were four towers. The office sat between the first two towers, so I went in, filled out paperwork, and accepted a key.

That was when they told me my room was on the sixth floor, and there was no elevator. There was also no air-conditioning. I carried my bag up the six flights, needing to rest twice, and feeling like I might pass out. My breathing was better than it had been, but still not great. By the time I reached my room, I dropped my bag on the floor and crashed on the bed, waking up a few hours later.

Aside from a lack of air-conditioning, it was a pleasant room, and I had it all to myself. The balcony offered a chair, a small table, and a breathtaking view of cultivated gardens. In the distance, I could see the university's centerpiece: the Great Court, surrounded by academic buildings.

There was a knock on the door, followed by a high-pitched voice. "Hello, are you awake?"

"I am," I said. I walked over and opened the door.

"Hi, welcome to International House. I'm your neighbor, Debbie." She was blond, tall, and bubbly. She looked at my duffle on the floor and added. "You haven't even unpacked."

"Hi, Debbie, I'm Ann," I said, following her gaze. "Yeah, I'm exhausted. I guess I'm not a great traveler." I didn't want to talk about being sick and spending two days at the infirmary.

"Yeah, the staff were talking about the student who showed up looking like death. Did you have pneumonia?"

"Just a bug. I'm okay. But I am tired."

"They expect students to have dinner and breakfast in the dining hall, but they'll understand if you skip tonight. I can bring you a tray of food."

"That would be great," I said, thinking about the stairs and hoping they would be easier to navigate in the morning.

After a few minutes, Debbie left me to the quiet of the room. I put a few things away, and by the time she returned with a plate of food, I felt almost human again.

The plate had some kind of pastry on it and a side of peas and mashed potatoes. I realized I was famished.

"Thanks, Debbie. I owe you. It smells great, but what's in it?"

"Meat pie. It's mince, vegetables, and gravy in pastry. We have it at least once a week."

"Thanks again. I'll bring the tray down with me in the morning. I'm going to put a few more things away, take a shower, and go to bed."

"I'm just next door. Call me if you need anything."

She left, and I sat at my desk and devoured a meat pie. Either I was hungry, or it was excellent. When I finished eating, I took my robe and toiletries down the hall and had a shower. The experience brought a pang of homesickness, thinking of my dorm days at USF. I was, as my mother had stated, as far from Florida as I could be, in a foreign country. But some things just seemed the same.

In the morning, I braved the stairs in search of coffee. By the time I reached the dining room, I felt like I was soaking in sweat. The lack of air-conditioning was a serious failing.

The food line had strange offerings. *Who eats lamb chops for breakfast?*

Eventually, I located eggs and toast. They seemed appalled that I didn't want the eggs on top of either steak or lamb chops. But I won, and the lady put the naked egg on my plate. I picked a table with a few empty seats and sat down.

"How do you do?" a student with a heavy British accent said. "Are you new?"

"I am," I said. The accent had me confused. I thought he and the other students at the table were American. Their dark skin and his features wouldn't have been out of place in Washington, DC.

"Welcome to International House, you're the new American?" he asked.

"Yes, I'm Ann," I said. "You're not Australian. Where are you from?"

"Uganda," He said. "I'm Robert."

"Glad to meet you, Robert. What are you studying?"

"Political Science," he said.

"And you came to Australia for school?"

"My country is in a bad state. Australia has been very welcoming. They offered me a spot at this university, and my family gratefully accepted."

"I know Uganda has been in political turmoil for a while. Do you think there is hope for things to settle down?"

Robert shook his head sadly. "Not until Idi Amin is gone. The man is a dangerous tyrant."

"I know. It's a mess. I'm glad Australia is helping."

He nodded. "They're a Commonwealth country, and so is Uganda. Commonwealth countries stand by each other. So, they allow many, many refugees seeking asylum."

I nodded, not really understanding what he meant by a Commonwealth country, and not wanting to look ignorant.

"Do they eat lamb chops for breakfast in Uganda?" I asked, looking at his plate.

Robert smiled. "No, but I'm learning to enjoy the food."

Like most Americans, I was myopic about world culture and governments. My application for graduate school was based on a desire to see the Great Barrier Reef and the allure of free tuition. My family encyclopedia provided a few details. Australians had a 98 percent literacy rate, and everyone spoke English. The country mined opals and raised sheep for wool. *What else did I need to know?*

When International House arranged a weekend tour of a wildlife sanctuary, I figured I could fix some of my knowledge gap. Feeling almost normal, and knowing I couldn't show up at the Zoology Department until Monday, I splurged and bought a ticket.

The sanctuary was home to koalas, wallabies, platypuses, and a variety of birds. On the drive to the coast, the driver played Slim Dusty over the bus speakers. Imagine Nashville country music, but with an Aussie twang! The coastal headlands offered breathtaking views. We finished the day at a rocky headland, watching waves crash onto a long stretch of white sand beach.

I ended up at International House because Mom and Dad wanted me to spend the first term on campus, even though it was expensive. Next term, I'd most likely find less expensive accommodation. For now, it was fun to play tourist and get to know the students in my dorm, many of whom were from all over the world. For now, I could put up with the six-flight walk up to my room, the lack of air-conditioning, and bizarre food choices.

Monday morning, I sat with Robert at breakfast. He hadn't gone on the field trip since he had already been. We joked about the Slim Dusty music and differences in Australian, American, and African holidays. Robert told how the Ugandan students petitioned International House to sacrifice a lamb for the Feast of Sacrifice, a Muslim holiday.

I was enjoying the company and was halfway through breakfast when my anxiety kicked in. At that point, all I could think about was my appointment to meet with my adviser in the Zoology Department.

I'd been communicating with Dr. Endean for almost six months. He was known for his work with the crown-of-thorns starfish, an organism that was currently devastating large parts of the Great Barrier Reef. He was a pioneer in coral reef ecology and a fierce advocate for the establishment of a national reef sanctuary. I was terrified that Endean would review my records and decide he'd made a mistake in accepting me. I hadn't been a stellar undergraduate student. So I was nervous about our meeting.

This time, I was well enough to appreciate the details while walking through the campus gardens. Jacaranda trees with brilliant purple flowers towered over the walkway. Gum trees with almost white bark hosting kookaburra birds, and ferns that made the gardens feel like a rainforest. The pathway ended at the entrance to the University Court—a large ellipse of grass circled by academic buildings clad in pink sandstone facades. It felt very Victorian with Arches and Pillars in the walkways outside the buildings.

I had to remind myself that while the buildings and campus looked old, they were actually only completed ten years ago. The architects used materials and design elements to create a Victorian atmosphere. It was an interesting contrast to USF, where every effort was for a sleek, modern, and futuristic presentation.

Inside the entrance to Biological Sciences, a majestic ceiling hosted a replica of a dugong, floating on wires above a granite stairwell. I walked up the stairs to the department office. A friendly receptionist walked me to Dr. Endean's office on the third floor. I wasn't sure what I was expecting, but a cramped, dusty room with little light and no air-conditioning made me wonder about what resources the university had to offer.

Dr. Endean wore crisp black slacks, a collared button-down shirt, and thick glasses. He opened the door.

"Dr. Endean, I'm so pleased to meet you. Thank you for agreeing to take me on as a student."

"We really like to encourage international students; it adds so much diversity. I'm glad you made it. I heard you had a rough trip. Come in," he said, and we talked. His accent made it hard to follow much of what he said.

We talked for about forty-five minutes. His accent made it almost impossible to be sure I understood what he was saying. I wasn't entirely sure he was speaking English. *How could English be almost unintelligible?*

It took a concerted effort to avoid saying "what" repeatedly, hoping I understood enough not to come across as an idiot. Despite our communication glitch, it was a productive meeting. We settled on topics for my qualifying year: marine biology, fisheries science, and coral reef ecology. The exam would take place roughly a year from now. The Australian system had classes like we had in the States, but graduate students undertook directed study, then sat for exams. It was a new and intriguing idea.

"We've set up a desk for you in the old library. It's temporary until we clear office space, but it will get you started."

"Sounds good."

"Follow me. Let me show you to your desk."

I followed and tried not to look disappointed. The "desk" was a ratty table in a very dusty, unused corner of an old library. The building looked like it might be slated for renovation, but certainly wasn't being kept up.

Dr. Endean approached a young man sitting at a nearby table.

"Howard, this is Ann. The American I told you would be starting in the program this week."

Howard looked up and smiled. "Welcome, it will be good to have another Yank here."

"Thanks, where are you from?"

"New York."

"Me, too, but a long time ago."

Endean said, "I'm going to show Ann around the department."

"Talk to you soon," Howard said. "Come back when you're done, and I'll show you how to access the journal stacks."

"Thanks," I said.

We toured a few labs and the department tea room. I was told the entire department took breaks at four in the afternoon and had an afternoon tea break. I wondered if coffee was allowed.

After the tour, I followed up with Howard. We chatted, and I discovered he was also Jewish. He was also starting this term and had only arrived two weeks earlier, so like me, he was still figuring things out.

I visited the campus bookstore and picked up a few supplies to make my table feel more like a work desk, and I took Howard up on his offer to show me the journal stacks.

I was ambivalent about my immediate task to research my topics and bring a reading list of papers for Endean's approval, but I started right away and soon gained some enthusiasm. It was cool being able to choose the focus of what I would read and study. And I had never loved my undergraduate zoology classes where the professor set the curriculum. It took a second and third meeting with Endean for me to really understand the process. I would select a topic and identify a book and current articles to read. Endean would look at my reference, approve what he thought was worthwhile, and suggest additional material to fill in the gaps.

At the end of the year, I would take three ninety-minute exams on consecutive days. Each exam would comprise a series of essay questions. Dr. Endean warned me that a panel of faculty members would examine my exam papers, and I needed to be prepared to show true mastery of the topics. Then, toward the end of the year, I would work on a proposal for a master's thesis topic on coral reefs.

My feelings were mixed and ambivalent. I was excited about working with Dr. Endean and the freedom to conduct my own studies. But, by American standards, the University of Queensland wasn't providing much—this was largely a Do-It-Yourself program. It was no wonder they didn't charge tuition.

# Chapter 43 ~ Culture Shock

I settled into a routine in the Zoology Department that was neither motivational nor exciting. I reported to my desk each day and pulled out my materials to study the topics Dr. Endean and I selected for my end-of-year qualifying exam. Sitting at a library carrel all day felt like my undergraduate years. By the end of the first month, I doubted whether I could stick with the program.

I didn't want to take more money from my mom and dad, particularly if it was likely that I would leave in my first year. Breaking my contract at International House, I took a flat in the West End, a modest neighborhood with a distinct Polish flavor. My flat was within walking distance of a ferry station that shuttled passengers across the Brisbane River to the university campus.

I missed my life in Washington, DC, both my friends and the ability to listen to folk music and perform. During my study breaks, I ventured into town. The Brisbane Folk Society held an open mic on Sunday mornings at a downtown park. I watched people sing Australian folk songs and play guitar on my first visit. The event was poorly attended and lacked the vibrant atmosphere I missed from the Red Fox open mic, but it was better than nothing. The following week, I returned with my guitar.

"Would you like to play?" the organizer asked.

"I would," I replied, and then I played a few Joan Baez and Tom

Paxton tunes, reasoning that as an American, I should play American songs. The set wasn't exactly high pressure—less than ten people were on the lawn—but it felt good to perform again. The organizer was Pam Gallagher, and she invited me to the local folk club, the Barley Mow, which met at a hotel downtown. I was confused until I learned that "hotels" are bars in Australia.

Back in 1977, Brisbane was called an "overgrown country town." It had a small-town feeling that I liked. And finding a group of people who, like me, played folk music made it feel like home. It didn't make sitting at my desk studying any less annoying, but my loneliness decreased. I felt better about life.

I began to get invitations to play American folk music at paid events. With no work visa, this under-the-table extra money enticed me to take gigs that I wouldn't have considered back in Washington, where tons of musicians were much more polished than myself. Sometimes, I would get off the stage feeling a bit shaky and wondering what I was thinking. But money was a strong motivator, and the local reception was positive.

It was an exciting and challenging time. I expected Australia to be like America—after all, they spoke English. What I hadn't realized was that Australians spoke Australian English. They also mumbled a lot. I understood about one out of every five words. Then there was the wildlife. I'd look up at sunset and see what I thought were birds, only to find they were bats.

Having cockatoos hanging out on a branch in front of my window and seeing a small wallaby hop across my front lawn reminded me that I wasn't in the United States. At Stradbroke Island, I stood on the headlands and watched the sharks chase the mackerel. The surfers didn't pay any more attention to the sharks than they did to the mackerel unless the lifeguard station sounded an alarm. Even then, some surfers refused to leave the water.

Most of the differences were subtle. Walking across the great court, students offered me "fairy floss" (cotton candy). They were from the Gay-Straight Alliance, an organization far ahead of its American counterparts. Walking down the streets, I saw women climbing telephone poles alongside their male coworkers. For all the talk of Australia being male-dominated, women were taking on diverse jobs, often closed to women back home.

There were other differences at the university, such as tea time and Communists. The biology department met at four p.m. in the "tearoom." They did this every day at the same time. During my first week in Australia, one of the younger faculty members, Ann Cameron, entered our dusty office.

"It's four, time for tea," she said.

Howard Silver, a fellow American and graduate student, joined me, and we left our dusty library behind, following Ann out the door and down the stairwell to the tearoom.

Australians brewed tea in a pot. While the tea brewed, they added milk to the cup and poured tea into the milk. No one back home had milk in tea. I poured myself a cup of tea (no milk) and sat down.

Howard sat beside a rough, heavyset young man with a dark complexion. He didn't look African American. But he wasn't white either, and he didn't look Australian.

"Hi, Ann, have you met Arthur Georges?"

"No," I said. "Pleased to meet you."

Ann said, "Arthur is our resident Communist."

"Are you really a member of the Communist Party?" I asked.

"Yes, it isn't illegal here in Australia," Arthur said.

I glanced at Howard, who looked uncomfortable. Back then, our high schools required a class called Americanism vs. Communism, which wasn't very complimentary toward communism.

"I know. Is it the Communist Party a major player here?" I asked.

Arthur shook his head. "No, but our political system differs from America's, and yes, the Communist Party is legitimate. Hey, would you guys like to join the food co-op?"

Howard suddenly seemed interested. "How does it work?" he asked.

Arthur Georges smiled and explained that he shopped at a food co-op where local family farms sold their produce. He then distributed food boxes to friends and coworkers for five dollars a week per box. It sounded good to me. Maybe Communists weren't all that bad.

Arthur became a good friend as well as a valued coworker. He, other coworkers, and Australian friends helped me develop a worldview without the United States at the center. I'd heard that international travel is good for personal growth, broadening perspectives, and fostering global understanding. This wasn't my purpose in going abroad, but it was a happy outcome.

# Chapter 44 ~ Brisbane Music

It was easy to be homesick when you're far from home. I missed music. It was more than just the music. It was the sense of camaraderie and belonging. Did Brisbane have a folk society? Was there anything like the Red Fox open mic? I didn't know, but once I settled into my dorm, I set out to find out.

The folk club in the Student Union was lame. College kids playing John Denver and James Taylor songs. It was more of a pop vibe than folk. I was polite, introduced myself, and asked if they knew of any less mainstream venues. One kid said there was an open mic hosted by the Brisbane Folk Society downtown on Sunday mornings.

I left, excited about contacting the local folk society. Looking forward to the event helped keep me positive, while sitting at my library desk reading books and papers on oceanography and marine biology. So far, Brisbane had been a disappointment. I was bored with a daily routine severely lacking in personal interactions. If I had known graduate school would mean sitting in an old dusty library reading books by myself, I might not have come. On Sunday, guitar in hand, I ventured to the Roma Street Station.

The stage was on a grass hill in a park behind the Roma Street Train Station. A handful of people milled around as an older woman with silver hair and a long skirt set up a microphone and tested the sound equipment.

"Welcome to the Brisbane Folk Society Roma Street Open Mic. My name is Pam Gallagher. We meet here every Sunday and have a few featured guests, then enthusiasts are welcomed to the stage. We ask that your music remain acoustic and folk. There are many venues for pop and rock music." She paused for a moment, then added, "Please join me in welcoming June Nichols to the stage."

The handful of spectators milling about clapped, and I joined them.

June was skilled at her guitar playing. She did a selection of English folk songs, then followed an Australian song, "And the band played Waltzing Matilda." I was impressed with her, and with the song, an evocative story set to music of a young Australian sent to Gallipoli in WWI, who returned home after the war without legs. I was in tears by the end of the song.

After June left the stage, Pam introduced a trio of musicians who delivered an Irish instrumental set using guitar, penny whistle, and violin. After each song, the few people in attendance gave polite applause.

There was silence after the trio left the stage. Pam pointed to the guitar beside me, still in its case. "Would you like to play?"

I nodded and took the stage. My set included a Joan Baez song, "The Wagoner's Lad," Pete Seeger's "Gonna Make my Garden Grow," and a traditional a cappella work song called "Captain." I picked the songs because I had performed them so much, I figured I couldn't mess them up. And it was a no-brainer that as an American, I should do American songs. When I finished, there was scattered polite applause.

Over the next few months, I explored every folk venue I could find. I still missed my community of folk musicians from DC, but I had an outlet to balance the monotony of self-study in a library. Soon, I was considered a "regular" and had a reason to practice in the evenings and places to play and sing to break up the dull grind of studying scientific papers in the library.

My exams seemed a long way off. I tried to keep to a schedule of daily study, taking copious notes, and meeting regularly with Dr. Endean to discuss my progress and to talk about potential topics for research on the reef.

A few months later, I was eating at a local café where a guy sat in the corner playing guitar and singing. I realized he wasn't any better than I was, and I wondered if he was being paid. Before I left, I asked the manager if they might be interested in an American guitarist/singer, and he asked me to come back and audition. The next week I started a regular Friday night gig. They paid me fifteen dollars cash and a meal for a three-hour set. The pay was minimal, but was also "under the table." That was important since I didn't have a work visa. After that, other paid gigs came my way. I'd still need to draw on Dad's account—but the gigs would slow down how often I had to pull money.

# Chapter 45 ~ Heron Island

Finding my footing in the music community gave my overall outlook a tremendous boost, and at almost the same time, the Zoology Department approved an exploratory visit to the Heron Island University Research Station. I was to explore the island and reef and to meet with other graduate students who had projects based on coral reef biology at the site. Dr. Endean felt that I was far enough along in my qualifying studies that it was time to develop a research proposal.

I wanted an ecological project on the reef. My focus wasn't biochemistry, embryology, or pharmacology—all hot topics for coral reef biologists. Dr. Endean suggested that I narrow my project to sites on the reef flat and lagoon. He'd had students working in deeper water who wasted weeks waiting for the weather to be calm enough to visit their study site. That wasn't a problem for students who grew up in Brisbane and were still living in their parents' house. I needed to develop a topic that I could expect to collect data for a year to eighteen months, then do my analysis and write a thesis. I agreed with Endean. I would work on the reef flat.

The trip to Heron would be a major excursion. Well, true, I'd already traveled from Florida—almost half a world away. But Brisbane was four hundred miles from Gladstone, and Heron was another fifty-seven miles off the coast in the Pacific Ocean. The Zoology Department would let me stay at the research station and would authorize reimbursement for gas or for a train ticket. I had a car now, but it was strictly a city car. To be exact, it was a Honda Zot with a 360 cc two-stroke engine. There were hills in my neighborhood that challenged its power. I took the train.

I was so excited I had trouble sleeping, and I was babbling to everyone who would listen. At last, I'd be doing more than sitting at my desk studying papers and books. One of the graduate students in my shared office space was sympathetic and spent hours talking to me about the island and reef.

Neil was also studying reef biology, and his father was the director of the research station. When I first met Neil, I thought he was from England—his accent was very British. Neil's family was from England, but his father had followed a career that took him to East Africa, Hong Kong, and then to Australia. It turned out all these places fostered an English accent. We quickly became friends, sharing a love of marine science and guitar. He invited me to dinner with him and his wife, Julie. He offered advice and a ride to the train station. Both were appreciated.

"Take your guitar," Neil said. "The evenings can be a drag. It really is a deserted island, without any entertainment other than what researchers plan for.

"I wouldn't go somewhere for two weeks without it," I replied, meaning it.

Of course, I was taking my guitar. Playing music was my way of relieving tension. My instrument was a cheap one from a used goods shop—the Australian version of a pawnshop. If I damaged it in travel or on the island, I would be sad, but it wasn't much of a risk.

"You're going to love the island. I'll see you in two weeks," Neil said after helping me load my things onto the train.

"Thanks for bringing me here," I said, looking at the mass of stuff and wondering how I would get it from the train station in Gladstone to the ferry landing. My dive gear was bulky. I think Neil read my mind.

"There will be taxis waiting when the train pulls in. You have cash with you, right?"

"I do. Thanks again."

I waved goodbye and boarded the train, finding a window seat and placing my guitar next to me. The train pulled out from the station at seven p.m., bouncing on the track and making me realize the seats were wood, did not recline, and had no padding. It was going to be a long night.

My excitement carried me through a bumpy, sleepless train trip. But when the sun rose, and the train pulled into the station, all I could think of was I'd soon be on the reef. There was almost a bounce in my step as I stepped off the train with my gear and transferred my luggage to a waiting taxi. The driver was kind enough to help me get my things loaded onto the ferry. I was almost done. But Neil insisted that I visit the local grocery and check my order. He said sometimes they get messed up. It would be bad to be on the island without food.

I checked in with the ferry, paid for a ticket, and walked up the street to the grocery. Everything was in order; my food and water would be delivered on the weekly supply barge tomorrow. I picked up food for today and tomorrow's breakfast.

The grocery clerk checked on my order and my basket of things I was taking with me. It had been intimidating to put an order for a full week, knowing that you couldn't run out and get something you forgot. I kept it basic—coffee, cereal, milk, bread, peanut butter, jam, dried fruit, fresh fruit, cans of tuna, frozen meat, and five gallons of drinking water.

"Did you pick up Dramamine?" he asked.

"No. I don't get seasick."

He smiled and shook his head side to side. "You look like a student. You're taking Attunga to Heron. You should get some Dramamine."

"Is that the name of the ferry?" I asked.

"Yes," he said. "We also call it the 'Achundra'"

When I didn't respond, he said, "To chunder is to throw up. Get it?"

"Okay, where is the Dramamine?"

"The chemist is two doors down. He'll have it. Make sure you take it at least half an hour before you board."

I picked up the Dramamine but didn't take it. I'd been on a ton of boats and had never been seasick. And I knew Dramamine would make me sleepy, and I wanted to experience the boat trip—not sleep through it. If I had trouble on the way to Heron, I'd use it on the way back.

As it was, I didn't need it. The ferry trip over was glorious. The water was royal blue, and while it had a bit of a chop, my stomach was fine. I stayed up on the deck watching for turtles and whales, seeing pelicans and dolphins, and had a wonderful morning. We pulled into the harbor at two-thirty in the afternoon and disembarked, walking off the pier onto the white sand of the island, eighty kilometers off the coast of Queensland, in a coral cay surrounded by a reef flat and lagoon.

From where I stood, I could see the reef crest and the open sea beyond. The sight left me feeling isolated from the rest of the world. The feeling was incredible.

I was the only student on the ferry. Everyone else was a tourist who would be staying at the resort side of the island. Walking off the boat, I couldn't believe the crystal clear, blue water and white sand. The island looked amazing. The ferry crew pointed out the path to the research station and showed me a cart they kept handy for researchers and students. I loaded my bag, dive gear, and guitar into the cart and headed down the path to the inside of the island. As I entered the island forest, I was startled by strange moaning sounds. I later learned these were the local "mutton birds," crested shearwaters that nest in underground burrows.

The research station had a few people in residence. As I approached the first building, a young man walked out to greet me.

"Sorry, I didn't meet you at the ferry. I got tied up in the lab. Let's get your dive gear stored, and I'll show you around."

"Thanks, I'm excited to be here."

The "tour" took ten minutes. There weren't a lot of buildings. I had a cabin to myself. It had two bunk beds, but from what I heard, rooms rarely had more than two researchers. The upper bunk was handy for attaching the mosquito nets that I was assured were necessary. The bathroom building was between my cabin and the kitchen/dining area.

I headed to use the facilities and thought about a shower, but decided it was too much work for right now. You had to heat water on a stove in the communal kitchen. The shower bucket was on a pulley. You lowered it to the ground to pour the water in, raised it, and pulled a rope to release water when ready. It was primitive, but it worked.

Speaking of water. There was no freshwater source other than rainfall. They collected rainfall from gutters on the buildings into rain barrels, but the roof was covered with bird droppings—so the water wasn't fit for drinking, and I'm not sure it was well suited for showering. But it was what we had.

I thought of my days in the Keys at Seacamp. Water pressure was always low, and a shower often meant sitting near the hose and rinsing off. In some ways, the "hot shower bucket" was an improvement. But maybe not—the water at Seacamp didn't smell of bird guano.

I put my clothes away and went in search of graduate students. It was a quiet time. The few researchers in residence were off the island on the reef. Sue, a researcher from England, was having tea in the kitchen. She offered me a cup, and we sat and chatted for a while. She offered to take a walk with me and show me the island.

Our unhurried forty-five-minute walk circumnavigated the small island, an elongated oval, with a harbor on one end and a sand spit on the other. Sue said she walked every morning while the temperature was still cool.

"The temperature feels fine," I said. "Do you find this too warm?"

"No, but this is May, wait until you're here in summer. Temperature hits thirty degrees by nine a.m. Most of us get up at four a.m., work in the lab for a few hours while it's still cool, and do a sunrise walk as soon as it's light enough.

Over my two-week stay, I fell in love with the island and the reef. Actually, my first dive left me a little disappointed. Heron Reef was beautiful, but seemed so similar to my Florida reefs that I wondered if it was worth traveling all this way. During my second dive, I began to see the differences. There were tropical fish I didn't recognize, and so many kinds of coral!

My companions confirmed my thoughts; for every type of coral on a Florida Reef, there were twenty or thirty different species here. I knew this from my library research, but now it was more than book knowledge. The same was true of the tropical fish. Everywhere I looked, I saw fish unlike any I'd seen before. By the time I left the island, I had four dives under my belt and had spent at least two hours a day walking the reef flat.

Some of my best memories of Heron Island were on the cool morning walks. I took Sue up on her invitation to join her on pre-dawn walks. The forty-five minutes often stretched a bit to include inevitable delays, like stopping to watch a turtle lumber up the beach to lay eggs, or watch a blacktip reef shark cruise the shallow water right off the beach, or the mandatory pause to watch the actual sunrise. We were here to work, but we made time to enjoy the island, too.

The cabins were in a thick strand of Pisonia trees near the island's center. The mutton birds were a hazard with their underground burrows. We used flashlights in the dark to avoid stepping into the nest holes—bad for us and the birds. In the open air, these birds flew with magnificent grace, soaring and gliding effortlessly. But they were so clumsy near the ground they sometimes flew right into people. Not that it ever happened to me. Yeah, they were bizarre birds.

We had a communal kitchen, which worked well to make sure researchers connected with each other, sharing ideas and often arranging times they would work together. Because I was a certified diver and had my gear from Florida with me, I was in demand as a dive partner when anyone needed to work off the reef flat on the slope.

By the end of my first trip, I had the seeds of a research topic in mind, and I was ready to start background research and to map out a proposal. It might have been the best two weeks of my life.

# Chapter 46 ~ Supervision

"You made excellent use of your time on Heron," Dr. Endean said.

"Thanks. It was an exciting trip. I can't believe the amount of life you find in a single colony of Tubipora. It's like an entire zoo in every sample."

"I think you have the makings of a fine project here. I'll compile a list of key references for diversity studies to help you get started with your literature search. You need to know the work that others are pursuing."

"Thanks. And you're okay with me restricting the study site to shallow areas in the reef flat and lagoon?"

"The reef flat is a habitat of its own; it would be too broad to include sample sites on the slope."

There was a pause while Endean fiddled with papers on his desk, and I had the feeling he was going to say something I didn't want to hear.

"Is something wrong?" I asked.

"The Reef Advisory Board has asked me to take on responsibilities at the national level. It means I'll be spending a lot of time traveling. I've asked Dr. Stimson to take over supervising your qualifying exams."

I felt like someone had hit me with a sledgehammer. I'd started communicating with Dr. Endean while I was still living in Washington, DC. His work with the crown-of-thorns starfish sparked my interest in pursuing graduate studies, and meeting with him weekly was the highlight of my academic experience here.

I turned away, trying not to let him see how upset I was.

"You should be ready next month. Stimson is likely to have very little responsibility. Do you feel ready?"

"I'll be ready. Will you still be supervising my research project?"

"I'll be here for you as much as I can and will certainly be part of your faculty evaluation team. But I talked with Dr. Stimson about taking over your field supervision. He has done extensive work in species diversity, and your project aligns well with his field of expertise. He's agreed to meet with you and see if it's a good fit."

I nodded, trying to keep the knot of anxiety from showing on my face. "I'll be happy to meet with Stimson."

We discussed briefly the work he would be doing, specifically securing support for the establishment of a National Reef Park. I left his office deeply disappointed and in a state of shock. I'd never even spoken with Dr. Stimson, and I would sit my exams under his supervision in less than a month. It was a lot to take in.

I limped back to my office and slumped into my desk chair, hoping it was empty. Neil was at his desk. I liked Neil. He was a good friend, but I wanted to be alone.

"What's wrong?" he asked.

"I just found out Dr. Endean is going to be traveling a lot for the next year or so. He's handing me off to Dr. Stimson for supervision."

Neil was reassuring and said, "I know you think Endean is God, and he's done some fine work. But he's more involved in politics now. Your project focuses on invertebrate diversity. Stimson is a good choice."

"I hope you're right. What can you tell me about his research?"

"He has a broad background in zoology, and he was one of the faculty members who pushed for establishing the research stations on both Stradbroke and Heron. His work is on pelagic swimming crabs. I know he's supervised several students with species diversity on mudflats."

"I guess I'll try to keep an open mind," I said.

I stopped by Stimson's office before leaving the department. It was after four on Friday afternoon. His secretary set an appointment for us to meet on Monday morning. I was glad he wasn't in. I'd have the weekend to get over my shock and come in with a positive mindset. It gave me the time I needed to get over my shock and adjust to the idea of a new supervisor. I brought photocopies of two of his papers to read over the weekend.

Monday morning at eight, I waited outside his office, chatting with his secretary, a friendly middle-aged woman. Stimson was late. I made a mental note to myself—he left early on Friday and came in late on Monday. Not the best work ethic. He showed up at eight-thirty and invited me into his office.

Our first meeting was reassuring. Dr. Stimson liked the idea of my species diversity project and was impressed by the preliminary work and proposal I put together during my stay at Heron. He was able to give me some ideas for statistical analysis. He suggested that I enroll in his undergraduate class on numerical classification, as well as a class in invertebrate zoology. The classes would start right after I took my qualifying exam so that they wouldn't distract me.

I wasn't against the idea of classes, but I wasn't thrilled either. On one hand, I was sick of sitting in the library studying on my own. But my experience with undergraduate classes back at USF left me apprehensive. Stimson reassured me that the grades wouldn't count for anything, but the knowledge would give me a significant boost in conducting my research.

Registering for classes brought home the fact that this was not the United States—there was no tuition. But there were sticking points. Despite Endean's reassurance, Stimson was *not* enthusiastic about supervising my reef project. He disliked the logistics issue of travel and weather restrictions that working on Heron presented. He tried hard to convince me to revise my proposal for a project on the mudflats of Morton Bay.

His concerns were legitimate, but from my perspective, they were crap. I'd traveled across the world to study on the Great Barrier Reef. It made little sense to undertake a project in an environment that I could have found in Florida. He argued, and I argued back. Endean had approved my proposal. Could Stimson now request that I make changes to it? I didn't know. We tabled the discussion for after my exams. We agreed that I'd been preparing for my exams for a year, and it was important not to get distracted.

I raised the issue of my dyslexia and my inability to write legibly on an exam. It took having records sent from the Office of the Registrar at the University of South Florida, stating I had a legal disability and had been given the option of using a typewriter during essay exams. The Zoology Department agreed to the accommodation, as long as I provided a typewriter, saying they did not have one they could spare. They would also permit extra time—four hours instead of the usual three. A visit to a pawn shop yielded a royal electric for only twenty-five dollars.

I took my qualifying exams over three consecutive mornings in late November. The first day covered general marine biology, fisheries, and oceanography. The second day focused on coral reefs, including their global distribution, environmental needs, and the symbiotic relationship between zooxanthellae and coral. The final day's topics would focus solely on the Great Barrier Reef, including studies of diversity, coral competition, and reproduction.

I used my typewriter for a first draft, then underlined each suspected misspelled word, checked it with my "word book" (a miniature dictionary without definitions) for spelling, and carefully retyped each essay to turn in.

The process made me think of individuals who unwittingly helped me prepare, like Mr. Groff, my high school English teacher, who would glance at my classwork and allow me to take essays home to correct and type before submitting them. I thought of my freshman English composition teacher in college, a graduate teaching assistant who introduced me to the word book for quickly checking my spelling.

I hated using my dyslexia diagnosis for special treatment, but without special accommodations, I would never have been able to meet the requirements of twenty pages per topic per day.

The exam committee took a week to review my work. They found my essays satisfactory, and my qualifying year was officially over. I spent the Christmas break trying to relax and prepare for my first year as a master's student. I'd be taking classes, teaching classes, and gathering data for my project.

The classes were helpful, especially Numerical Classification. It provided a solid foundation for my thesis. However, Stimson wasn't keen on my returning to Heron Island. He pressured me to shift my diversity study to the local estuary, and we had some pretty heated arguments. Then, in one meeting, he sat next to me and put his hand on my knee.

"I could be of great help on the right project," he said.

I lifted his hand from my knee, stood up, and left the office. I walked outside to the courtyard and began walking, unable to return to my office or face anyone in the department. I was angry. I was embarrassed. I was confused. Most of all, I didn't know what to do.

Eventually, I walked home to my flat in St. Lucia. Dr. Endean was out of town. Who could I go to? I knew I couldn't continue with Stimson as my supervisor. Hell, I couldn't even face him again. If I could have, I think I would have gotten on a plane and gone home to Florida, and not come back again.

The next morning, I was late going to the university. When I stepped into the office, Neil said Dr. Stimson had come by looking for me. I sat down and cried. I hated myself for doing that.

"Okay, what happened?" Neil asked.

So I told him. He laughed. "He does that to everyone. I guess I should have warned you."

"Does it ever work?" I asked.

"I don't know. I doubt it."

"I can't work with him," I said.

Neil didn't say anything, and my anger grew. I no longer wanted to get on a plane and go home. I wanted to hit someone. The situation wasn't something to laugh about.

"He's harmless," Neil added.

"That's easy for you to say," I said and walked out into the corridor.

I had been the only girl in my high school Physics class. Back then, students only had to take one year of science. It didn't occur to me I was doing anything weird.

But the people at NOAA hired me because no males applied. They waited until the last minute to offer me the job. The men had cut-out pictures of semi-nude calendar girls posted on the walls, and they told crude jokes while they worked on the boats and docks. I knew they resented me because I made them feel uncomfortable. When I started, the pictures came down, and the men cleaned up their language around me. Eventually, I developed friendships, and I think of that term working with NOAA as a golden period.

*How would I have felt if someone at NOAA had treated me like Stimson just did? Was I left alone because I was only seventeen?*

I'd seen no sign of sexual harassment or inappropriate behavior at NIH. However, I had to consider that my supervisor, Dr. Gibbs, treated his students as if they were his children. No one would have insulted him by putting the move on us. He was a religious man, and to do so would have been career-limiting.

Did I want to work in science if it meant dealing with people like

Stimson? It was the first time I questioned how determined I was to work in science. Would I be battling sexism and harassment my whole life? The more I thought about it, the more I realized that, sexism or not, I wanted to work in science.

And for now, I wasn't about to give up and go home. If I had to fight to keep my degree, then that was what I'd do. I just had to figure out exactly what I could do. What I couldn't do was go back to my office right then. I was too mad.

I grabbed coffee and lunch at a nearby shop before heading back to my apartment, where I could think things through and try to weigh my options. After I'd managed to relax, I made two calls looking for advice.

First, I phoned my best friend in Australia. Helen was a former medical student who transferred to hospital administration. I wanted her input as a woman and someone who understood the bureaucracy of the university.

The second call was long-distance to a friend and colleague at NIH in Washington, DC. I trusted Lon, and he was older. I wanted his perspective on sexism in research. Both Helen and Lon strongly advised me to go to the university administration, file a formal complaint, and request a new supervisor.

My friends both stressed a crucial point. Stimson wasn't remotely interested in me. The sexual harassment was aggressive, a way to assert dominance. It took me three days to figure out what I wanted to do. While I did go to the university for my teaching job and spend some time in my office, I avoided talking about the incident. On Thursday, three days after Stimson had accosted me, I walked into the administration building to file a complaint.

Helen told me to ask for the vice chancellor, so that was what I did.

"I'd like an appointment with the vice chancellor," I said to the receptionist.

"I'll need your name and a few details about what you are here for."

"I'm a graduate student in zoology." I paused before continuing, and I was sure I was blushing. "My name is Ann Rudnick, and I need to request a change in supervisor."

"Wait here," she said and went into the inner office.

It was only a minute or two before he came out and greeted me.

"Come in and have a seat," he said, as he took his place behind the desk. He asked a few questions about my topic. We waited for his assistant to return with my exam results and grades.

"Your exam results are impressive, and your topic sounds fascinating."

"Thank you."

He tapped a pencil against the desk, and I tried to keep my knees from shaking. *How would I explain the situation? I hadn't rehearsed what I would say before coming.* I expected to just make an appointment for later.

He nodded, closed the file, and said, "Why do you need to change supervisors?"

"Dr. Stimson behaved inappropriately, and I feel uncomfortable in his presence. I'd like to file a complaint and ask for a new faculty supervisor."

"I'm sure he didn't mean to make you uncomfortable, but I know Stimson. The man is brilliant, but his behavior can be more than rude at times. What exactly did he do?"

"He sat next to me on the couch in his office. He put his hand on my knee and suggested he could be helpful to me with my project." My face felt hot, and tears were forming.

He handed me some tissues. "I'll talk with him," the vice chancellor said.

*Was that all?* I didn't want this man to "talk" to Stimson. What I wanted was Endean back as my supervisor. Well, I couldn't have that, but I didn't want to work with Stimson. I didn't want to talk to Stimson, ever.

"I appreciate that you will talk to him. However, the situation is awkward enough that I need a change in supervision. I've invested considerable time and energy into this program, and I can't see a way forward without a change of supervision."

"I understand, but I need to talk to him first. There are always two sides to the story; he is my responsibility. At the same time, I'll look into placements with a different supervisor."

He stood, opened the door for me, and added, "Let's plan to meet tomorrow morning at eight. I should have some answers for you."

"Thank you," I said.

I left with mixed feelings. He had carefully manipulated the meeting so that my "concerns" would be addressed, but hadn't given me the opportunity to file an official complaint. All I could do was wait and see. Not that I needed "justice," although it would be nice if Stimson had more than a talking to. But it burned me that he did this to women before me, and would do it again.

What I needed was to have someone supervise my project and keep his hands to himself, so I could complete my master's. As long as the vice chancellor arranged a change of supervisor, I'd be alright.

I went back to my office to get some work done.

"Are you okay?" Neil asked.

I nodded, not wanting to talk to him about it.

"Stimson was looking for you again," he said.

"That's nice," I said.

I worked in silence, reworking my research proposal and timeline, in hopes that I'd be presenting it to a new supervisor.

When I returned to administration the next morning, I found Dr. Hailstone with the vice chancellor.

"Ann, come in and have a seat," he said. "Have you met Dr.

Hailstone?"

I nodded. "Good morning," I said.

"After reviewing your research proposal, I believe Dr. Hailstone would be an excellent supervisor. I've invited him to our meeting to discuss it further."

Dr. Hailstone had my proposal in hand. "I'd be glad to help you refine your plans. Your project on soft coral associations seems very promising," he said.

"Thank you. I've done some more work on the details and the timeline," I said.

Hailstone said, "Let's plan to meet this afternoon, say at one p.m., to go over details."

We chatted for a bit longer, and then they said I could go.

I'd met Dr. Hailstone a few times around the department, and he seemed nice. I was also familiar with his taxonomic work on mollusks of the Great Barrier Reef. Some of my anger eased. Hailstone wasn't Endean, but he was someone I respected and could work with.

While I was pleased with the outcome, it bothered me that the vice chancellor never mentioned his talk with Stimson. It was abundantly clear from Neil's reaction, and now from the vice chancellor's reaction, that I wasn't the first graduate student to have difficulty with Stimson.

The vice chancellor "fixed" the supervision issue, and he must have talked with him at least to explain that he was changing my supervision. But was it a reprimand? I'd never know. And, I suspected if anything, it was a mild verbal warning. Would there even be a record of my complaint?

In the end, I swallowed my anger and moved on, comforted in knowing I'd passed my exams, finished my coursework, and launched my research project. While I lost Dr. Endean as my supervisor, I now had someone I respected and who seemed enthusiastic about my work. For the first time, my crazy plan to pursue a master's in Australia felt achievable.

I finally agreed to visit my family in Miami—something they'd been wanting for six months.

# Chapter 47 ~ Home Visit

After eighteen hours crammed in a metal tube up in the air, I wondered if visiting Australia was such a good idea. It was literally on the other side of the world from Miami. The longest stretch was from New Zealand to Los Angeles. The other flights were not short hops either, and by the time I walked out the last gate in Miami, I'd been traveling twenty-seven hours. I needed a shower and then a bed.

Even with the excitement of seeing family, I felt my exhaustion and strained to keep my eyes open. Mom waved as I came through the gate into the terminal. She wore fashion jeans and an art-print top. Dad wore his silk shirt and slacks, a thick gold chain, and a big smile. I had on a University of Queensland T-shirt and discount jeans. I was their daughter, and they had to live with my lack of fashion sense. Some things hadn't changed.

Dad put my bag in the trunk of the Cadillac, and we drove to the house in North Miami. The car was big by American standards and huge compared to the Australian ones I had grown used to. I had to get used to the steering wheel being on the right-hand side and highways filled with vehicles traveling way too fast. I was happy I wasn't the one driving.

Dad pulled into the driveway in front of the olive green house. Ours was a typical Florida suburban house: one story, no garage, with palm trees in the garden bed. I walked into the house, enjoying a cool breeze from the central air-conditioning. Brisbane gets hot in summer, and almost no buildings were air-conditioned. I walked through the living room with its wall-to-wall carpeting and the large projection TV on the wall, and a fake fireplace in the corner. My black cat, Charlie, was asleep on the couch.

My bedroom was at the back of the house. A *Welcome Home* banner over my dresser greeted me. Yeah, my folks were making a big deal about their daughter coming "home." It felt surreal. My younger brother had left for college, and Richard was married and living in Hawaii. I guess the house felt empty.

A few years earlier, Jim and I visited Richard in Hawaii. I met his wife Debbie and their two-year-old daughter, Cora. Richard worked as a bellhop in a fancy hotel. Debbi stayed home taking care of Cora. The island was strikingly beautiful, rich in lush foliage and amazing lava flows. The view of the ocean from his living room picture window took my breath away. Jim and I slept on swimming rafts covered with sleeping bags. Well, we were young and flexible back then.

The five of us were visiting over dinner when Debbie said, "Richard says the two of you aren't very close. Can I ask why?"

"Well, he used to beat me up for my allowance," I said.

She was wide-eyed and glared at Richard while she spoke to me. "He told me that, and I thought he was kidding."

Richard looked embarrassed. "I was an ass growing up. I really am sorry."

I smiled and said, "I survived, and hey, you taught me how to fight."

Richard laughed. "She actually beat up some bullies in junior high. I was proud."

Now, it was my time to blush.

The memory of that visit brought a sense of melancholy, and I wished he were in town. Yes, he was a pain as a teenager, but he grew up to be okay. I missed him and wondered how he, Debbie, and Cora were doing. Maybe we could fit in a family phone call.

Dad poked his head into the room. "It's great to have you home."

"Yeah, the house feels kind of empty. You guys are empty nesters now that Jim's at college."

"The house does feel empty. You know, I had no idea how expensive college was until he went to FSU. He's spending a lot more money than you did. Not that it's a problem."

"I had a co-op job, which helped."

"Yes, you did. I notice you're not drawing much from the account I set up. What are you living on?"

"The Zoology Department gave me a part-time teaching job, and I play guitar in a restaurant. I make enough to get by. But Dad, it's great that you set the account up. It's nice knowing it's there if I need it."

Mom came to the door, too. All I wanted to do was close my eyes for a few minutes.

"We want to hear all about Australia and what you've been up to," Mom said. "But you look tired. We'll let you get settled and rest."

"Thanks. I'm here for a week. We have time. I could use a nap."

It had been a long, long time since I'd been in my room. I lay down on the bed and felt for the hole in the box spring where it had caught fire. Yup, it was still there. The furniture was stuff I'd picked out when I first got my room. It had a bookcase headboard, and we added a second bookcase. The room was filled with my old paperbacks and felt like home.

When I woke up, I heard sounds in the kitchen. Mom was fixing dinner. I joined her and peeled the carrots. We talked about my work on the reef, my classes, teaching, and music. It felt great to talk and not have long-distance phone charges putting a shadow on how long we talked.

At dinner, the three of us talked about my class in numerical classification and collecting samples on the reef. When I talked about statistics and programmable calculators, Mom's eyes glowed. She used an old-school mechanical adding machine at work.

Dad noticed and asked, "Can we buy you the Texas Instruments calculator you are using?"

"Thanks, but the department has one for me to use. No one buys their own. They are really expensive."

"Okay, but we would like to buy you something nice that you can use."

"Dad, how would you feel about buying me a guitar? I'm playing in nice restaurants, and I could use a better instrument."

"Sure, shop for one and let me know what you need."

"How much longer do you think you'll be in Australia?" Mom asked.

"At least another year. It may be as long as two."

"What comes after that?" Dad asked.

"Find a job."

"Back here in the States?" Dad asked.

"Yes."

They both nodded approvingly. It was good they had confidence in my ability to find a job. I didn't.

The week in Miami went by fast. Jim came in from Tallahassee, and he was taller than I remembered. We talked about his studies in business. Clearly, Mom and Dad were more comfortable with his choice of major than they were with my choice of zoology. And I could understand their feelings. He had a girlfriend, and they were serious. I shared that I was also seeing someone who rode a big motorcycle.

"Don't tell Mom and Dad," he said.

"About what?"

"The motorcycle," he said, and we both laughed.

Jim had grown up a lot in the last eighteen months, and I enjoyed getting to know my grown-up younger brother. He said he was thinking about law school when he graduated.

"You know," he said. "When you went to college, the house felt empty. I really missed you."

"Sorry," I said.

It hadn't occurred to me that when I left, he'd feel a void. I should have been a better sister. I should have come home more often, or at least called and talked with him.

I took Dad up on his offer of a guitar. The shop had a beautiful Martin 00028 with a scratch along the back. They would have sent it back to the factory for refinishing, but the Martin workers were on strike at the time. Because of the scratch, the shop owner sold it for $475, a great price. It was a beautiful instrument. I felt wholly inadequate to own it, but I was determined to improve my skills.

I'd arranged two weeks off at the university. With travel time, I had ten days in Miami, and they disappeared quickly. It was hard to say goodbye and get back on the plane. It hadn't felt like I'd been gone from home a long time, but a lot had changed. Jim was in college. Bob was married!

I hadn't spent much time with my parents lately, and I was sensitive to the changes. Mom was dyeing her hair a dark blond to hide the gray. Dad, who had always been heavy, was bigger than I'd ever seen him. They were both getting older. I wasn't a kid anymore either, and I wondered what they thought of the changes in me. I needed to go home more often.

# Chapter 48 ~ Mate

When I arrived in Brisbane, I was socially inexperienced, a classic late bloomer, a former tomboy who had missed the memo that I was supposed to be interested in boys and dating. Well, I "went steady" with Allen in junior high, but we hadn't even kissed. Gordon at Seacamp was my first serious interest in the opposite sex. But I was seventeen and he was twenty-seven, and aside from fear of legal issues, Seacamp had little privacy.

Then there was Jerry in Washington, DC. He was an enlisted man and a great guitar player. And he introduced me to the delights of sex. In Australia, I took up with another guitar player, Mick Bourne, who also happened to be married. That was it. Considering that I was now twenty-six years old, I was woefully inexperienced when I first met Ken.

Ken and I met on Heron Island. He had long hair and a quick smile and (of course) a great Australian accent. The first time I saw him was in the research station kitchen. He had long hair, a bushy beard, and was thin as a rail, and his right hand was heavily bandaged.

"What did you do?" I asked.

He smiled and shook his head. "I was making tea and let the pot boil dry. When I added water, the steam hit me." He held his hand up. "Third degree burns."

"Oh wow." I couldn't think of anything else to say.

"Yeah. Hurts like hell. I'm smoking a lot of weed."

I looked closer at his eyes and saw he was indeed quite stoned. I laughed.

"Are you a graduate student?" I asked.

"Naw, I'm still an undergraduate. I come here when a researcher needs another pair of hands. But right now, I'm not much use to anyone, and I'm stuck here another week."

"Know any invertebrate taxonomy?" I asked.

"Sure, what do you need?"

"My project is on invertebrate associates of the soft coral, *Tubipora musica*. Each piece is like an entire zoo on invertebrates. I could use help with identification."

"Sure, I can help," he said.

Ken was good to his word and showed up in the lab the next day. Even if a lot of what he said wasn't quite right, he said it convincingly. I had to remind myself that he was stoned. Even so, I found him charming and enjoyed spending time with him in the lab. And he was cute.

He asked about life in the United States, and I talked about Washington, DC. He talked about growing up in Brisbane and how it differed from life in the United States. Ken favored rock music but was intrigued by my description of the Barley Mow Folk Club and seemed overly impressed that I was confident enough to play and sing in public.

Ken left Heron later that week. I stayed on another ten days. The lab felt a bit empty, and I wondered if I would run into him back on campus. I hoped so.

So, when I did see Ken weeks later at the library cafeteria, I asked him out to the Barley Mow Folk Club. I'd been seeing someone else, and we had broken up. But Mick wasn't getting the message that we were done. I asked Ken if he would show up as my date to help strengthen the message.

Ken did a fine job of playing up that we were "together." Mick got the message, and really, Ken and I did have a good time. He was living in a student house, Sherwood, and I was living in a student house in Yeronga. The two suburbs were quite close together. Ken was finishing his program in zoology. My office was in the Zoology Department, so we crossed paths a lot. Soon, we were arranging to meet for meals, movies, music, and outings to the rainforest.

Ken was smart and fun. I enjoyed riding pillion on his motorcycle, especially the scenic trips to Mt. Coot-tha, where we could look down and see most of the city skyline, or even better, the thrilling hour-long ride to Mt. Glorious, followed by a rainforest walk and Devonshire tea.

About six months after we started keeping company, both of us were unhappy with our current living conditions, and an opportunity for a shared house close to the university. It was a two-story house with five bedrooms, a spacious living room, and an old-fashioned kitchen, complete with a terrifying gas stove.

The two large front bedrooms each opened onto a huge veranda via French doors. Though we shared with another couple, the high rent meant we tried to find a fifth roommate, but we struggled to keep a stable fifth housemate. It didn't help that the landlord dropped by weekly for rent and never asked for the same amount. He was shady enough that he only accepted cash.

Ken and I each had our own bedroom, but living together in the same house marked a significant step in our relationship.

# Chapter 49 ~ Diver Down

I'd been on Heron for ten days and was looking forward to catching Tuesday's ferry and heading back to Brisbane. Fate had other ideas. We were in the kitchen making dinner when John rushed in with the news.

"We're missing a diver. Mandy didn't come up."

The room went silent. John had tangled, wild hair, and his face still showed marks from his face mask.

"How long has she been down?" Sue asked.

"It's been close to an hour."

I didn't know Mandy well, but I knew her dive partner, Rick. I assumed they had been diving together.

I asked, "Was Rick with her? Is he okay?"

"He's with the resort doctor," John said.

"Was he with her on the dive?" I asked.

"Yeah. Rick went down looking when Mandy didn't come up and ran his tank dry."

I couldn't imagine ending a dive and having my partner not surface. We left the plates on the table and turned the burners and oven off. Dinner would wait. We all raced to the harbor.

The doctor sat with Rick on the pier. A blanket was thrown over the diver's shoulders. Rick sounded awful. His sobs filled the air, and he was shaking. In the distance, even in the dim light, I could make out a dive boat returning from the Bommie.

"Should we get our equipment?" I asked.

"There isn't enough light," the dive master said.

I looked at the sky. It was after sunset. It would be getting dark on the reef.

"How long has Mandy been missing?" Sue asked.

"Two hours," Jerry said.

"We could use lights," Sue said.

Jerry shook his head. "The light levels are too low. She has to be on the surface. The Coast Guard is on the way. They'll take over for now."

What he hadn't said, but meant, was that if she wasn't on the surface, she was dead.

They flew Rick to the hospital in Gladstone. The doctor gave him a heavy dose of sedation and wanted him off the island.

I joined the certified divers the next morning for a meeting. They wanted all of us to work in teams and search the reef slope. I was certified, and although I didn't need to dive for my project, I had been quick to volunteer when any of the researchers needed a spare pair of hands. Now, it looked like I'd be joining the search for Mandy.

But the dive master looked at my equipment and said, "Hell no."

My equipment was old and simple: a single regulator, no pressure gauge, and a tank with a J-valve for safety.

He handed me a modern dive setup, gave a quick explanation, and sent me to the boat. We anchored off the reef crest. We spread out, three meters apart, and traveled in a line, working our way around the island.

I started diving at fourteen and fell in love with it. But this was awful. I could never master the buoyancy compensator and constantly struggled, pushing off the bottom and scraping against sand, rock, and coral. I finally got the hang of it by the end of the second day, though I still missed the simplicity of my old setup.

We searched for three days and came up empty. When they went through Mandy's belongings, they found asthma medication. Everyone assumed she had suffered an asthma attack and drowned.

But I wasn't convinced. Asthma was an easy answer, but it could have been anything. During the search, I had a flashback to an incident at Seacamp when I was seventeen. One afternoon on a dive at the base of a coral head, I brushed my hand against a long-spined black sea urchin. I woke up back on the boat. Evidently, the sea urchins have a neurotoxin in their spines, and I blacked out.

*If my partner hadn't seen me, I could well have drowned. Most teenagers are convinced they are invincible. I wasn't a teenager anymore, and I had a serious case of the willies. Did something like that happen to Mandy?*

Since I missed Tuesday's ferry, I was stuck on the island until the following Tuesday. For three days, I sifted through my samples and worked on taxonomy. Everyone wanted to get back to their normal routines, including doing fieldwork. I declined two requests to help out as a diver. While I sympathized with their need for backup, I felt it was too soon. I wanted to stick to the shallows for a while. The questions about my equipment and my difficulty with the modern gear added to my anxiety. I wasn't sure I even wanted to continue diving.

And, for the first time since coming to Australia, I felt like I needed a break from the reef.

I'd been on the island longer than usual. We searched for five days. I really wanted to get off the island and back to Brisbane.

Tuesday morning came, and I was the first passenger on the boat. As the sunrise drifted over the horizon, the morning light was just enough for me to make out a large shovel-nose ray swimming in the harbor, silhouetted against the sand. As the island disappeared into the distance, I felt lighter, like a weight had been removed.

The island disappeared into the distance, and four hours later, the boat pulled into Gladstone harbor. Unfortunately, I had an entire afternoon to kill before my train would leave at seven-thirty, and Gladstone had little to offer.

*How to kill five hours?*

I hadn't been sleeping and had a case of agitation that made me want to punch holes in something. Instead, I went into a hair salon for a cut and a perm. They said it would take about three and a half hours—perfect. It was wild and stupid, and I thought it would help me feel better.

For future reference, Gladstone isn't the best place to get your first perm. That might not have been the best move I could have made. When I left the salon, my hair was a frizzy mess.

By the time I got on the train, I fell onto the seat in exhaustion. The trip was a red-eye, but the seats had little padding and no sound insulation. I dozed off a few times, but by the time I reached Brisbane, I was not in the least bit rested. What I wanted was to get home and go to bed. So, I wasn't pleased when the train pulled in, and Ken wasn't there to pick me up. He lost track of time and missed the fact that I would be home today.

I took a cab home. It wasn't a great homecoming. When I walked into our house, he actually didn't recognize me. Well, aside from the weird hair perm, I'd been out in the sun and was darker than I'd been when I left for Heron. A lot darker. Or, he might have been stoned.

When he figured out I wasn't breaking in—I lived there and was actually his girlfriend—he apologized. He tried to tell me the haircut was kind of cool. He had just been caught by surprise and said that I shouldn't cry. I hadn't even realized I was crying until he said that.

Ken knew Rick, and we talked about the accident and the search diving. The next morning, I was doing better, but it felt weird to be back in our student shared house. It took about a week for me to get used to the wild hair and not freak out when I looked in the mirror.

And I was wondering when I'd feel all right about diving again. I still had a bad case of the willies. *What if I didn't get over it?*

# Chapter 50 ~ Making Plans

Being back at the Zoology Department made Heron Island and the diving incident feel a world away. I had meetings with Dr. Hailstone to go over my data and progress, and we talked about the diving incident. The whole Zoology Department was pretty shaken. I hadn't known Mandy well. So for me, it was more the realization that ocean work and diving could be dangerous. People could die. People had died.

I mentioned I was going to take a break from scuba diving. Dr. Hailstone said it wouldn't be an issue, as my project was focused entirely on the shallow reef flat. He offered to talk to the other graduate students and ask them to back off. Graduate researchers always helped each other out, lending a hand and extra eyes on work dives. I hated to say no, but I wasn't ready to dive again.

Ken was sympathetic. He didn't dive and was not comfortable in deep water. I was empathetic. His grandmother had died from drowning during an epileptic seizure.

But Ken wasn't planning to work in marine biology, and I still dreamed that I might. The diving incident didn't change that. *What if I couldn't go back to diving? Could I still work in marine science?* There had been another researcher who had thrown in the towel after a boating accident. That wasn't me. I would continue my research. Maybe I would go back to diving, but not now, and probably not while still in Australia.

Full-time researchers at NOAA had to retrieve fish traps in deep water. They used scuba and earned hazard pay because of the Bull sharks. Had a shark taken Mandy? No one knew.

My project was going well. Traveling to Heron every second month and spending a week collecting samples gave me ample opportunity to run a transect line from the beach to the reef crest, collect samples of my soft coral Tubipora at set distances, and take them back to the station lab. Each small boulder held fifty to one hundred invertebrates. After sorting and storing my samples in alcohol, I brought them back to Brisbane.

The work was satisfying. It gave me an excuse to spend time on the reef flat, and I found the lab work and taxonomic identification of the samples back in Brisbane enjoyable. The goal was to determine if the invertebrates were true commensals or opportunistic generalists, and whether the soft coral was impacting diversity on the reef flat. The range of invertebrates was so large, it felt like I was working my way through a complete invertebrate textbook with most samples.

My teaching duties at the university were enjoyable and, along with my guitar gig, generated enough income to cover rent and buy food. I felt at home in Brisbane, no longer getting lost when I ventured off campus. And the serious relationship with Ken gave me a warm glow of acceptance and love.

I'd come a long way since my chaotic qualifying year. Life was good.

Ken and I loved the old Queenslander house we shared, but when the other couple moved to their own place, we decided to find a smaller unit we could afford on our own. Ken asked me to find a flat (apartment) since he was completing his thesis, an overwhelming process. I found a cozy two-bedroom duplex near the university. It was perfect! The kitchen window overlooked a plum tree, and a kookaburra often serenaded me as I made coffee.

We lived like typical impoverished students, buying groceries from a co-op and occasionally splurging for a cheap meal out. Our favorite place was called Hungry Years. It was a casual cafe with bar-height tables, fake plants, and canned music that appealed to college-age clientele. They had a five-dollar Wednesday spanakopita special. The serving was large enough to feed both of us, so we went almost every week. The conversation often included thoughts about what we wanted in our futures.

It was on one of these date nights that Ken asked me, "Do you want kids?"

It was a question I hadn't really given much thought to. *Did I want kids?*

When I was a kid, lots of girls played with dolls, but I didn't. Was I missing that drive? *Some maternal gene?*

"Do you want kids?" Ken repeated.

"Honestly, I haven't thought about it. But someday, I'll want my own family, so I guess, yeah, I'll want to have kids."

Ken looked relieved. I wondered how long he'd been wanting to ask that question.

"Me too, someday in the future," Ken said.

"We both have a lot to do before we consider having kids."

"I know, but it's important to know we both want kids," he said. "We're talking about staying together. We should work out what that means for both of us. To me, being on the same page about kids is important."

"We're on the same page," I said.

He pulled out a silver ring and gave it to me.

I took it and smiled, thinking how sweet he was being. "A promise ring?" I asked.

"I guess so, a promise that we'll stay together. I guess I'm formally asking if you'll marry me. If you will consider making a life and having a family with me."

We had talked about the issues of me being American and Ken being Australian. We knew that for very practical reasons, we should get married. Tonight, this was different. Did I want to make a life with Ken?

Ken was as close to perfect as anyone I could hope to meet. We hadn't been together all that long, but he was the smartest man I'd ever met. He was kind and loving and a genuinely good person. *But was I ready to get married?*

"Yes," I said and immediately began to worry about the commitment, but I didn't take it back.

We finished our meal, each feeling a little awkward.

And for now, we found time for fun. Ken would stop by my cafe when I was playing. I'd picked up a scooter and had Ken give me lessons on riding. He liked the scooter too and got a kick out of dressing in his motorcycle protective gear and hopping on for a ride. His long hair and black leather motorcycle gave him an alarming look, and the staff at the cafe worried about my choice in companions.

I thought the "bad boy" look was part of his charm.

I knew that we were moving faster than we would have because I would be ending my master's work and would need to leave the country. Ken wanted to study in North America, but would have difficulty with tuition and a student visa. If we wanted to stay together, getting married seemed the logical thing to do.

I felt better because of our dinner conversation and Ken's proposal. I did love Ken, and we wanted to spend our lives together. There were millions of people who got married with less of a foundation. We would be fine.

# Chapter 51 ~ Dad

I normally called home on Sundays, at a time that worked with the sixteen-hour time difference. So when one of the graduate students opened my office door to say I had a phone call, I was confused. I hadn't given the department phone number out to anyone.

The phone was in the hallway. "Hello," I said.

"This is Mom. Your father is in the hospital; he's had a stroke."

I glanced at my watch and did a quick mental calculation. It was six o'clock in the morning in Miami.

I felt an ache form in the pit of my stomach. Dad was obese and in terrible health. Jim and I talked about "a heart attack waiting to happen." Still, the news hit me hard.

"How bad was it?"

"He's in the hospital, and he's stable," Mom choked out. "He's paralyzed on the right side and isn't talking. The doctors are hoping for some recovery. But, they don't know how much."

"Mom, I think I should come home."

"Jim is on his way in from Tallahassee. I called him last night," Mom said. "Australia is so far away that I'll understand if you can't come in. I can keep you up to date over the phone."

That wasn't going to happen. Mom wouldn't say it, but she needed me home.

"Let me see if I can get a flight," I said. "I'll call you back soon."

"Okay, sweetie. I love you."

"I love you too, Mom." I hung up and went to Dr. Hailstone's office. He was in and listened as I explained the situation.

"We can find coverage for the labs you teach," he said. "Let me know as soon as you have travel plans arranged."

"Thanks."

Half an hour later, I was explaining the situation to Ken. He called Qantas for me and asked about special compassion rates for air travel, when the Qantas agent asked if it would be a round-trip or one-way ticket.

"I don't know exactly when I'll be coming back," I said.

"Since you aren't sure of your return date, it's best to book a one-way ticket; it's slightly more expensive, but you won't have a change fee."

I pulled money from my emergency bank account to pay for the ticket. I'd be leaving in just over twenty-four hours. When I got home, I called Mom and let her know my travel plans, so she could have someone pick me up at the airport.

***

Once I had the trip booked and had a second conversation with Mom, I felt a bit better. Dad was in the hospital, but he was out of immediate danger. *Did I have to go?* Maybe not, it was a long trip, and I couldn't do much for Dad. But I wanted to be there for Mom.

Ken drove me to the airport.

"I guess this is goodbye for a while," he said.

It felt like we'd been saying goodbye too often. I'd only been back from Heron for a few weeks.

"Goodbye for a while," I said. "I'll call from Miami."

"Let me know when you have an idea on how long you will be gone."

I nodded, reached over, and gave him a bear hug and kiss. Then I watched as he drove our tiny, two-seater Honda away.

The trip seemed surreal. Well, I don't think anyone is in the best shape after a sixteen-hour flight. I stayed up watching movies. By the time I was in Los Angeles to go through customs and change planes, I was exhausted.

The customs agent looked at my overnight bag and asked, "How long are you staying in the United States?"

"As long as I like, I'm an American."

He stamped my passport, and I was now back in the USA. Two more hours in the airport, another six-hour flight, and I'd be in Miami.

I settled into my seat and thought about Dad, about how I used to sit on his shoulders at Jones Beach when he would jump up to keep me "safe" from the waves. I thought about trips to pick up bagels and smoked fish for family brunches, and how he'd let me pick out a paperback. Most of the time, Dad left dealing with the children to Mom, but he was always there for me. I wanted to see him and was glad I was on my way home.

As the plane taxied to the gate and came to a halt, I stood and retrieved my bag. I wondered if I should have packed more and checked a bag. It had been a last-minute decision not to. I wanted the travel to be simple. Mom would have clothes I could borrow.

Mom was waving at me from the gate. She looked tired, and her eyes looked sad. I walked across to where she stood and hugged her. She gave a soft sob and hugged me back.

"I'm glad you came," she said.

"You look tired. How's Dad doing?" I asked as we walked through the terminal toward ground transport.

"He's still in the hospital. We can see him tomorrow."

"Can you tell me what happened?" I asked.

"You know your father has heart issues. Well, a bit over a week ago, he went into the hospital for a heart procedure meant to clear a partial blockage. They kept him for observation for three days."

She stopped as she opened the trunk, and I put my bag in.

"We thought he was fine. They checked him over and released him on Monday. He was on blood thinners because the procedure increases the risk of stroke. Tuesday, he took a nap in the afternoon. I checked on him after about a couple of hours and couldn't get him to wake up. So I called 911 for an ambulance."

I nodded, trying to think of something I could say.

"It was a massive stroke, and I don't know how long he had been in bed when it happened. I should have been checking on him more often."

"Mom, you didn't know."

We went to the hospital the next day. His room was drab and smelled of disinfectant. Half a dozen flower arrangements crowded the counter next to the window. They didn't make the room cheery, but they added color and reminded me that Dad had people who cared about him.

Dad was lying flat in bed. He waved and tried to sit up. Mom used the control and raised the back of the hospital bed. She adjusted the pillows and helped him to an upright position. He smiled and gave me a thumbs-up with his left hand. A nurse came in and thanked Mom, saying they were short-staffed on weekends.

"Whenever you come in, help Bernie sit up. Too much time on his back, lying flat, can lead to lung problems," she said.

Mom and I agreed that we would have someone with Dad on weekends since the hospital was understaffed.

I stayed for five weeks and mostly didn't think about Australia. It was hard to see Dad lying almost motionless in a hospital bed. I went every day, looking to see signs of the man I knew from childhood, the larger-than-life figure who threw an open house every New Year's Day for his birthday. The big TV would be showing a football game, and the place would be filled with cheers, laughter, and good times. That was Dad in his element. This was a shadow of who he had been, and I worried about what his future would be. I worried even more about Mom.

The nurse had been right about under-staffing only; it wasn't just on weekends. They would bring a tray of food at mealtime, but Dad couldn't eat on his own. It could be hours before a nurse came in to cut food up and feed him.

The hospital sent a physiotherapist to work with Dad on sitting up, standing, speaking, and using his left hand. But no one came to work with him on weekends. If we weren't there, he spent the whole day lying flat, so we made sure that didn't happen.

I was spending almost every day at the hospital, and one time, the occupational therapist came in to work on "life-skills." I watched while she tried to teach Dad to write cursive with his left hand. She wanted him to sign his name.

I said, "You know, he didn't write cursive with his right hand. I don't think he knows how."

"You spoil all my fun," Dad said in a halting mumble.

Two weeks later, they released Dad from the hospital. Mom had returned to working as an office manager at Monday Classics, a garment company similar to Dad's. They hired Mom when Dad's business downsized in the recession. They were thrilled to get an office manager with over fifteen years of experience in the garment industry. While they were giving her flexibility, Mom needed to work, not just for money. She needed a place to be herself. While I was home, we interviewed and hired a retiree who would come to the house and help Dad while Mom was at work.

We found a rhythm. Dad had physical therapy twice a week, and it was obvious his recovery would be slow. It seemed unlikely he'd fully regain use of his right side or his speech fluency. The damage was simply too great.

Mom was certain that if she had discovered the stroke sooner, Dad would have had less brain damage. I told her we didn't know how long Dad was without care, and that we had to deal with reality. I pointed out that she thought he was having a nap. She could have easily left him longer.

Five weeks was more time at "home" than I had spent in years. Jim had long since returned to Tallahassee. As an undergraduate, he couldn't miss very many classes.

We talked about Mom and Dad, about the downsizing of the company, and Mom taking a job with Monday Classics.

I said, "I'm so used to talking about Mom and Dad together—at work, at home, out to dinner. I'm just used to them being together as a pair."

"I know."

"Do you think he'll get better?"

"Mom thinks so," Jim said.

"Mom hopes so," I said.

We sat quietly at the breakfast room table, sipping coffee, each lost in thought about how much had changed since we'd both lived in that house. Our lives were different now, yet we'd somehow expected things to remain unchanged, here, with Mom and Dad. What came next would be very different. The business was small, but still operational. Would Dad continue to be a partner? How much recovery could Dad expect from therapy? None of us had answers. The future was one big question mark.

I took a gulp of coffee. "I'm glad Mom has a job. She'd go crazy if she stayed home taking care of Dad every day."

"When are you going home?" Jim asked.

"I'll be here another week."

"Are you still seeing the motorcycle guy?" he asked.

"I am."

He smiled. "Going to tell Mom?" he asked.

"Not now," I said. "She doesn't need anything complicated right now."

Jim didn't say anything, but nodded.

As soon as Jim left, Mom started fussing, saying it was time for me to go back and complete my program.

What she said was true, but it didn't help me. I felt guilty that I'd been gone for so long. Not only while I was in Australia. I moved out at seventeen. I rarely came home or spent much time with them. For five years, I bounced between Tampa and Washington, DC, and now three years in Australia.

Now, I regretted the time I'd kept my distance. Time I could have spent with Mom and Dad while they were both healthy. I could never get that time back. So how could I go back to Brisbane now?

I'd spent little time in the house. Both of them drank all the time, and I found it uncomfortable. Dad wasn't drinking now. He was on far too much medication for more than an occasional, small drink. But Mom still was. I couldn't change who they were.

It was unlikely that I'd accomplish anything by staying longer. Jim was right to go back to Tallahassee, and I needed to get back to my life, too. Mom pressed me for a timeline.

"I know you have your own life, and I want you to earn your degree. But I'd feel better if you were back in the States. It's just travel from Australia is so complicated. Even phone calls are hard. Can you tell me when you will be moving back?"

"It's complicated. I'm not taking classes. It's a research project. I need at least a full year of data collection. That means I need another four months for fieldwork."

"Could you be home in six months?" she asked.

"I doubt it. Mom, I don't know how long it will take for me to complete my analysis and write a thesis."

"Can you do this in a year?" Mom asked.

"I think so, but I can't promise."

"Good enough. Start making plans. We'll be fine."

I should have talked to Mom about Ken. We had been living together for almost two years, and it was absurd that I hadn't said anything about a boyfriend. And now, we were making plans to get married. So not having a conversation would be really wrong.

Sometime soon, I would need to tell my family that when I came home, I wouldn't be coming home alone. I told myself, Mom had so much on her plate, she didn't need me complicating things even more. I told myself I needed to wait, at least until Mom and Dad were in a stable routine.

But I was chicken. It would be safer to do it by phone.

.

# Chapter 52 ~ Timeline

The trip from Miami to Brisbane took twenty-seven hours, and the conditions were cramped and uncomfortable. I couldn't sleep. I'd told Mom I'd try to be back in the States in twelve months. *Could I?* I needed to talk with my faculty adviser soon. And I needed to talk with Ken about our plans.

It took a few days to recover from jet lag, but soon, I'd resumed teaching and returned to playing Friday nights at the café. I made an appointment to meet with Dr. Hailstone first thing Monday morning.

We went over my data, and I showed him what I'd written: the introduction and research methods section.

"I'm trying to establish a timeline for the project. Do you think it's reasonable to complete my project in twelve months?"

He took his time looking at my field notes and data tables. Then he read the rough draft that I'd given him.

"You need at least two more visits to Heron for sampling, and there should be a month between them," He said.

"I agree. That will give me eighteen months of sampling."

He nodded. "Then it's a matter of how focused and productive you can stay. Your analysis needs to identify which invertebrates are commensals, which are opportunists, and whether the diversity in the colonies differs from what you see in rock rubble. I would think a year should work—if you push."

"I'm motivated. My mom would like me to be in the States."

He said, "From the university perspective, I'd like to see you stay on as a teaching assistant for the January to March session, and plan on submitting before the term ends on March twenty-third."

"This is helpful. Thank you."

"Your project is worthwhile, and I'm eager to see the results. I'm sure you're folks want you to earn your degree."

"I'm going to do my best to make that happen."

"Good. Let me know if I can help."

I shared the timeline for my thesis, and Ken pointed out that once I turned in my thesis, I would have to leave Australia. We had talked about getting married, but it had been in the abstract "someday." Were we ready for that someday to be now? We had been living together for two years now, first in a student share house and now in a place of our own. How much would it change if we were married?

It wasn't a romantic discussion. We were both being practical. I couldn't stay once I turned in my thesis. Ken wanted to study in the United States or Canada, and while he could get a student visa, it would be easier if we were married when we were ready to leave Australia. We decided we would make it "legal," but we would keep it simple. After our non-romantic conversation, it hit home that I hadn't even told Mom about Ken. Yikes!

We were broke students and decided on a civil service wedding at the registry office. When we called to schedule an appointment, we discovered that you had to wait six weeks to advertise the marriage in the newspaper. That was to give notice for anyone to raise objections. We made our appointment for February sixth, a Friday afternoon. Friday was five dollars cheaper than Saturday. We also applied for a marriage license. I was going to have to call home and let Mom know.

Mom had jokingly told me I wasn't to get married before I was twenty-eight. She had married very young and felt she had missed out on parts of life. Well, I was twenty-seven now. Close enough to satisfy that silly promise.

I wasn't entirely sure I was ready to get married, but I suspected I wouldn't be the first person to get married while still having some doubts. Ken seemed confident he was ready, which might have been a difference in our personalities. Then again, keeping it simple was a logistics decision that eased a lot of our concerns. Still, I worried about what Ken would think of my family when he met them.

The first time I ate dinner with Ken's family, I realized how different his family and my family were. I walked into the kitchen, and Ken's younger brother and girlfriend were in the breakfast nook. June was at the stove.

"Can I help with anything?" I said.

"Sure, take over this," June said, pointing to a piece of meat in a fry pan.

I moved over to the stove and accepted the offer, figuring she was searing the meat. It looked to be some kind of steak, but she was boiling it. I guessed she assumed I knew what to do. *Who boils steak?*

Evidently, June boils steak, but most Australians do not. I did the best I could at the stove, and dinner was, well, not uneatable. The steak was tasteless, and the vegetables were mushy. Ken later told me his Mom was a brainiac, but one of the world's worst cooks.

Phil and Liz worked for the Department of Surveying and Land Management. They sat in a breakfast nook at the end of the kitchen, talking about a job they were on together, surveying the site for a new international airport.

"How's it going?" Ken asked. "Have the mosquitoes carried anyone off?"

Liz groaned. "No, but I have little blood left."

"You should see Liz in her stylish wading boots," Phil said.

The breakfast nook was small and best suited for feeding young children, which I was certain was its intended use, and I wondered why they used it instead of the dining table.

"I'm sure you both look stylish," June said.

June was a professor of metallurgy at the university. She sat down next to Liz, and I squeezed in next to Ken. The talk at the table was technical and of a level that I had difficulty following. June was also a bookbinder, a deacon at her church, and a volunteer with Meals on Wheels.

Ken's Father died when he was only nineteen. His dad had been a professor of physics and had met June when he was studying at Cambridge, where she was a graduate student. None of my family members had attended college. They were too busy trying to pay bills and raise a family to volunteer. I felt that anything I said would show how ignorant and provincial I was, so mostly I listened.

I thought about what the conversation would be like if it were my mom and dad at the table—it would be business, garment shows, prices, and distribution centers. Maybe they would feel as lost as I did.

We shared our timeline with June, and we planned a simple registry ceremony in February.

"Who will be at the service?" she asked.

"Helen and Graham. We want to keep it to a minimum, and we need two witnesses."

"Let me take you two out to lunch and drive you downtown," June said.

"That would be great," Ken said.

It made me feel so good that she was on board with us getting married.

We wanted to keep everything simple. I was juggling long days on my thesis, teaching two labs a week, and still playing at the café one evening a week. I called home and told Mom; she cried because she couldn't come.

My brother Jim had told her about Ken, so it wasn't entirely out of the blue. I told her we were keeping it simple, with our two best friends as witnesses at the registry office. She felt better, less like she was being excluded.

June planned two parties in the month after the wedding; one for our friends and the younger members of the family. The second party was for relatives to "meet the bride."

We really were both busy and didn't take time to make a lot of plans for the day. On Friday, February sixth, Ken was walking up the stairs in the Zoology Department to pick me up for lunch and to go to the registry office.

Professor Greenwood noticed the tie and said, "You're looking sharp. You getting married or something?"

"As a matter of fact," Ken said, "I am."

We hadn't told anyone in the department.

When I came back to the office, the department had bouquets waiting for us. I was so overwhelmed, I cried.

\* \* \*

Helen wore a pale blue dress. Graham wore a suit. I had on blue corduroy jeans and a borrowed Hawaiian shirt.

"You still have time to run," Graham whispered to Ken, just loud enough for me to hear.

Helen carried flowers and hugged me.

I hadn't given much thought to what the registry ceremony would be like. But it was lovely. We had the room to ourselves—Ken, me, Helen, Graham, and the official. He took his time, talking to us about the importance of marriage as a part of civilization, about our duties to each other, and the covenant we were undertaking. It was a sweet and touching ceremony.

Graham and Helen drove us back to our duplex, and we all had tea and cake. We said goodbye and headed to Stradbroke Island, where we planned a mini-honeymoon. Ken had to be back at work on Tuesday morning, so we had two days to ourselves.

The island was as beautiful as I remembered. Ken was taken aback when a young surfer called him "sir." The only "fly" in my ointment was the lack of screens on our guest cottage, and that several hundred unintended guest insects (flies in the day, mosquitoes at night) kept us company.

Looking down from the headlands at the clean sand and the crystal blue waters took my breath away. But when I stood on the sand looking out to the ocean, the waves were alarmingly large.

I wasn't sure I wanted to go in at all. As I stood watching, a young boy took a surfboard and dashed into the water. He looked like he was an eight-year-old. He paddled like a professional and caught a wave like he'd been surfing all his life. Well, he had probably *been* surfing all his life.

Ken said the waves were perfect.

"Come on, let's go body surfing," he said.

When I didn't respond, he added, "Have you gone body surfing?"

"When I was a kid in Florida, but not with waves this size."

"You'll be fine. I've seen you in the water. You're like a fish."

Ken was telling the truth. I was a strong swimmer and had always felt comfortable in the water. I nodded and followed Ken into the wild blue water.

The wave lifted me higher and higher until it felt like I was on top of a tall building. The beach looked insanely far away, and I wondered how much water was below me and what was swimming in it. The wave passed, and I felt myself slowly drift downward. My relief was short-lived; another wave arrived in a matter of seconds.

"When I say go, swim as fast as you can."

"I know."

"Remember, when you feel the wave push, hold still. Keep yourself in a dive."

At first, it was fine, exciting, and exhilarating. Then the wave tumbled me over. I landed face down on the sand. One wave was enough. Ken apologized and accepted my desire to enjoy the beach but stay dry. We went out to dinner at a local café.

It was a wonderful weekend. It made my mind spin to think that when we left the university to go to the registry office, we were two individuals who were living together, and now we were a married couple. We would be facing the world together. It was a strange thought, but a nice one.

# Chapter 53 ~ America

I held the letter for Ken to see. "They want me out of the country by June," I said.

"What?"

"I guess immigration was informed when I submitted my thesis."

"I guess we need to let them know we're married and see what paperwork we need to fill out," Ken said.

It wasn't unexpected. We knew that once I submitted my thesis, I'd have a limited amount of time before immigration would pull my student visa. Although we had already made plans, the letter still came as a shock. After all, the thesis was submitted, not accepted. It was likely I'd need to make revisions. I guess they figured I could do that from the United States.

It was nice to focus on the wedding, the party, and the short but romantic "honeymoon." Now came the mundane, practical details we needed to take care of. We filed for a spousal visa and residency. When they found out we were heading to the United States in May, they filed an extension of my student visa instead, saying the spousal visa would be void if I left the country. It was all complicated, and honestly, I wanted to go home and be there for Mom and Dad. It was time to leave Australia.

We packed a steamer trunk with our heavier items and shipped it ahead to travel by sea. Since shipping was costly, we had to be selective in our choices. Music was important, so all our vinyl records made the journey. We sold the apartment's contents for two hundred dollars, which was more than we'd paid for the furniture, television, and refrigerator.

Well, our bed had been a piece of foam on the floor. Even so, it felt strange to walk away from everything that wouldn't fit in our trunk or the suitcases we could take on the plane. Ken sold his beloved Laverda 1000 motorcycle. I sold my car. The two sales brought in enough money for our plane tickets. Our cat, Billy, would travel to the new country in a cat carrier.

Back in April, Ken took the Graduate Record Exam and applied to doctoral programs at the University of Florida and in Newfoundland, Canada. I was pushing for Florida, but was open to Canada. We would have the summer to work out where we were going. In the meantime, we would stay with my parents.

Ken gave notice at work, and we spent the month visiting with people and places that we might never see again. Brisbane had become dear to me, and for Ken, he was leaving his birth city. We walked through the rainforest of Mt. Glorious, wondering when and if we would be back. I felt tears form at the Point Lookout headlands. Even walking down the stairs to our duplex, looking at the ferns and iridescent spiders filled me with a sense of loss. I thought of the cockatoo that often sat in the tree outside my kitchen window. Brisbane had become a special place.

"Don't be silly," Ken said. "We'll be back."

"I hope you're right."

Ken was beyond eager. He had traveled with his family on his dad's year-long sabbatical, first to England, and then to Seattle. His memories were remarkably clear for someone who had traveled at the age of nine. Now he would experience North America as an adult. The excitement carried him easily over the sadness of leaving.

I was more conflicted. I knew the pain of leaving places I loved and missing them. I lacked Ken's innate belief that we would be back. Oh, I figured we would visit, but I doubted I'd live in Brisbane again.

So now I would miss Washington, DC, and Brisbane. For the first time, I hungered to live somewhere with no intention of moving on.

June drove us to the airport, and we said a tearful goodbye. The flight took us to Sydney, where we spent a night with Ken's relatives, who were faculty at the University of New South Wales.

The next day, he dropped us off at the airport. Between us, we had two suitcases and a large pet carrier. When we tried to check in, they questioned us about the carrier, saying it was the wrong size. We had followed the airline instructions exactly, and now, they were turning us away.

Ken said, "This is the carrier the airline told us to get. What do you want us to do?"

"Take him away."

Ken was pissed. "No. We're getting on a plane. If you won't let him on the plane, he's your problem."

They let us on the plane with the carrier.

We flew from Sydney to Los Angeles via Fiji. The stop in Fiji was in the pre-dawn morning. They had to refuel, and we waited on the airplane tarmac, watching the sunrise. The sunrise over the mountains was beautiful, and I thought it might be nice to visit Fiji sometime.

Our next stop was Los Angeles, where Richard was supposed to meet us. We got off the plane and waited, but Richard was nowhere to be seen. It turned out he'd gone to the wrong airport! He finally arrived, and we went to the house Debbie's father had helped them build. Richard and Debbie had married when they were just teenagers, and they had been through tough times. Debbie took Cora and left Richard, returning to California. Richard followed her back to the mainland, and they tried to rebuild their family. They now had a second child, their son Avery.

Richard was selling cars for a living. He seemed to be a good salesman, which didn't surprise me. He'd won a lot of awards.

"Have you been to Bondi Beach?" Richard asked Ken.

"Sure. It's in New South Wales; it's beautiful."

"The surf's great in Australia. One day, I'll get there."

Richard had to work the next day, so Debbie suggested the zoo. We had a fine day with Cora and Avery. Cora was five now and had a real personality. Avery was a toddler, but fun to have with us. It was nice to have a break in air travel. We wouldn't be nearly as exhausted and jet-lagged as I had been the last time I arrived in Miami.

Three days after leaving Brisbane, we arrived at Miami International Airport. Mom picked us up. Ken was worried about meeting Mom. He was concerned that his "bad boy" look wouldn't go well. Mom didn't hesitate. She hugged me first, then turned to Ken and gave him a welcoming hug, treating him like royalty. There was no hesitation, no glances at his shoulder-length hair or bushy beard. Mom was great.

"You both must be exhausted. Let's get your bags into the car and get you home!"

"Thanks, Mom."

Ken was holding the pet carrier with our cat, Billy. I was glad Billy had settled down. When he came off the cart, he was yowling piteously.

Mom peered into the case. "What's his name?"

"Billy," I said, giving Mom another hug. "It's great to be back in the States. Thanks for getting us."

"Like I wouldn't. I'm so glad you're home. "

"How's Dad?"

"He's better than when you visited, but he's still not himself."

"Can he walk?"

"With a walker, for short distances. We use a wheelchair if he needs to go far."

Mom had a job and had hired a caregiver to help in the house. John was an older gentleman. He came in the morning, about half an hour after Mom left for work, and stayed until five-thirty in the afternoon. Mom got home shortly after that.

The last time I saw Dad was in the hospital. The stroke had left him paralyzed, unable to get out of bed, and with very limited speech. So if Dad could use a walker, this was progress. We walked in the side door and crossed the breakfast room and kitchen. Dad was sitting on the living room couch. He turned his head when her heard the door, and I saw a big smile on his face. My heart ached when I saw the distortion on the right-hand side of his mouth. The paralysis was quite evident.

"Hi, Dad," I said and sat next to him.

"Hi, pumpkin."

He put his hand on my knee and looked directly at Ken, saying nothing.

"Dad, I want you to meet Ken. I know you've heard a lot about him. We were married in February."

Ken came over and took Dad's hand. He said, "Nice to meet you."

Dad's smile was wide. "Glad you're here," he said.

Dad paused, with a pensive look. I could tell he was working to find the right words.

He took my hand again. "We're going to have a big party."

"That will be fun," I said. "We're going to put our stuff away. We'll be out in a little bit."

I nodded to Ken and led him down the hall toward my bedroom.

The house was just as I remembered it. I took Ken to my old bedroom. Mom had replaced my twin bed with a sleeper sofa, but otherwise, the bedroom was just as it had been when I was in high school.

It was Memorial Day weekend. The next day, Mom announced she wanted us to take advantage of the Memorial Day sales and pick out a car. We were still jet-lagged, and the idea of taking a large sum of money and buying a car was intimidating.

They were adamant, so we went car shopping—for an actual new car.

We bought a bare-bones Honda Civic, with no electric windows and no air-conditioning. We needed a car. And I loved that they wanted to buy one for us, but I didn't want to take what we didn't need. We would later regret the lack of air-conditioning.

We sat at the breakfast room table, each of us nursing a cup of coffee. Dad sat in his wheelchair.

"Okay, I'm planning the meet-the-husband party. I need to let people know the date," Mom said.

Ken and I looked at each other.

"Okay, when did you want to have it?" I asked.

"I need your travel plans." She looked directly at Ken.

"I'm going to Newfoundland to talk with the Parasitology faculty. Ann said she doesn't want to go with me until I decide I'm serious about their program."

Mom nodded.

"We're both going to Gainesville so Ken can talk to the Parasitology faculty at UF."

Mom said, "UF is closer. That's good. When is it safe for me to schedule a party?"

"Mom, why don't you give us the month of June? That way, Ken will have decided on a program, and we'll be able to share the news at the party."

Mom smiled. "We can work with that. A July party!"

"Can we not go crazy with this?" I asked.

Mom said, "June told me she hosted a meet-the-wife party; this will be the same sort of thing."

Ken said, "My mom baked a cake and invited our relatives over to her house."

Mom said, "We're Jewish, so there has to be lots of food. But we will have a cake too."

I rolled my eyes. "Mom, it sounds good, but here in the house, right?"

"Right," she agreed.

Later that week, Ken went to Newfoundland and immediately realized the program wouldn't work for us. They required him to have thirty thousand dollars to prove he could support himself, and neither of us would have work visas.

Gainesville was far more viable. Since I had been a student at the University of South Florida and went to Brisbane on a student visa, I retained my Florida Residency. We were married, so Ken would pay in-state tuition. And, of course, as a United States Citizen, I could get a job immediately. So, we were Gainesville-bound!

While Gainesville was over three hundred miles from North Miami Beach, it was a lot closer than Brisbane. We were in the same time zone and only a six-hour drive away. Mom and Dad were thrilled that we would be close.

Mom invited the high school and college friends I knew were in town and our local relatives. We were a big family, and it was a festive affair. A Jewish deli called Corky's catered the party. We even had a guitarist playing music.

Ken mixed with my friends and seemed to have a good time. I was happy to be among friends and family. I hadn't seen some of them in years. Grandma Ester and Grandpa Harry were all dressed up. They were "old school." Weddings were formal. It was great to see them and to have Ken meet them.

Before we cut the cake, Mom offered a toast. "Here's to the bride and groom, who saved us a fortune by having a registry wedding in Australia."

People chuckled, but Mom was serious. She explained later that buying a car and putting a down payment on a house would still cost less than what many of Dad's partners spent on their children's weddings. It wasn't the reason for our small, private wedding, but

I wouldn't deny that the unexpected financial perk was a welcome surprise.

A week later, we drove to Gainesville. The town felt comfortably familiar. I knew the campus inside and out from all those college weekends visiting Bob and Phylece. We settled into a motel for five days, hoping to find a short-term rental by the end of the week. Billy wasn't thrilled about being stuck in a small room, and I felt off-kilter as well. It was a strange feeling, being unmoored and without a home. I hoped it wouldn't last long.

# Chapter 54 ~ New Life, New Plans

While Ken met with advisers, I visited the university employment office and filled out an application. I listed my cooperative work positions at NOAA and NIH. I hoped that in this university town, I'd be able to find a lab job similar to ones I'd held before. To my relief, research laboratories contacted me for interviews almost immediately.

We signed a contract for a one-month stay in a short-term apartment on Tuesday. On Wednesday, I had my first interview, and Ken met with an adviser to work out the details of his studies. When he returned from the meeting, he wasn't happy.

"They want me to take a year of Chemistry and Physics," he said.

"Didn't you have them in your bachelor's program?"

"No, in Australia, they expect you to take stuff like that in high school; they don't make you do it again."

I felt for Ken. Really, I did. However, I had doubts that even in Australia, high school Chemistry and Physics were equivalent to college-level classes.

"Well, in that case, you'll find the classes easy. And, hey, they made me do a qualifying year with exams when I got to Queensland."

He sat down on the couch, obviously unhappy. "I never liked chemistry or physics, but you're right, I don't have a choice."

Two weeks later, I started my new job as a research technician for the veterinary school. While I was at work, Ken unpacked our clothes and belongings into our one-bedroom rental and connected with a realtor to look at houses. The apartment was small and expensive. We had it for a month, but if we needed it longer, we would need to take it for at least six months.

I agonized at the thought of buying a house. Ken hadn't even begun his program and wouldn't be a formal graduate student for another year. I would be working as a low-paid research assistant in a contract position that would last for twelve months. To make matters worse, we were in a recession, and interest rates were at an all-time high of 18 percent. *What were we doing? Were we insane?*

Mom was adamant. "Buy a house. If you stay in Gainesville for at least two years, you'll be able to sell it for a profit. And it will be less expensive than renting."

Our apartment was $250 a month and was tiny. We met with a realtor. He convinced us that, with our down payment, we could afford to buy a house and keep our monthly payment under $250. So we shopped for houses. We visited over twenty houses in the northeast. It was exciting, but also nerve-racking. Buying a house was a significant decision, and none of the houses we saw gave me the feeling that I wanted to make it ours.

The realtor was patient. A big part of the problem was that interest rates were very high, so we were looking at houses that had assumable mortgages or owner financing.

He said, "The important thing is to get into your first house. It doesn't need to be perfect; it needs to be acceptable and affordable."

He was right, and I tried to be less judgmental.

We found a place about two miles from campus. It was a small Florida-style home with jalousie windows throughout. In some ways, it reminded me of the rental I lived in when my family first moved to Florida. Well, it was the terrazzo floors and jalousie windows that reminded me of my old home.

The kitchen was small, with terrazzo floors. All the floors were terrazzo, but the living room and dining room floors were covered in green carpet. But the backyard was huge, and it had three bedrooms. And the owner offered financing at 8 percent (the going rate was 18 percent). We could work with it.

After Mom and Dad put the down payment in for us, we could afford the mortgage even on my salary. Mom was right. It was less than our one-bedroom apartment. And it was ours. We were in a new city and had a new home that we were buying. I had a job, and Ken had started in graduate school. So much had happened in the last two months that my head was spinning.

As summer gave way to fall, the trees displayed brilliant reds and oranges before shedding their leaves. Ken built a garden bed, and I planted impatiens. We got a bed and dining set from a thrift store. Ken built a couch frame, and we used Mom's old cushions after she redecorated.

Right after we moved in, our neighbor, a silver-haired woman in her seventies, came over to introduce herself.

"Hi, I'm Betty, and this is my granddaughter Susan," she said.

"Hi, I'm Ann, and this is Ken."

Susan, a blond teenager, said, "Welcome to the neighborhood."

"Thanks, it's good to meet people. Are you a student?" Ken asked.

She smiled and shook her head. "I graduated last year. I work at Publix now."

"That's nice," I said. "I work at the university, and Ken is a student."

Betty said, "Oh, that's nice. We have another student about halfway up the block. It's nice to meet you. We'll talk again soon. I need to finish making dinner."

They both went inside. Eventually, we met the other student. The neighborhood was pleasant, but truly working-class. Our neighbors included air-conditioning repairmen, construction workers, and grocery clerks. But I felt safe walking at night; they seemed like good people.

As winter settled in, the house was cold; there was no way to really seal the old Florida windows. Over time, we made changes to make the house our own. We removed a wall to eliminate the wasted space in the long hall and expand the living room. Ken replaced the awful green carpet with oak tiles. I grew to love the house.

While I missed Brisbane, I was happy to be back in the States. Gainesville was not entirely new to me. I enjoyed reconnecting with family and friends. That might be why I handled the changes in our lives better than Ken did. He was on his own, except for the support I could offer. We'd been married less than a year, and I was still trying to figure out the support angle.

He missed being able to drop in on friends he'd known all his life back in Brisbane. I wanted to help, but didn't know how. One of the research assistants in my lab was a long-haired hippy. I thought they would hit it off, and they did. Ken often dropped by for lunch.

"Hey," Ken said.

I walked over and kissed him.

Mark waved from the other side of the lab. "Hey, Ken,"

"G'day."

The three of us took our lunch bags and headed for the elevators. There was an outside picnic table that we liked.

"Chemistry still giving you problems?" Mark asked.

Ken glared. "Can we talk about something else?"

Mark shrugged and dropped the topic. He and I had talked at length about the seriousness of Ken's struggles. These classes were mandatory for admission to graduate school.

Ken disliked the large auditorium-style classes of the undergraduate program and struggled to maintain focus, which led to poor exam performance. I hoped he would adapt, but he was taking a long time.

He failed the first test and only just passed the second.

Ken was the smartest person I'd ever met, so I assumed he would meet the challenge, but it worried me. I'd seen many students fail chemistry. For as long as I'd known Ken, he'd talked about graduate school. *What would happen if he didn't qualify?* What I couldn't understand was why I seemed more worried about it than he did.

But I had my own issues; my job required daily surgery. Part of me enjoyed the challenge. It required a steady hand and good eye-hand coordination to insert a breathing tube into a guinea pig's trachea and administer drugs intravenously. I was measuring the effect of anti-asthmatic medication. The research was important, but it always ended badly for the guinea pigs. I'd kept guinea pigs as a kid, and killing them bothered me. It was a way of earning a living, but I didn't like it. I was happy that it was a contract job that would only last one year. I promised myself that for the next job, my highest priority would be avoiding killing animals.

* * *

Our lives revolved around work and study from eight to five, but we still had a city to discover. For Ken, it was an entirely new experience. My frequent college visits to see Bob and Phylece gave me some familiarity with the town and helped me feel at ease. It was fun showing Ken old favorites, like the Devil's Millhopper, a massive sinkhole that resembled an upside-down mountain with a rainforest at its base. It reminded us of our walks on Mt. Glorious and stirred up a bit of nostalgia.

And of course, we had to look for music, and we were in a good place to do so. Gainesville was Tom Petty's birthplace, a fact that made the locals quite proud. There were bars and restaurants with live music everywhere. I briefly considered finding a paying gig, like I had back in Brisbane, but there were far too many people playing for free or for tips. I'd made decent money back in Australia and wasn't tempted to compete with the college kids.

We didn't find a folk club in our town.It was a fact that dismayed me until I realized it was an opportunity. Gainesville needed a folk club, and I was experienced enough to start one. Ken was skeptical at first, but warmed to the idea as we started scouting out likely locations.

We were having dinner at a favorite Chinese restaurant near our house, enjoying orange chicken, beef with snow peas, and a pot of green tea. That evening, the world felt *right*; I realized Gainesville had become our home.

# Chapter 55 ~ Gainesville

Gainesville had a charm of its own. The streets had hills and trees that changed colors in the fall. We both bought bicycles to get around. I'd never had a ten-speed before, and it was a lot of fun. I worked from eight to five Monday to Friday. Ken had classes most days. On weekends, we tried to have fun exploring Gainesville and the surrounding areas.

Everything was new to Ken, and it was tremendous fun showing Ken the local springs, parks, and towns just outside of Gainesville. Our house was in a suburb, and like many new homeowners, we had fun fixing it up and planting a garden. It hurt that we lived in the middle of the state. I'd always loved the beach and was used to going to the ocean in summer. While I loved the springs, fresh water wasn't the same. Crescent Beach, south of St. Augustine, was almost a two-hour drive, and it was our closest beach.

Mark asked us to go to the beach with him and his girlfriend. I enjoyed working with Mark, and I was glad he and Ken got along so well. The four of us had a lot in common. We all had science degrees and were figuring out our paths in life. We said yes to the invite. Mark and Ann-Marie came to our place early Saturday morning, and we drove to the coast together.

We spent about three hours at the beach. It was a beautiful, sunny day with a clear sky. The beach, while busy, had clear blue water, white sand, and dunes covered in sea oats and other plants. I felt nostalgic for the ocean, and I thought about my time on Heron Island, wondering if I'd ever see that reef again.

When we first arrived and were staying with my folks, Ken and I did road trip to the Florida Keys. We stopped by Seacamp, and I loved introducing Ken to one of my absolute favorite places and having him meet people who were important and dear to me. We snorkeled my favorite reef—Looe Key. But Ken didn't dive, and I wasn't diving either. Gainesville was in the middle of the state, and I missed being near the ocean.

After a picnic lunch, we headed into Old Town, St. George Street in St. Augustine. As we approached the Castillo, it became obvious a civil war re-enactment was in progress.

"This is so cool. How often do they put on reenactments?" Ken asked.

"I think it's a once-a-year event," Mark said.

"I play music with Lisa Johnson in Gainesville. She and her husband are really into this stuff. I bet they're here," I said.

Ann-Marie looked curious. "What kind of music?"

"Lisa and Jonathan do old-time music. He plays fiddle. She plays the guitar. When I play with Lisa, we do standard folk music."

"Wow," Mark said. "Hey, there are bars with live music on St. George Street. We can find one for food and beer and cool off before we head back to Gainesville."

We ended up at an open-air bar called The Prohibition Kitchen. It had great food and music, and we all concluded the day had been a success. We headed back to Gainesville, tired but happy.

That was the first of many trips to the beach. Well, I'd always loved the beach, and it hurt that it took two hours to drive from Gainesville. But I developed a love for Crescent Beach, and we went at least a few times each summer.

And at least once a month, we drove the 325 miles to North Miami Beach to visit my parents. The trip took over five hours, and our Honda Civic was not meant for touring. By the end of the summer, we regretted our decision to buy a non-air-conditioned car.

In many ways, working in the pharmacology lab of the vet school reminded me of my time at NIH. My coworkers were educated and congenial. The lab benches had a familiar feel to them as well. I tried not to get too attached, as I knew my grant-funded position would end after a year.

We were testing anti-asthma drugs using guinea pigs as test subjects. The subject interested me. My grandfather and my older brother had asthma. But I cared little for the day-to-day routine: sedate my animal, hook the poor little creature to a breathing machine, administer drugs to trigger an asthma attack, and collect breathing data. In the late afternoon, I would kill the guinea pig, collect the lungs, and send the tissue to pathology for testing.

We had used animals at NIH, and I'd come to terms with the need for animals in research. But I also had my doubts about the value of the results and the ethics of spending animal lives casually. It did not help that the accepted method for killing the animal was a quick blow to the neck with an iron rod. It also hurt that guinea pigs were cute and friendly. I was determined that my next position would not have me directly involved in animal testing.

Ken's struggles with chemistry intensified. He hated the large class setting and resented the class, saying it had nothing to do with parasitology. He complained that the textbook was overpriced and poorly written.

In my experience, the subject was used to weed students out of selective programs. Most professors expected half of those who enrolled to fail. But I couldn't convince Ken to take it seriously. He had always been bullheaded, insisting on doing his own thing, and he skated by with a D in Chemistry for his first semester. Physics proved even more discouraging. The professor unexpectedly required Calculus, despite the course description omitting it.

After two terms of poor grades, it was obvious graduate school would be on hold, and Ken was not in a mind to try repeating the classes.

"What do you want to do?" I asked.

"Find a job," Ken said with a shrug. "At least, we're in a town at a research university."

I must have looked dubious. Ever since I met Ken, he'd talked about doing a doctorate in Parasitology. I expected more backlash.

"Hey, it won't hurt me to have some research lab experience. Your job is kind of cool."

I nodded, glad that Ken's first reaction wasn't talking about going "home" to Australia. But then, he knew I wouldn't go.

"You know, both of my parents worked in science. While my dad had a Ph.D. My mother didn't. It will work out."

It was true. Ken's dad had been a professor of Physics, and his mom a professor of metallurgy. What I didn't say was that they were a different generation. In today's world, the lack of a doctorate restricted your work choices to being an assistant—a pair of hands.

And Ken might think my job was "cool," but I didn't. I was glad the grant was ending. I hoped to find a job that didn't involve killing animals every day.

In the end, I let Ken's assertion go unchallenged. Ken was smart and capable. He was right; things would work out. For now, I was enjoying showing Ken part of the United States. We had a home and were comfortable in Gainesville.

So, as our second summer in the United States came to a wrap, we were both looking for jobs.

# Chapter 56 ~ Two-Income Family

The country was in a prolonged recession, and that had us worried. It was July 1982, and my position would end August 1. Ken was seeking his first employment in the United States. But we were young, healthy, and optimistic as we searched the university research listings. I had an easier time than Ken and had a new position before my contract job closed.

It helped that I was already in the system as a current employee and had years of experience working in research laboratories ranging from NOAA to NIH, and now, the pharmacology department at the university vet school. One week after I contacted human resources, asking for employment listings, they contacted me for an interview.

The job listing asked for applicants with five years of experience and a master's degree. Well, I only had about four years' experience, but I guess they figured that was close enough and called me in for an interview. When I arrived at the lab, the principal investigator was sitting at a biological isolation hood working with tissue culture flasks. It reminded me so much of my old lab at NIH that it flooded me with nostalgia.

The head investigator was a young woman from England. She was thin with jet black hair, and she wore a crisp white lab coat. She didn't stop working, instead asking me to take a seat on a stool at the nearby counter. The interview was brief and to the point.

"Tell me about your experience with biohazardous materials."

"Well, I worked with Dr. Gibbs at NIH. They had me handling tissues and tissue culture from animals and humans. We worked with Kuru, scrapie, and Creutzfeldt-Jakob disease."

"Did you do primary culture?" she asked.

Primary culture is when you take a small piece of tissue, place it in growth media, and dice it up with sterile scissors. Once in a tissue culture flask, the cells adhere, grow, and multiply.

"Yes, they had me do explanting, then passaging and freezing. I'm excellent at cell culture."

She paused with her work, closed the microplate she had in hand, pushed away from the hood, and looked me over. I felt a bit uncomfortable.

"How long ago were you at NIH?" she asked.

"From 1972 to 1976. After that, I went to Australia and did a master's degree."

She nodded. "Neurological slow viruses have an incubation time of seven years. You're still alive, so you must have been taught the necessary safety techniques. My work is with lymphocytes, so the tissue culture is suspension, not adherent cells. But the sterile techniques don't change. Tell me about your other duties."

"I made laboratory solutions, cleaned and sterilized glassware, prepared trays for animal autopsies, and assisted with the autopsies."

"What animals?"

"We worked with chimpanzees for Kuru and mice for scrapie."

She got a far-off look for a minute. "Chimpanzees and Kuru. Did you work with Dr. Gajdusek?"

"My lab was headed by Dr. Gibbs, but they worked together. We had lab meetings with the combined teams. He's eccentric. I was there when he was awarded the Nobel Prize. We threw him a pizza party."

Lindsey took her gloves off, turned the fan off for the hood, and stood up. "Let me show you around."

I left the interview enthusiastic. It would be good to work in tissue culture at biological safety hoods again. And I liked her no-nonsense approach. I was offered the position the same day. It paid better than my old job and didn't require killing animals.

I came home bubbling over with excitement. Ken was pleased with my success and frustrated by a lack of interview offers.

"I'm thrilled at least one of us has a job. It would be nice if I got called for an interview."

He wasn't the only one frustrated. I'd been supporting the two of us for more than a year, and I was eager to share the burden. But I wanted to be supportive.

I said, "I know it's frustrating. It's a recession. I expect Professors are being told they have to hire people in the system."

"Yeah." He ran his fingers through his shoulder-length hair, looking thoughtful. "I guess I can look for temp work to hold us over."

I thought about suggesting a haircut and beard trim, but I didn't say anything. That would only help if he had an interview offer. Shortly after September I when I started working for Lindsey, Ken was placed by a temp agency for construction work on a wing of the hospital on campus. He was installing windows. It wasn't what he wanted, but Ken had built our living room set, bookshelves, installed ceiling fans, repaired plumbing, and kept the car maintained. In short, Ken was an excellent handyman. Working on a construction site suited him for temporary work.

After a few months, he got a trickle of interview invitations, but it wasn't until the end of November that he had a job offer working in pulmonary pediatrics as a research assistant. Maybe it was only a coincidence that the job offer came in shortly after Ken got a haircut and a beard trim, but I think that might have had an impact. We were now a true two-income family.

We splurged and bought a stereo so we could listen to our albums, which had been carefully transported from Australia. And we no longer had to eat split pea soup for most meals.

I considered taking a music gig, particularly when finances were tight, as they were for most of that first year. The problem was that Gainesville was a college town filled with students willing to play for free or for tips. I'd been spoiled in Brisbane, often earning "union" rates for playing in restaurants. When I thought about it, I realized it wasn't just a financial need. Performing, playing guitar, and singing had been a central part of my life for over ten years. While I was still working on my guitar skills in the evening, I missed having a venue like the Red Fox in DC and the Barley Mow in Brisbane.

We talked it over. Since there wasn't a local folk club, we would start one. I had in mind finding a place like the Red Fox—a bar that had a house band on weekends and might enjoy hosting an open night to bring in business on a weeknight.

When we came across a corner coffee shop/restaurant called the Reality Kitchen, it felt perfect. The owner, Jim Evangelist, was an idealistic, long-haired hippy and a mural artist. The place was artistic.

We discussed folk music, singer-songwriters, and the philosophy behind open mics and how they help musicians gain performance experience. Jim was keen but also apologetic about not having a sound system. Then, he offered us twenty-five dollars a week to host an open mic, provided we brought the equipment. I said yes.

We picked up a small portable amplifier, two microphones, and two stands from a local music store, financing the purchase with a four-hundred-dollar loan from the credit union. We were excited to launch our new business as we began putting up fliers around town and the university.

Thursday came, and we set up the stage in the empty Reality kitchen. It was seven p.m., and the place was all but empty. Jim Evangelist propped the door open and had a sign positioned on the sidewalk advertising *Open Mic All Welcome.*

I walked onto the stage and started a song. The empty room didn't faze me. It reminded me of my old cafe back in Brisbane. Ken was at a table with a signup sheet. A few people trickled in, but I didn't see any guitars. I played for fifteen minutes, then announced a break, suggesting people sign up with Ken for either tonight's open mic or next week. No one budged. But as I began my second set, I saw several people chatting with Ken. By the time I finished, we had two more performers for that night, and one for the Thursday after.

I was thrilled when the first volunteer, David, brought out a dulcimer and played it beautifully. Next was Paul, who took the stage with his guitar and sang two British folk songs. By the end of the night, I was exhausted and happy. We'd hosted our first open mic, and I could stop worrying about finding a folk club—we were building one.

# Chapter 57 ~ Crises

It was nice being a two-income family, but then we were hit with the dreaded health emergency, and things fell apart for a while. Ken worked at a remote research lab called the "Farm." It was only two months into his new job when he had a grand mal epileptic seizure.

I knew Ken was epileptic; we talked about it a lot. His seizures started when he was thirteen and seriously messed up his high school education. But he hadn't had a seizure in over five years, and his doctors took him off the medication. They felt he had grown out of them. We both found out the hard way that wasn't a great decision.

"They need you downstairs in the emergency room. Ken had an epileptic seizure." Lindsey walked to the hood where I was in the middle of an experiment. "Go ahead. I'll take this," she said.

"Thanks," I said, turning the flame off and leaving everything in the hood. I hung my lab coat up, walked from the lab, took the elevator to the first floor, and rushed inside the emergency room.

The staff at the Shands emergency room didn't waste any time. They had me in the room with Ken within five minutes. He was on a gurney. Four men were holding him down. His sneakers were on the floor, and his boss was standing by the side. She came toward me.

"He was working at the lab on the 'farm' when he started seizing. I waited with him, but when he kept seizing, I called for an ambulance."

The gurney was bouncing around as Ken thrashed. They had

strapped him to the gurney, and a doctor inserted a needle for an IV bag.

The doctor took a blood sample and walked over to me.

"Are you Ken's wife?" he asked.

"Yes. Ken had epilepsy in his teens," I said. "His doctors thought he had grown out of it. It's been more than five years since he's had a seizure."

A doctor motioned for me to follow him into an office and had me take a seat.

"He's been seizing for over an hour. I'm giving him medication to stop him from convulsing, and checking his blood oxygen level, which is low. Has Ken been using drugs?"

"What do you mean?" I asked.

"Does Ken use recreational drugs?"

"Well, I know he's smoked marijuana, but I don't think he's done that in the last week or so."

"I'm asking about anything harder."

I said no. I was still not sure what drugs the doctor was asking about.

Five hours later, they had Ken sedated, and the seizures were over. They wanted him in intensive care, saying he was at risk of a heart attack. Shands, the university and regional hospital, didn't have a bed for him, and transferred him to Alachua General, a local private hospital. And so began my education on the horrors of the American medical system.

They transported Ken in an ambulance for the second time that day. His first was from the "Farm" to Shands Emergency Room.

I followed a few hours later in our car and visited Ken's room. He slept through the night. I know, because I sat there the whole time while Ken slept. It was a fitful rest interrupted by groans and coughs, but he never woke enough for me to talk to him.

I was scared for Ken. While I knew about epilepsy, this was the first time I'd seen anyone in a grand mal seizure, and it was more than disturbing. Gradually, my fear morphed into anger at the hospital staff. Not one person walked into the room to check on him. They had a heart monitor on him, but I did not feel that it took the place of a human being. I walked out to the nurse's station and asked if a doctor had been by. They checked his charts and said no, but it should be soon.

Around noon, Ken woke up, and I pushed a button to call for the nurse. She came in, went to his side, and asked, "Do you know where you are?"

"Shands emergency room?" he said.

His answer surprised me. I didn't think he had been awake enough to know he was even at the Shands emergency room.

"No, they transferred you over to Alachua General. Do you know why you are in a hospital?" she asked.

"From how I feel, I'm guessing I had a seizure."

"You seized for over five hours. That puts a strain on your heart, so the doctors want you here for observation."

"Can I get something for a headache?" Ken asked.

The nurse looked at Ken's chart. "The doctor will be in to see you soon. We need his approval to give you anything."

She left, and we sat.

"How are you feeling?" I asked. "It was quite a seizure."

He was silent for a minute. "I'm cold. Can you ask for a blanket?"

I went to the nurses' station, and they gave me a blanket.

"I've never seen a seizure," I said. "It was scary."

"Well, they aren't fun for the person having one either."

I had a cup of coffee from the cafe with me, and Ken was looking at it. "Do you want me to ask if you can have something to eat or drink?"

"Yes, and something for a headache."

I asked the nurse, and she came in with a cup of water for Ken.

295

"Can I have some Tylenol?" he asked her.

"Sorry, the doctor should be here soon. I can't give you anything other than water until he checks on you."

I said, "Ken hasn't had anything to eat in over twenty-four hours. Didn't they write orders on him when they admitted him?"

"Well, for someone with an epileptic seizure, they need to be seen by a neurologist. When Ken arrived, Dr. Feussner wasn't at the hospital."

Ken said, "It's okay. My headache isn't that bad."

He looked at me. "How long have you been here?"

"Since they brought you here yesterday."

"You haven't been home?"

"Nope."

"Oh, wow. Yeah, go home. Feed the cat, take a break. I'll be fine. This isn't the first time I've had a seizure."

I went home and took care of a few things, grateful that it was Saturday and I wasn't missing a day of work. Thinking about it, I was grateful that we both worked for the state, had sick leave, and insurance.

I came back after letting the cat in, feeding him, and having a bite to eat myself. By the time I walked into Ken's room, it was almost four in the afternoon.

"What did the doctor say?" I asked.

"He hasn't been in yet. It sucks because they won't give me anything to eat or anything for the headache until he checks me over."

We visited, and I realized Ken was really fuzzy in how he was talking. I wanted the neurologist to get there already. Five o'clock came and went. Still no doctor. At five-thirty, I asked them to get him on the phone for me.

"Hello, this is Dr. Feussner."

"My husband, Ken McNicol, is at North Florida Regional. The nurses won't let him have any food or anything for a headache until you fill in his paperwork."

He told me to hand the phone to the nurse.

"I can't do that," she said into the phone.

"Good, we'll see you soon," she said and hung the phone up.

"He'll be here in half an hour," she said to me.

It was more than half an hour, but he got there in a golf shirt and shorts—and pissed off.

"It's after hours," he said to me.

I was more pissed off than he was. "They said Ken can't be given anything to eat or drink, or anything for a headache unto you see him and approve it on his chart."

He looked over Ken's chart, glanced at the monitor, and made a few notes on the chart. "He can have whatever he wants to eat. Tylenol for the headache. I'll look in on you tomorrow. After that, we can move you out of intensive care."

Then he left.

I was speechless, but not as I was eight days later when they pulled me into the business office before releasing Ken.

Ken spent almost eight hours at the emergency room at Shands, three days in intensive care, and four days in a regular hospital room. The business official wanted me to write a check for the estimated hospital bill before they would discharge him.

I was earning about twelve thousand dollars a year. Ken was earning slightly less. The bill was over fourty thousand dollars."

"What about insurance?" I asked.

"This is the estimated amount we don't expect insurance to cover. Ken's insurance covers 80 percent. The bill is an estimate, and it may go down. If that happens, you'll get a refund."

I looked over the list. Each of the ambulance rides was two hundred dollars. Dr. Feussner charged three hundred dollars for an after-hours visit to the hospital. The list of charges was three pages long.

"We don't have this kind of money," I said.

"We take credit cards but prefer checks," she said. "Do you want to come back after you talk with your bank?"

"If I write a check, it will bounce all over this room. We've been in the country less than eighteen months, so we have no real credit history. This bill is outrageous. But if it is what we owe, you're going to need to come up with a payment plan."

She came up with a payment plan, and it felt like we had two mortgage payments to make. Adding to the financial pain, Ken was off work for the next two months, far longer than the amount of his accumulated sick leave. We would be back to being a one-paycheck family for a while. It also hurt that Ken wouldn't be allowed to drive until he was seizure-free for six months.

We adjusted. Gradually, Ken came back to himself. He was getting restless, so I suggested we take a road trip to break up the time before he could go back to work. We drove south, stayed with my folks for a few days, then continued down to the Florida Everglades and into the Keys. We made it all the way to Key West. I loved every opportunity to visit the Keys, and was happy Ken seemed to like the place almost as much as I did.

By the time we were back in Gainesville, Ken was doing much better, with far fewer "fuzzy" moments. He took to using a ten-speed bike to get to work. Life returned almost to normal.

# Chapter 58 ~ Living Life

Now that Ken was back at work, things felt normal. He was seeing a neurologist and taking his Dilantin again. I stopped worrying so much about his epilepsy. Aside from not being able to drive, we just fell back into our routine.

"This is my research assistant, Ann," Dr. Hutt-Fletcher said.

I waved from the tissue culture hood. Her visitor nodded in response, and I continued with my work.

"We need blood," Dr. Hutt-Fletcher said.

"Give me a minute," I said, finishing loading the centrifuge and turning it on before hanging my lab coat on the rack and sitting at the bench where she waited with a syringe to draw blood. Lindsey was adept with the needle, and giving blood never hurt much. Usually, we had volunteers, but if no one was available, lab techs were the backup.

I looked at my lab bench, and not for the first time, I longed for NIH and my old lab team. The equipment and work were so similar, and it was hard not to be reminded of DC. The skills I'd learned included handling biologically hazardous materials, calculating and mixing solutions, and keeping records, which meant I had no difficulty adapting to my new job. But this laboratory lacked the excitement I'd experienced working at NIH. Maybe I was just older and jaded.

But I think it was the difference in the experience and accomplishments of the people I worked with. At NIH, the researchers were established professionals at the top of the scientific community. The chatter in the lab was on breakthrough science in our lab and in others. The love of discovery and science was palpable.

Here at the University of Florida, the chatter was about budgets, cost of materials, and pressure to get articles published. I missed the easygoing banter and inclusion that made me feel like I was part of the team. My former boss, Dr. Gibbs, was a former Navy SEAL, a world-renowned virologist, and treated his student assistants as future research scientists. Dr. Hutt-Fletcher was friendly, but treated me like a pair of hands who would never be more than a low-paid lab assistant. I wasn't unhappy, but the work felt like something I did to bring in a paycheck.

The Reality Kitchen filled the void and helped me find a feeling of self-worth. I lived for Thursday nights.

"Is the mic live?" I asked.

"Give me a minute," Ken said.

I sat on a stool placed on a small corner stage, while Ken worked the soundboard. It was six forty-five, and we had this part down to an art form. We arrived at six-thirty and set up the equipment. At seven p.m., I did a fifteen-minute opening set, while Ken opened the ledger for people who wanted a spot.

Tonight, my set included "Artesian Waters," "And the Band Played Waltzing Matilda," and "The Newsboy." While I had centered on American folk while I was in Australia, it was fun to play Australian folk to our American audiences. I had a large enough collection of songs that I wasn't worried about running out of material, but my goal was to spend the evening as the host of an open mic, not as a solo performer. I rarely had to play more than one set. The town was filled with talented and eager artists.

Ken took charge of keeping sound levels appropriate during performances and relished his role as "roadie" and sound engineer as much as I enjoyed being the host.

Stephanie, one of our regular guitarists/vocalists, came off her set to the usual enthusiastic applause right before our mid-evening break.

She walked over to the counter where I sat and said, "Can I talk to you?"

"Sure."

"Nancy and I are forming a folk group. Are you interested in joining us?"

I didn't hesitate. "I'd love to."

The words came out without hesitation. I loved all forms of playing and singing with other musicians and was thrilled with the invitation.

Stephanie, a guitarist and vocalist, was tall and thin with wavy brown hair. She had a down-to-earth voice that was rich with emotion and played the guitar as if she were born to play. Nancy was still in college and would graduate with a teaching degree later that year. She was five foot two, a ball of energy, and accomplished on the hammered dulcimer, a strikingly beautiful and unusual instrument. Together, the three of us became Cypress Lake. We played at the Reality Kitchen (of course) and at several local concerts. I branched out and added the Appalachian dulcimer to my instruments.

What we had in common was a love of American folk music, singing harmonies, and experimenting with instrumentals. We weren't stellar musicians, but together, we put on a performance that was pleasing to us and to the audience. That year, we performed at the annual Florida Folk Festival at White Springs. It was so much fun. The stage was just off the Suwannee River, and we all camped there for the weekend.

# Chapter 59 ~ Old Life Meets New

Ken and I were really getting into "adulting." We had jobs, and we were handling a mortgage, household bills, and scheduling doctor and dentist appointments. We were figuring out how to navigate life.

Ken had recovered both from the emotional hit he took when he dropped out of graduate school and from the crises of a major epileptic seizure. He was driving again and seemed content to be working in pulmonary pediatrics. Both of us enjoyed the music scene we were helping to build. Gainesville was a mecca for road bike enthusiasts. Ken taught me to use a ten-speed, and we joined a bike club. We were in a house and were making mortgage payments and trying to stay on top of the hospital debt.

Sometimes, it felt like my two lives, the one before Australia and the one after, were colliding. Usually, this happened when people from my old life before I moved to Australia came to visit.

I hadn't seen Phylece since I stayed with her in California. Her sister, Robin, lived in Gainesville, giving her a reason to visit frequently. When she did, it was as if we'd never been apart. Phylece had visited me in Washington, DC, and in Tampa, and we'd even traveled through Hawaii together. She was truly my sister, even though we weren't related by blood.

Gainesville was Phylece's college town, and when she was a student, I'd drive up from Tampa to visit on weekends. We had a great time, revisiting old haunts and showing Ken around. She and Ken bonded over some weed, and he took her for rides on his motorcycle, a Suzuki 400 that he bought because he felt he was missing part of his identity without a bike. To my amazement, Phylece loved riding on the back of the bike, and they had a great time zooming around Gainesville.

Phylece had a complicated relationship with her parents, who still lived in South Florida. It was better now that she was an adult and independent, but we both vividly recalled the night she came to my house after a huge fight with her father. She had run away from home, seeking refuge with me, and my parents let her stay.

"What's your latest project?" I asked.

"I'm laying tile in Linda Ronstadt's house?

"Oh my God, you're kidding!"

"Nope, it's a very cool house."

When I lived with Phylece in San Francisco, she worked in an office job she couldn't stand. She had a psychology degree, but finding work in her field seemed impossible without a master's. Eventually, she landed an internship with a tile setters' union and ran her own tile-setting business. I thought it was the perfect career for her. In high school, she took art as an elective, and I recalled how detailed her work was. She loved working with her hands. Tile setting seemed like a natural fit. Later, she would win awards for her amazing mosaic tile work throughout the city.

For now, I was delighted that her sister lived in Gainesville. Phylece had multiple reasons to visit Florida. We could visit each other often.

While I was in Australia, I was focused on finding my way in academia and in life. But while I was away, life continued for those around me. Uncle Bob got married, had a home of his own, and a full-time job as an elementary school teacher. They lived in South Florida, near my parents. But he and Nancy liked to camp in the Ocala National Forest—not far from where we lived in Gainesville.

So there were times we found Bob and Nancy with their camper in our driveway, waiting for us to get home. They joined us for Ken's very first Passover dinner. I cooked, and we read through a short Passover Haggadah in our living room.

Of course, I forgot to warn Ken about horseradish, and he spilled wine all over the table. It was a fun evening.

My younger brother, Jim, had huge life changes while I was away. He was married, owned a house, and had started a title insurance agency. He and Lenoir married as soon as they graduated college—ridiculously young. They had a son and were living in Tallahassee, a city in northern Florida, about a three-hour drive from us.

Richard and Debbie split up, at least for a while. She hated the isolation of living in Hawaii. I'm sure there were other problems, too. She took their daughter and went back to California. To his credit, he followed them back to the mainland, and they reconciled. They were living in Carlsbad California. Richard worked selling cars at a dealership and seemed to be trying to be a good father and husband. I was proud of him and hoped they would make it as a family.

The big change, the elephant in the room, was Dad. When I left for Australia, he was a larger-than-life figure, joking, laughing, hustling, and always the life of the party. I knew he was massively overweight, and I worried about his health. But even so, the change was a terrible shock. Like Mom, I had hoped he would recover more mobility and more ability to communicate. It didn't happen. Since the stroke, progress had slowed, and he was a shadow of his former self.

Ken and I drove down to South Florida about once a month. Sometimes, Mom would bring Dad up for a visit. He used a wheelchair outside of the house and a walker for movement indoors. His speech was slurred, and he could manage only a few words at a time. It would not have changed a thing if I had not gone to Australia. I knew that and felt guilty anyway. Mostly, I regretted the time I could have spent with him before the stroke. Now I would spend as much quality time with him as I could.

My Uncle Mike's family was growing up, too. When I left for Australia, they were all high school students. Now, his oldest child, Audrey, had graduated high school and was a freshman at UF. Life went on.

"Audrey called," I said. "She could use a hand at her apartment."

"Okay," Ken said.

I'd known Audrey most of my life, but when I knew her, I was also a child. She was Mike and Barbara's oldest child. Now, she was a freshman at the University of Florida, and she looked to us as her adult relatives here in town. It felt weird to be thought of that way, but also nice.

Audrey was eight years younger than me, a gap that clearly made her think of us as adults. I was also now married, and we had a home. She was no longer a kid living in her parents' house, and our relationship adjusted nicely. Ken and I genuinely enjoyed having her over for dinner, hearing about her classes, and catching up.

We went over to her condo and helped with moving furniture. It felt good to play the part of an adult in her life.

# Chapter 60 ~ Then We Were Three

At the end of October, while riding my bike home, a car bumped into me. I didn't even fall, but the tap from his car caused a fracture in my bike frame.

"You're pregnant!" the man said, jumping out of his car and staring at me.

"I know," I said, thinking it was hard to miss. I tried not to obsess over my figure, but it had been a long time since my body felt at all "normal."

"I hit a pregnant lady," he said.

"I'm okay," I said. Then, looking at my bike with a broken frame, I added, "But my bike isn't."

He looked at my bike, pulled out his wallet, and handed me a business card and a one-hundred-dollar bill. "If it comes to more than this, call me. Do you need a ride?"

"My husband will come and pick me up," I said, pointing to a phone booth. "I can give him a call."

"I'll wait until he gets here," the man said. He moved the car off the road and waited with me while I made the call.

Ten minutes later, Ken came with the car, looked me and the bike over, and tossed the broken bike into the hatchback.

"I don't want you riding to work anymore."

"Yeah. Probably not a great idea," I said, getting into the passenger side. It was late, and I was hungry. "Let's get home. Do you think we can fix the bike?"

"Not likely. But for one hundred dollars, we can replace it. We didn't pay that much for it."

I would miss riding the bike to work, but I was in my last trimester. It had been a near miss, and the accident could have been serious. I'd take the hint and stop riding.

* * *

Back in Brisbane, when Ken asked me if I wanted children, I answered yes, someday. The big question we faced was when our "someday" would be the right time. I wanted to wait until we were stable. I didn't want my kids to move around like I had. Mom had her first child when she was twenty years old. I was now in my thirties. We had a house and jobs. *Was it time?*

Bob, Richard, and even my younger brother Jim had all started families. Mom didn't pressure us too much about when we'd have kids, but I knew she was hoping for another grandchild, this time, from her daughter.

Telling Mom that I was pregnant on Mother's Day was a nice touch.

"Mom, Happy Mother's Day," I said into the phone receiver.

"Thank you," she said. "One day I hope to say the same to you."

"That's part of why I'm calling," I said. "Mom, I'm pregnant."

She shrieked. "For real? Oh my God, Congrats. This isn't a joke, is it?"

"Mom, for real. Happy Mother's Day, you're going to be a grandma."

"Hang on, I have to tell Dad."

I waited. Mom was the first person we told about the pregnancy, and now, it felt like it was real. It was still early. I would have waited until I was further along, but I wanted to share the news on Mother's Day.

Ken was sitting across from me at the table. I waited a minute, and then they were both on the phone.

"I'm happy for you," Dad said.

"Can I tell the family?" Mom asked.

"Yes, tell anyone you like."

The official due date was December 25, but after December 8, my pregnancy would be full term and not require a hospital birth. Those were birth center rules, and I respected them. But I didn't want a hospital birth.

It had been a difficult pregnancy. My morning sickness was so bad in the first trimester that I lost weight and had to drink protein shakes. I struggled with anemia for eight months, taking prenatal supplements and eating iron-rich foods to meet the birth center's requirements. If I failed to stay within their health guidelines, they would turn my care over to a doctor, and we'd need to plan and pay for a hospital birth. Once we made it to December 8th, the pregnancy qualified as full term and low risk. We were cleared for a birth center delivery.

We celebrated crossing that threshold by hosting a "coming out" party instead of a lame baby shower. We made it, and people had been arriving since late afternoon.

"Where do you want the cheese platter?" Paul asked.

Ken looked at the kitchen counter, already covered with dishes of wings, chips, cookies, and an assortment of dips.

"Put it on the table. We're running out of space."

The doorbell rang, and I called, "I'll get it!"

Nancy came in, hugging me before putting her hammered dulcimer case down. I was glad that Nancy and Stephanie came. I missed playing music with them. We performed at White Springs, Florida, back in November. It was a blast, but they said they wanted the group to take a break until after the baby was born. I wasn't sure if it was because they were nervous around me or because they didn't like the optics of a pregnant lady on stage.

I'd cried when they told me they wanted the band to take a break. It was a lot more fun to perform with a group than solo, and I didn't want that part of my life to end. It felt unfair. "We" were having a baby, but it was *my life* on hold. I had tried to argue my case, but they were adamant. There wasn't anything I could do about it. We announced that the band was taking a break and would no longer be accepting invitations to play.

It was encouraging that they didn't find a new member and go on without me. Music had been an essential part of who I was. I didn't want to give up that part of me. I made a vow to continue working on guitar and singing on my own over our "break."

The house was small, and by eight p.m., people filled every chair, couch, and most of the floor space. They even lined the long hallway leading from the living room to the back bedroom. At one point, we counted eighty people in a house that was just over one thousand square feet.

Ken and I weren't party people. The last big party we'd had was when Mom and Dad hosted the "meet the husband" for us when we first came to the States. We'd never had a large circle of friends, but we did now. Running the Reality Kitchen open mike put us at the center of the folk and pop music community of Gainesville. And it felt like all of them were in our house tonight.

Things started winding down around eleven, and slowly, the house emptied. Ken and I packed the food away and cleaned up. I looked at the baby blanket from Ken's boss, an assortment of "baby's first Christmas" ornaments, pacifiers, and jumpers. The gifts were mostly from people we worked with. Our music friends took us at our word and brought us food. I wouldn't need to cook for the rest of the week and was pleased at the prospect. But the gifts were lovely.

Then, the next day, my boss pulled me aside. "Ann, even if your baby isn't here, I want you to take next week off," Lindsey said.

"Why?" I asked. "My due date isn't for another two weeks." While I had enough sick leave accumulated to take seven weeks off, I wanted the time with our baby after the birth.

"Ann, I'm looking at you, and I don't think you're going to make it to your due date. And, if you go into labor here, where you are essentially at the hospital, this is where you will deliver. Seriously, it's time to stop working next week."

I told her I'd see how I felt closer to the weekend. So, of course, Thursday night I went into labor. The contractions started at dinner-time. They were intense enough that we cleared the kitchen and headed to the birth center. The contractions had eased, and Edith, my nurse practitioner midwife, checked me over. She'd overseen my prenatal care, and I felt my anxiety ratchet down during the examination. She was warm, friendly, and professional. I felt like I was in excellent hands.

"It's six o'clock," Edith said. "You're at the start of what is likely to be a long evening and night, and looking at your cervix, you have hours before anything will happen. Would you like to go home and come back in a few hours?" Edith asked.

"I don't think that's a good idea," Ken said.

"How about we take a walk in the neighborhood?" I suggested. Like Ken, I didn't want to be far from the birth center.

Edith nodded approval. "Walking is always a good idea. Movement helps."

So, Ken and I stepped outside into the cool evening air. The birth center was a converted old Gainesville house in a lovely northeast neighborhood. The houses were mostly two-story affairs with brick facades and elaborate porches. The yards had trees and gardens. For the first ten minutes, I almost relaxed. Then the next contraction came, and all I could think of was pain. It was crippling, and I couldn't walk.

All I could do was stand and hold onto Ken.

Then the pain left almost as quickly as it had arrived. We continued our walk. Thirty minutes later, another contraction hit. This one caused me to double over, and it lasted longer.

"That's it. We're going back," Ken said.

I had a few more on the way back, then as we started up the birth center entrance stairs, I felt water running down my legs. My pants were soaked.

We walked inside.

Edith looked at my wet pants. "That was fast," she said and ushered us into the exam room. "It's still going to be awhile, but it is time to get you settled."

The birthing room had a queen-size bed, comfortable sitting chairs, and a freestanding bathtub. I smiled at the sight of an old-fashioned beanbag chair. It didn't feel anything like a hospital room. That was good. I hated hospital rooms.

I sat down in a chair, trying to calm my nerves. This was it. We were here to have our baby. Not for the first time, I wished I could have a glass of wine. But it wouldn't be a good idea. I'd been avoiding alcohol during the pregnancy.

"Can I have some tea?" I asked.

Ken said, "I'll fix you a cup." He headed to the kitchen.

Edith said, "I'll want to check on you frequently. You're welcome to lie down on the bed if you need to, but we usually see mothers do better when they stay active and change positions."

"Thanks," I said.

Ken returned with herbal tea, which made me feel better. I think Ken was glad to have something to do. He was as nervous as I was.

The pain came and went with the contractions. The beanbag chair gave me some relief. Nothing was *comfortable,* but the beanbag was flexible, which helped. Most of the time, I paced the room, only sitting or lying down during contractions.

Around midnight, Ken asked if I minded if he took a nap. I hesitated, but didn't have the heart to say no. He lay down on a couch in the room next to ours. Edith stayed with me. My contractions were frequent enough that I couldn't doze off. I moved from the beanbag chair to the bed and paced around the room.

At two in the morning, the contraction pain was intense, and I asked Edith to wake Ken. I wanted him by my side. He came in, held my hand, and said all the encouraging words that should have been comforting. But all I could think of was how much it hurt and how long I'd been suffering.

It was the first and only time I regretted not being in a hospital. If I were having a traditional hospital birth, they would give me something for the pain. It was too late now, and I cried.

"It hurts so much."

"You're fully dilated. It won't be long now."

"Can I do anything?" Ken asked.

Edith and I looked at each other.

I said, "Next time, you have the baby."

That made everyone laugh.

"When you feel the contraction start, push as hard as you can. Don't let up. You're almost there."

Edith was right. When the next contraction came, it forced an agonizing scream from me. The contraction and the scream continued for what felt like an eternity. Ken held me, and then everything came to a stop. When the final push ended, and my daughter gave her first cry, all the pain disappeared. Robin Pauline McNicol made her entrance at seven-thirty a.m. on Friday, December 14th.

We looked in wonder at this tiny human being we made. I rested, holding her, and Edith helped me position and encourage Robin to nurse. She was a natural.

We were home by mid-morning. When Robin was asleep in her crib, we couldn't tear ourselves away. She was so tiny, smaller than any baby doll, with black hair. She weighed just over five pounds. After the first few hours, I tried to get some sleep, and Ken brought her to me when she was hungry, about once an hour. Robin wasn't shy about letting us know she was hungry. I didn't mind.

But by eleven at night, we were worried. Robin's breathing seemed labored. We listened to the noisy, uneven sounds as she drew air in and then released it. *Was this normal?* Ken and I missed the memo that newborn babies have noisy, uneven breathing. Maybe that would have been in our birth center training if she hadn't rushed things and come two weeks early.

Around midnight, we both grew so concerned that we bundled her up and drove to the emergency room. They made a fuss over our beautiful baby and assured us her breathing was normal. When Ken mentioned he worked for pulmonary pediatrics, they teased him a bit.

"You work in pulmonary pediatrics? And you don't know what newborns sound like?"

"I work in research with sheep, not with infants," Ken said.

We took Robin home and tucked her into bed with us.

The next day, Ken called Mom and handed me the phone.

"How are you doing?" Mom asked on the phone. "Do you need help?"

"Mom, I'm good. Exhausted, but feeling good. Robin is beautiful."

I knew Mom wanted to get in the car and see me and the baby. And I wanted her to come, but I needed a few days to recover. I wanted a few days with just the three of us.

"Mom, I'd love you to come up and see her, but how about waiting for next weekend?"

"That sounds perfect. Listen, we'll stay at the Sunshine Inn, and we won't intrude. But I really want to meet my granddaughter. Are you sure you don't need help now?"

"Ken is taking a week off work," I said. "We are all fine."

When we hung up, Ken called his mother and shared the news. She expressed joy and regret that we were so far away.

Saturday and Sunday disappeared in a blur. There was no night or day, just intervals between feedings and watching our baby.

We had an appointment with our pediatrician on Monday morning. Our pediatrician's office was in the same building as my lab. So, after our appointment, we went to my lab to show Robin off.

Lindsey insisted on the team coming out into the hall to see her, saying there were chemicals in the room.

"I'm starting my maternity leave now," I said.

Lindsey laughed at the joke. "She is just beautiful."

I had seven weeks of sick leave to use for my "maternity leave."

Robin was always hungry, and I was breastfeeding through the day and night, so it was good that I was off work. The longest I slept was ninety minutes. Ken and I became adept at changing diapers and holding and comforting a crying baby. It was December and cold out, but we bundled Robin up and took her for walks in a stroller. We set up a mobile over her crib and a baby swing. I sang songs to my baby and enjoyed being a new mom.

It was a magical time. Ken was happier than I'd ever seen him, and I felt bad when he had to go back to work.

Mom and Dad came up to see Robin after a few weeks. They came on the weekend and stayed at a motel near our house. Dad was using a wheelchair, and he was struggling to talk. But when he held Robin, his smile stretched from ear to ear. Mom told me that after his stroke, Dad said he wanted to die. Watching him hold Robin, I think he was happy he was alive and able to meet his granddaughter.

Mom already had two grandchildren, but you wouldn't know it. She fussed over Robin as if our baby were a long-awaited miracle. Mom always said daughters were special. I think Mom was afraid that her only daughter might drop the ball and not have kids. Well, it took a long time for me to develop an interest in boys. I guess I gave her reason to worry.

Week six of my maternity leave brought changes. We visited a daycare center and signed paperwork for Robin's first day. It left me feeling empty yet determined to make the most of the last week of my leave. Lindsey dropped by to see Robin and to confirm that I was ready to return to work.

"She is beautiful," Lindsey said, holding Robin and making faces at her. "Ann, are you ready? I can approve more leave. Your job will be waiting for you if you want another month."

What Lindsey didn't say, and I knew, was that the "leave" would be unpaid.

"Thanks, but I'm ready. Ken's been back at work for over a month now, and I'm getting restless."

Lindsey didn't have children and wasn't planning to have any. Her reaction made me wonder if she felt that women working in science shouldn't have kids. No one questioned that Ken was ready to go back to work.

*Was I ready to return to work?* Robin wasn't sleeping through the night, and I was suffering from sleep deprivation. Going back to work would mean no daytime naps to catch up. And I was enjoying breastfeeding. While I had a pump and had built up a supply, I worried about being able to pump at work. Mostly, I knew I'd miss being with Robin while I was away. It was tempting to take another month off. I was sure I would have taken *paid* leave if it were available. But, we had no choice. We couldn't afford for me not to work. And so, a new chapter began.

# Chapter 61 ~ Epilogue ~ Science Teacher

As soon as the bell rang, I connected the vacuum pump to the bell jar and turned it on. The pump was an ancient piece of equipment and noisy enough to attract the attention of my students, who quickly eyed the balloon inside the bell jar as it expanded.

"WHOA," Jason called out. He was excitable all the time.

"Cool," Mat said.

I had Mat in a seat off to the side. He was hyperactive and literally bounced his desk.

I turned the pump off and opened the valve to equalize pressure in the chamber. The balloon returned to its relatively small size.

Pointing to a rough drawing of the bell jar and balloon on the whiteboard, I asked, "Who can explain the science behind this demonstration?"

"That's a pump, isn't it?" Terry said.

"It is," I said.

Terry, a petite girl with red hair and freckles, rarely spoke up. It was good to see her join in.

Next, I drew another picture, this time with the bell jar and a blown-up balloon inside. I used evenly spaced dots again, but there were fewer this time, further apart.

I pointed to the compressor. "Terry was right. The pump removed air molecules," I said, pointing to the first diagram.

Now, I added another drawing with the expanded balloon.

"Notice the difference between the drawings. The first shows the jar before turning the compressor on. The second shows the jar after removing air."

I paused, making eye contact with students and giving them time to process.

"Why is the balloon in the second drawing larger?"

Then, I waited, knowing that if I waited long enough, I'd get an answer or two.

Sarah, the blond cheerleader in the front, waved her hand in the air. I nodded to her. "Tell me what you think."

"The dots inside and outside the balloon have to be the same distance. The pressure inside and outside the balloon has to be the same."

"Excellent! Good thinking, Sarah."

She beamed.

"The balloon is elastic rubber. When I lowered the pressure by removing air molecules, it expanded until the pressure inside was the same as the pressure outside."

I pulled my next demonstration into view: a really large graduated cylinder filled with water. It had a glass dropper floating upright. I had very carefully adjusted the dropper so it had neutral buoyancy. I secured a cut balloon over the top of the cylinder and placed it on the desk in front of Tyler.

"Watch the dropper carefully," I said and pressed down on the rubber dam. The dropper slowly drifted to the bottom of the cylinder.

"Oh my God. That is cool!"

Tyler's response was very gratifying.

I nodded my agreement and pointed to the lesson title on the board. "Today's lesson is on gas behavior."

It had taken me years to develop the materials and techniques I needed to make science exciting and connect with students. My arsenal included demonstrations, animations, silly drawings, and an understanding that teaching is a performing art. I loved teaching and never regretted the unconventional path that led me to the classroom.

I often reflected on how someone who struggled so much in her early schooling became a teacher. When I was in high school, I could never have imagined teaching. But by the time I was working at the University of Florida, the idea wasn't so strange. I had taught lab lessons at the University of Queensland, and I enjoyed interacting with the high school students working in our lab.

But when I shared my goal with my mother, her reaction was that of disbelief and shock.

"Would they let you do that, be a teacher?" She asked.

I tried not to be insulted and decided I wanted to see what it would take. After Robin was born, I knew I needed to change; I needed work that would be satisfying. Why not try teaching?

That I loved being a mom was a wonderful surprise. I never played with dolls as a kid, but I absolutely loved being with Robin. Ken and I would watch her sleep, marveling at this miracle who was ours. Of course, there were challenges, like her flinging food all over the place at dinner. And, we didn't have family nearby in Gainesville. It was tough to find a babysitter, so Ken and I rarely had time alone.

Like many new mothers, I suffered from a lack of sleep and mild depression that comes with a radical change in life. But part of my depression was dissatisfaction with my work and a feeling that I was underappreciated. I spent most of my workday sitting at a tissue culture hood engaged in repetitive tasks. Sometimes, I felt like it was more of a factory job than science research. Robin was the first infant to arrive at daycare and the last child picked up. And my boss, Lindsey, showed her resentment when I left lab meetings at five-thirty to pick my child up before the daycare closed.

I needed a different job. I wanted to work, but I didn't want to look for another lab job. With only a master's degree, I would always be a pair of hands in someone's lab. My interest in science never wavered, but I questioned my choice of working in a research lab. *What else could I do that would keep me in* science?

*Could I teach science?*

Brazenly, I called the education department at UF while I was on a break at work.

"I have a bachelor's and a master's degree in Zoology, and am currently working in a research lab here in Gainesville. What would it take for me to become a science teacher?"

"We have a program just for people like you. Give us a year full-time, and we will have you in the classroom," she said.

"Can I get information?" I asked.

She took down my information and said that an adviser would be in touch.

I hung up the phone and sat for a minute. *Could I do this? Be a teacher?*

I met with the adviser that week, and she suggested night classes for the rest of this academic year. I was already past the deadline to apply for the 1985-86 school year, but luckily, as an employee, I could still take classes without paying tuition.

My first course was Sociological Foundations of Education. The professor, Dr. Webb, used our first meeting to set expectations. He explained the class would be run as a student-led seminar. The topics were riveting to me: the impact of poverty on family dynamics and school performance. How work instability and frequent moves disrupted education, and how parents who had experienced difficulty in their own schooling were often uncomfortable visiting schools, or being involved in their children's schooling. The class struck home in so many ways and helped me put my elementary experiences in perspective.

My father left school after eighth grade. He was uneasy attending teacher-parent conferences and left that to Mom. For the first time, I wondered if he had experienced something similar to my humiliation in Mrs. Maxwell's class. I wished I had talked to him about it. He was gone now, and I doubted Mom would know.

My second evening class was Psychological Foundations in Education. It was every bit as fascinating as my previous class. All my life, teachers told me to memorize words, and no one ever told me there were techniques that make the task doable. No one had explained that if you cluster numbers into groups of four, that makes it easier to memorize. Information about learning styles and types of intelligence was unbelievably cool. By the end of the semester, I knew this was what I wanted to do, and I felt ready to jump back into being a full-time student.

The university program, "Pro-Teach," integrated observation in classrooms, college lectures on effective classroom techniques, and a full-time semester internship. To qualify for the program, you had to have at least a bachelor in science and want to become a science teacher. I applied for financial aid and started full-time in the fall of 1986.

My classes focused on science instruction methods. Right away, I knew I'd found my niche. I was essentially studying the *science of teaching.*

We were all assigned to a classroom for observations and to keep detailed journals to use in a seminar class, where we talked about everything from levels of content, methods of questioning, and teacher-student interactions.

At Gainesville High School, Pat Baxter welcomed the two of us for our observation placement. She was an enthusiastic woman in her forties. From day one, we were amazed that she knew every student's name and so much more. Pat knew if each student played volleyball, basketball, or football. She knew their interests, such as dance or anime. She greeted each student by name as they entered the classroom, and their affection for her was clear through their playful and friendly interactions.

Cathy and I quietly watched, absorbing everything. The first class was about animal cells. Pat had drawn a detailed factory on the blackboard. It included a fuel-burning furnace, conveyor belts for moving materials, and a wall to separate the inside from the outside. She explained each cell organelle, connecting it to the diagram. That diagram must have taken her ages to create.

"If the mitochondria are a furnace, why isn't the cell hot?" a student asked.

"It is hot," Pat said. "Feel your forehead." She paused while everyone put their hands to their foreheads. "See, you feel warm. The mitochondria are where the heat is made."

* * *

In the College Methods class, we had lessons on how to present science principles using clear communication and when and how to question students to engage their active attention and check for comprehension. We learned about using laboratory activities to foster critical thinking and an appreciation of science inquiry. What was wonderful was to see what we learned in our college class, in action, in Pat's Biology classroom.

I was genuinely enthusiastic about my classes, more than I had ever been before. *Why had I never considered teaching before?*

We had observations in the middle school as well, and it was exciting. The teacher had us bring a lab activity for the students. We chose "Electric Breakfast," a lesson on static electricity using Rice Krispies cereal, Saran Wrap, and plastic cups. Students counted out thirty pieces of cereal, placing them in the cup and sealing it with the wrap. They then rubbed the wrap against their sleeves and tested how many of the cereal pieces would cling to the plastic. The kids, in their early teens, were enthusiastic and appreciative. I had such a good time. I thought about asking for a middle school internship.

My college professor dissuaded me, saying my academic background and research experience would be more suited to high school. To my delight, Pat Baxter accepted me, and in the spring term of 1986, she introduced me to her students as their new intern teacher. These were the same students I'd observed earlier in the fall.

"If she's going to be teaching us, where will you be?" one student asked.

"Observing and providing feedback. Don't worry. You'll get me back again."

For a few days, Pat observed my lessons, offering feedback after each one. Eventually, she'd leave the room, giving me full control. Within a week, Pat was gone for longer stretches, and I was teaching solo.

It was the way it had to be; an intern has to learn to handle the classroom. But it was sink or swim. One day, a young girl asked to use the restroom and didn't come back. After ten minutes, I was worried. There were no phones in the room, and I couldn't leave the classroom to check on her. Another five minutes passed. I used the button on the wall that connected to the front office.

"Can I help you?" a voice came from the speaker.

"This is Ann McNicol in Mrs. Baxter's room. Can I have an administrator come to the room?"

Within a few minutes, Mr. Hayward was at my door. I explained why I had called, and he watched the room while I checked the bathroom. Jill was passed out on the floor. She had taken an overdose. Ten minutes later, she was in an ambulance on the way to the hospital. Gainesville High was an inner-city school, where student overdoses were not uncommon.

I was shaken—more than shaken. *Did I take too long to call for help? It never occurred to me that teaching could be a matter of life and death.*

Pat talked with me at length about the incident, telling me that I had acted swiftly and correctly.

"Lots of these kids have problems bigger than studying for tests," she said.

"Do you know what Jill was dealing with?" I asked.

"She was upset that her boyfriend broke up with her," Pat said.

"Is that all?" I was incredulous.

Pat sighed. "It's hard to know where to start. Some of our students are living in homes with no electricity. Some of them, particularly boys, have fathers and grandfathers serving time in prison and think prison is their destiny."

"What does this have to do with Jill?" I asked, thinking about the well-dressed, white girl who had been hauled off to the hospital.

"Maybe nothing," Pat conceded. "But these kids grow up too fast. It's likely Jill had been sleeping with her boyfriend for some time, maybe even years. Breakups can be intense. Teenagers are hormone-driven and very emotional. It could also be something else, too. I just don't know."

I nodded, understanding why Pat wanted to know as much about the students as she could and realizing how important it is for a teacher to be a positive, approachable human being.

For sixteen weeks, Pat Baxter regularly observed my lessons and offered feedback. As my mentor, she was always available to discuss teaching and answer my questions. The most important thing I learned wasn't about lesson plans, but about connecting with students. Pat was their teacher, but she was also their volleyball coach. Students on the team resented my internship the most. One girl, Kelly, seemed to hate me the most.

"What can I do?" I asked Pat.

"Make it your mission to make her like you. I will consider your internship a failure if she isn't sad when you leave."

I was horrified. This was huge. But I accepted the challenge and every day, I worked hard to connect with Kelly. I noticed what she wore. I commented on her drawings, went to volleyball games, and talked about the game before class began.

Pat was right, and Kelly's resentment faded. Connecting with challenging students was possible, though it wasn't always simple. At the end of the term, the students created a banner to thank me for being their intern, which I still have.

They each wrote personal notes. Kelly said she was sad at first to lose Mrs. Baxter, but that I was the "best intern" she'd ever had. I learned how to teach at the University of Florida. I learned from Pat Baxter what kind of teacher I wanted to become.

\* \* \*

My internship ended, and I had a full load of classes for the summer to complete the pro-teach program. It had been an intense three terms of full-time study, and I figured substitute teaching would work for a while until I found a full-time position.

Dan Boyd, the principal of Gainesville High School, called me to come in for a last-minute interview. It was Friday morning, and students were starting school the following Monday. I'd applied to Alachua County Schools, but I knew the main hiring push was likely over.

I'd met Mr. Boyd while I'd been interning. The interview went well. We talked about my science background and my internship. He told me that Mrs. Baxter spoke highly of me. As I was leaving, he asked a strange question.

"How do you feel about math?"

"Math is very important. I try to integrate math into my science lessons whenever I can."

"Excellent answer," he said. "I have a few more interviews, but one way or the other, I'll call you soon."

What I hadn't said was that math had always been my favorite subject at school, and that I'd taken a ton of math at college as electives. It didn't feel like that was something I should say at an interview for a science teaching position.

I had a few errands I needed to run, and by the time I got home, the phone had a message from Mr. Boyd offering me the job and asking me to call the county office to accept the job as soon as possible.

They were expecting my call and asked me to come in and fill out the employment paperwork. By the time I'd finished, it was too late to go over to the school and pick up textbooks or see my classroom. I had to wait until Monday and would start the same day as the students.

Monday morning, I discovered I didn't have a classroom. I had four rooms spread over two wings of the school. My schedule was Earth and Science, Physical Science, Biology, and Algebra I. It was when I walked into the last classroom and saw the math books that I understood Dr. Boyd's question.

I would have taken the job anyway. By the time my second child was born, I had completed a specialist in education degree and my first year of teaching.

There were struggles and triumphs. My first year of teaching, I took a knife from a student who was threatening someone at least twice his size. Mr. Hayward told me never to do that again. One day, Mr. Hayward had to console me when a student ripped up my attendance book.

"These things happen," he said.

Then there was the day, as I sat in a dentist's waiting room, a woman approached me and said my Environmental Science class changed her daughter's life, that she majored in environmental engineering and

325

worked at the Suwannee River Water Management District. She made me smile because I remembered her and her daughter. There had been a meeting with the guidance counselor and seven of Sarah's teachers. Each one said Sarah didn't seem engaged in class and wasn't doing well. I was amazed. Sarah often had her hand up in my class. She loved the labs, contributed, and performed well on her tests. I was glad to hear she survived high school and that my class made a difference.

Teaching was my second career. I built a firm foundation at the University of Florida and with Mrs. Baxter, and I never stopped learning. I went to educational technology conferences and submitted grant applications to bring modern tools to my classroom, attended state and national science teaching conferences, and earned my National Board certification in chemistry education. There were workshops to take and even more to give. I loved mentoring new teachers. While I might have been bored as a lab research assistant, I was never bored with teaching. I retired in 2020 after thirty-eight years in education, wanting to slow down and pursue other interests.

A long time ago, I was a college student in an elective writing class at the University of South Florida. My professor, Dr. Saunders, said, "Everyone has a book in them, maybe only one book, but make sure you write it."

So I did. After a lifetime as an avid science fiction fan, I used my freedom as a retiree to take an online science fiction writing class from the Gotham Writers Workshop in New York. My first piece of fiction, *Charlie's Story*, grew from a short story to a novel, and then to a four-book series. Maybe Mr. Saunders would consider me an overachiever.

I found that writing science fiction gave me an outlet for creativity and a way to stay connected to science. My books focus on marine biology, coral reefs, and climate change.

It's been more than half a lifetime since I became "Mom," and I've enjoyed revisiting the earlier "me." Not too long ago, Uncle Bob asked me if I had my life to do over, what would I change. We all have regrets, but I don't have many. And there aren't any major parts of my life I would do differently.

Ken and I live in a small town in Florida, where we settled almost forty-five years ago. My children are grown. Neither of them had an interest in science. Robin works in the music industry in New York, and Bernard is a pastry chef in Tampa. Both are wonderful human beings. I'm as proud of them as a mother could be. Life is good.

# About the Author

I've been a jack of all trades of science. I worked in the field and laboratories for NOAA, NIH, and the University of Florida Veterinary School. But for most of my career, I taught high school science, community college science, and science education. In 2019, I retired and have been enjoying writing and publishing science fiction, and now a memoir..

When I'm not writing, my husband and I walk along Tampa Bay, ride our bikes, camp in state parks, visit our adult children and play with our attention-demanding cats. Life is good.

**You can connect with me on:**

 http://mcnicola.com

 https://www.facebook.com/ann.mcnicol.98

# Also by Ann R McNicol

Charlie's Story (2021)
  The Nest (2022)
  Tentacles (2023)
  Cyanea (2024)

Connect with me at http://mcnicola.com
  or at mcnicola@gmail.com